SMART Board® Interactive Whiteboard

FOR DUMMIES®

D1501876

SMART
Board®
Interactive
Whiteboard
FOR
DUMMIES®

by Radana Dvorak

 **WILEY**

A John Wiley and Sons, Ltd, Publication

SMART Board® Interactive Whiteboard For Dummies®

Published by
John Wiley & Sons Canada, Ltd.
6045 Freemont Blvd.
Mississauga, ON L5R 4J3
www.wiley.com

Copyright © 2012 by John Wiley & Sons Canada, Ltd.

Published by John Wiley & Sons Canada, Ltd.

For general information on John Wiley & Sons Canada, Ltd., including all books published by Wiley Publishing, Inc., please call our warehouse, Tel 1-800-567-4797. For reseller information, including discounts and premium sales, please call our sales department, Tel 416-646-7992. For press review copies, author interviews, or other publicity information, please contact our marketing department, Tel 416-646-4584, Fax 416-236-4448.

For technical support, please visit www.wiley.com/techsupport.

Wiley publishes in a variety of print and electronic formats and by print-on-demand. Some material included with standard print versions of this book may not be included in e-books or in print-on-demand. If this book refers to media such as a CD or DVD that is not included in the version you purchased, you may download this material at http://booksupport.wiley.com. For more information about Wiley products, visit www.wiley.com.

Library and Archives Canada Cataloguing in Publication Data

Dvorak, Radana

    SMART Board interactive whiteboard for dummies / Radana Dvorak.

Includes index.

ISBN 978-1-11837-668-3

    1. SMART Board (Computer file). 2. Interactive whiteboards.

3. Teaching—Aids and devices. I. Title.

LB1043.5.D86 2012   371.33'4   C2012-904784-8

ISBN 978-1-118-38742-9 (ebk); 978-1-118-38740-5 (ebk); 978-1-118-38741-2 (ebk)

Printed in the United States

1 2 3 4 5 RRD 16 15 14 13 12

WILEY

About the Author

Radana Dvorak holds a PhD in computer science from the Queen Mary, University of London, a master's degree in artificial intelligence from the University of Sussex, and a BA from the University of Michigan. Radana has been involved in eLearning since 1989, when her research in human computer interaction focused on computer-based training. She has been a researcher and a university instructor in the United Kingdom, the Cayman Islands, and the United States. She also has spent time in the software industry. Currently, she's an associate dean at Saint Martin's University in Lacey, Washington, where she heads an office charged with providing the general oversight and strategic planning for the improvement, growth, and development of Saint Martin's online and off-campus learning opportunities. Her focus is combining her love for technology and education to help organizations with the transitions impacted by the enormous changes technology has brought to education.

Dedication

I dedicate this book to my children, Anna and James, and to my dear Paul, for encouraging and believing in me.

Author's Acknowledgments

I want to go back a number of years and thank three professors: Professor Mike Sharples supervised my master's thesis at the University of Sussex and was instrumental in developing my interest in human-computer interaction. Professor Peter Johnson accepted me into the computer science PhD program at Queen Mary, University of London. And Professor Stephen Summerville was instrumental in my research interests and supervised my PhD. His enthusiasm, dedication, and research interest, combined with the way he always made time for his students, made him a great role model. I'll never forget his preaching that the best research questions are the simplest, those for which the question itself helps the learner to search for possible solutions and answers.

I want to thank the Saint Martin's University community I have grown to adore. Special thanks to Dr. Joe Bessie, the provost, for bringing me to his team, and to Leon Chickering for embracing new technology and getting his MBA and BBA students excited to use the newly installed, state-of-the-art SMART Board interactive whiteboards. Dr. Joyce Westgard, the dean of the School of Education, was instrumental in making sure the university had the new technology for the graduate programs. The Instructional Technology Services team installed and looked after the interactive whiteboards for both the main campus and the extended campuses. Thanks also to all the faculty and students who have shared their experiences and provided feedback.

This book owes a great deal to Blair Munro at SMART Technologies. He came onto the project as a technical editor and created the screenshots and graphical components. Blair, I am indebted to you for your dedication and for promptly answering my e-mails filled with questions and scheduling phone calls before 7 a.m., so we could talk before the phones started ringing at work. Anam Ahmed, from John Wiley & Sons in Toronto, gave me the opportunity to write the book and was professional and supportive throughout the process. Elizabeth Kuball, the project editor, kept us on track and made sure the book was crafted in the *For Dummies* style.

Lastly, I am grateful for my children, my husband, and my parents for being so patient and understanding and putting up with my nocturnal working hours, stress, and abandonment while I was trying to meet tight deadlines.

Publisher's Acknowledgments

We're proud of this book; please send us your comments at http://dummies.custhelp.com. For other comments, please contact our Customer Care Department within the U.S. at 877-762-2974, outside the U.S. at 317-572-3993, or fax 317-572-4002.

Some of the people who helped bring this book to market include the following:

Acquisitions and Editorial

Project Editor: Elizabeth Kuball

Acquiring Editor: Anam Ahmed

Copy Editor: Elizabeth Kuball

Technical Editor: Blair Munro and SMART Technologies

Production Editor: Lindsay Humphreys

Editorial Assistant: Kathy Deady

Cover and interior photos:
© SMART Technologies

Cartoons: Rich Tennant (www.the5thwave.com)

Composition Services

Project Coordinator: Kristie Rees

Layout and Graphics: Jennifer Creasey, Corrie Niehaus

Proofreaders: Melissa Cossell, Rob Springer, Penny L. Stuart

Indexer: BIM Indexing & Proofreading Services

John Wiley & Sons Canada, Ltd.

    Deborah Barton, Vice President and Director of Operations

    Jennifer Smith, Publisher, Professional and Trade Division

    Alison Maclean, Managing Editor, Professional & Trade Division

Publishing and Editorial for Consumer Dummies

    Kathleen Nebenhaus, Vice President and Executive Publisher

    Kristin Ferguson-Wagstaffe, Product Development Director

    Ensley Eikenburg, Associate Publisher, Travel

    Kelly Regan, Editorial Director, Travel

Publishing for Technology Dummies

    Andy Cummings, Vice President and Publisher

Composition Services

    Debbie Stailey, Director of Composition Services

Contents at a Glance

Table of Contents

Introduction

*O*dds are, years ago, you used chalk and a blackboard. Then you progressed to a whiteboard. And now you're moving to the SMART Board® interactive whiteboard. This book is the resource you need to make this transition a smooth one.

You're probably familiar with the SMART Board interactive whiteboard. You may even have sat through a workshop and realized that you need more guidance, but you don't want to spend hours reading online manuals or spend more time in training sessions. You just want a reference that you can keep by your side, something that'll help you use the interactive whiteboard to accomplish your goals. You want a book that cuts through the vast amount of information out there and gets to the nuts and bolts you need.

About This Book

SMART Board Interactive Whiteboard For Dummies is a reference book. You don't have to read it straight through, from beginning to end, to get what you need out of it. Instead, you can use the table of contents and index to locate the information you need when you need it. You don't have to commit anything to memory — you can return to it anytime to make using the interactive whiteboard a breeze.

Conventions Used in This Book

I don't use many conventions in this book, but I do use a few to make information easier for you to find:

- ✔ When I introduce new terms, I *italicize* them and define them nearby, often in parentheses.
- ✔ Numbered steps you need to follow and characters you need to type are set in **bold.**
- ✔ Web addresses and e-mail addresses are set in `monofont`. ***Note:*** When this book was printed, some web addresses may have needed to break

across two lines of text. If that happened, rest assured that we haven't put in any extra characters (such as hyphens) to indicate the break. So, when using one of these addresses, just type in exactly what you see in this book, pretending as though the line break doesn't exist.

What You're Not to Read

You can safely skip text in gray boxes — those are sidebars, and although they're interesting, they're not critical to your understanding of the subject at hand. You also can skip anything marked with the Technical Stuff icon (see "Icons Used in This Book," later, for more information).

Foolish Assumptions

I make a few basic assumptions about you as the reader:

- ✔ You've used a whiteboard and an overhead projector and presented in front of a crowd or a classroom using applications such as PowerPoint.
- ✔ You're an educator, involved in some kind of training, or you work in the business sector where you're required to give presentations.
- ✔ You have basic computer skills and access to the Internet.

How This Book Is Organized

SMART Board Interactive Whiteboard For Dummies is divided into five parts. Here's an overview of what each part covers.

Part 1: Getting Started with Your SMART Board Interactive Whiteboard

This part is a great place to start if you want to find out everything there is to know about your interactive whiteboard. Here, I present the hardware, show you how to identify which model of interactive whiteboard you have, explain the software, and demonstrate a few tricks.

Part II: Creating Lessons and Presentations with SMART Notebook™ Collaborative Learning Software

In this part, I fill you in on SMART Notebook software. Here, you start creating fabulous lessons and presentations. You find out how to use cool objects, animate your content, and create new content with your finger, pen, or keyboard.

Part III: Adding Interactivity Tools and Collaborating Activities

In this part, you get an introduction to interactivity, how to use multimedia features, Bridgit® conferencing software, and SMART Meeting Pro™ software. When you know how to use these SMART Board interactive whiteboard capabilities, you can impress all your colleagues and (more important) your audience with your newly acquired knowledge and interactive whiteboard skills.

Part IV: The Part of Tens

This part is where to go if you're short on time but want a heavy dose of useful information. Here you find answers to ten frequently asked questions; ten cool SMART accessories; ten tips, hints, and shortcuts; and ten creative ways to involve your audience in your presentation.

Icons Used in This Book

Icons are those little pictures you see in the margins throughout this book. Here's what the icons mean:

When you see the Tip icon, you're sure to find information that'll make your job easier.

When you see anything marked by the Remember icon, pay attention — you'll need to use this information again, and it's worth remembering.

When I channel my inner geek, I mark the text with a Technical Stuff icon. You can ignore these paragraphs if all you want is the information you absolutely need — but if you have your own inner (or not so inner) geek, read on!

When I give you a heads-up about something that could cause you a real hassle or headache, I flag the text with the Warning icon.

Where to Go from Here

If you're just getting started with the interactive whiteboard, you can start at the very beginning — a very good place to start. If you're trying to figure out how to set up your interactive whiteboard, turn to Chapter 2. If someone else has already set up and configured your interactive whiteboard, skip Chapter 2 and head straight for Chapter 4. Or, if you just want to figure out how to do something specific, use the table of contents or index to find the information you need.

Part I
Getting Started with Your SMART Board Interactive Whiteboard

The 5th Wave   By Rich Tennant

"Here's your SMART Board. Want me to set it up for you?"

In this part . . .

Here you find out about all the capabilities and possibilities available with your SMART Board interactive whiteboard. Chapter 1 gives you an overview of the interactive whiteboard, briefly explaining its conventions, terminology, and tools. Chapter 2 fills you in on the hardware and how to identify what product versions you have; I also walk you through setting up the interactive whiteboard if you're in charge of this task for your organization. Chapter 3 shows you how to configure your interactive whiteboard so that it performs exactly how you need it to. Finally, in Chapter 4, I cover the nuts-and-bolts information that gets you started using the interactive whiteboard and designing your first project.

Chapter 1

Unveiling the SMART Board Interactive Whiteboard

Congratulations! You've decided to get serious about using that great big interactive whiteboard standing proudly in your classroom or meeting room. You've seen others use it. You've heard students talking about how cool one of your colleagues is because he does the wildest things with it. You've heard your boss praise one of your co-workers, saying how well she was able to explain the new workflow using the interactive whiteboard. You want a piece of that action!

In this chapter, I introduce you to all the capabilities of the SMART Board interactive whiteboard. I explain how it works, what you can do with it, and the tools you'll be using to get the job done.

Exploring the Interactive Whiteboard: The Big Picture

You may be thinking, "I've seen one of these interactive whiteboards, but what exactly is it and how does it work?" Well, you're about to find out. The SMART Board interactive whiteboard is a digital whiteboard that gives you all the capabilities of your computer on a whiteboard. Plus, you can use your finger to write on the screen in digital ink. Then you can save, print, or distribute your notes at the touch of a button; access multimedia files; collaborate on activities by allowing two or more people to write on the screen at the same time; access the Internet; and teleconference.

Some teachers have held lessons with classrooms of students spread across the world. How cool is it to be able to write on the screen in the United States and have students in Canada or England seeing what you've written and participating in your class?

How it works

The interactive whiteboard (see Figure 1-1) connects to your computer and a projector. Your computer desktop is projected on the interactive whiteboard surface. You control the desktop by touching the screen with your finger, a pen, or an eraser, or you can use a keyboard and mouse. The display is touch sensitive, allowing your finger to become the mouse to control writing on the display and control your computer.

Interactive whiteboards versus electronic whiteboards

You may have heard people talking about electronic whiteboards and wondered if those are the same as interactive whiteboards. Here are the differences between an interactive whiteboard and an electronic whiteboard:

✔ The interactive whiteboard displays your desktop.

✔ You can write directly on an interactive whiteboard with your finger or various tools and then save your note from the screen to your computer.

✔ On an interactive whiteboard, you can use all the features and software on your computer, including the ability to access the Internet.

With an electronic whiteboard, all you can do is use your dry-erase markers on the board and save the notes to your computer. You can't use gestures on your desktop or access any software.

Electronic whiteboards are pretty limited. You're better off using your laptop connected to an overhead projector than using an electronic whiteboard. Of course, the best option is an interactive whiteboard, which takes your laptop's functionality to a whole new level.

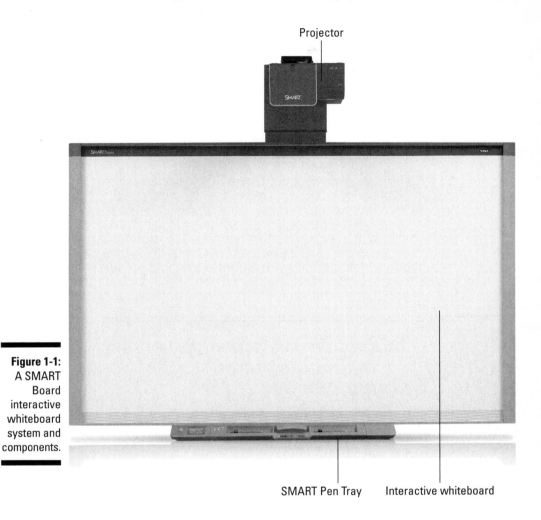

Projector

SMART Pen Tray   Interactive whiteboard

Figure 1-1:
A SMART Board interactive whiteboard system and components.

Originally developed in 1991 by SMART Technologies, interactive whiteboards have been around for over 20 years and continue to incorporate the latest hardware and software.

The term *SMART Board* is actually a brand name owned by SMART Technologies; it isn't a generic term for an interactive whiteboard. (This book focuses on the SMART Board interactive whiteboard, not just any old technology.)

Any software and programs on your computer you use day to day can be used with your interactive whiteboard, including the following:

- Laptop and desktop computers
- Video cameras
- Digital cameras
- Projectors
- DVD players
- Tablets such as the iPad (through web conferencing only)

The great advantage of the interactive whiteboard is that you can engage every type of learner or member of the audience and deliver your message or learning activity to capture their attention. Your participants can interact with information on a different level than they could in the past. Remember the groans or wide eyes when you opened a PowerPoint presentation? Your audience won't experience "death by PowerPoint" when you fire up the interactive whiteboard. Instead, you'll be able to mix content with rich graphics, sound, video, text, and 3-D images. You can even give your audience a kinetic experience by involving them in working with the interactive whiteboard. The next section explains how.

What you can use it for

You can use all kinds of tactics to deliver your message to your audience. Here are some ways you can use your interactive whiteboard:

- **Brainstorming and editing:** Let your students or team members work in a group to brainstorm on a specific topic and record their ideas, and then drag and drop them to other areas of the interactive whiteboard. You can add their notes to pages and save them (see Part II of this book for more information).

- **Real-time collaboration:** You can share your screen with anyone at a computer anywhere in the world and let them take control of your desktop to collaborate on files and projects.

- **Diagrams:** Using diagrams in your presentations and projects livens up the material.

- **Teaching/training aids:** You can use your interactive whiteboard to teach math, vocabulary, and grammar interactively using notes and games. Use a blog or other social network as a classroom exercise; the class can work together on an e-book or blog. Use the record feature to narrate the text.

✔ **Portfolios:** Encourage your audience to create interactive project portfolios and share them with a department. Students can demonstrate their work at parent-teacher conferences.

✔ **Games:** An abundance of games (including Scrabble, Jeopardy!, and Who Wants to Be A Millionaire?) are available to break the ice for workshops or educational purposes. Check Appendix A for resources.

✔ **Streaming:** You can stream video through sites such as Discovery Education (`http://streaming.discoveryeducation.com`) or free videos for teachers from PBS or the BBC. Most are free, but you'll need to create an account. Schools have used multimedia to teach everything from language skills to safe rugby and football tactics.

✔ **Sharing:** You can save all your presentations and show them to students or team members who weren't present.

✔ **Group activities:** Websites enable you and your students or team members to create worksheets, posters, and flyers. Try setting up a group activity and create a worksheet to use on the interactive whiteboard. One teacher used the conferencing capability to work with another school across the country to plan a lesson.

✔ **Access to education aids on the Internet displayed on the large display:** For example, a biology teacher can access 3-D hearts, rotate the images, and add her own notes while explaining the heart's function.

Touring Your Interactive Whiteboard System

The interactive whiteboard system is made up four different components:

✔ **The hardware:** The hardware consists of the following:

- The interactive whiteboard
- A projector (see the nearby sidebar)
- Your computer
- A keyboard
- A USB cable
- A VGA/RGB cable

I discuss how to identify your hardware components in the next section and how to connect them in Chapter 2.

✔ **Interactive devices:** The interactive devices are the following:

- An on-screen keyboard

- Loads of on-screen tools

- The SMART Pen Tray, which includes two or four color-coded slots for pens (depending on which model you have) and one slot for the eraser

The pens and eraser work by interacting with the place setting. Each pen sitting in a slot has an optical sensor to identify it. When you pick up a pen, the sensor sends info to the interactive whiteboard, enabling you to write with the pen by applying pressure with the pen or your finger. (I discuss the functionality of these tools in more detail in Chapters 3 and 4.)

If you misplace one of the pens, you can add any object to interact with the sensor. When you remove the object, use your finger or another marker, and that particular color will be activated. *Note:* The 800 series has a feature called Object Recognition, which can identify whether you're using a pen or your finger, so if you do replace the pen with another object, make sure you use that object each time you want to use the "pen."

✔ **Software:** SMART Notebook collaborative learning software, SMART Meeting Pro software, and SMART Ink™ software (or Ink Aware software) are a few of the many packages included with the interactive whiteboard enabling you to work with some of the coolest applications. I cover these software packages in Part II.

✔ **Resources:** SMART Technologies offers an abundance of material for you to download for free. SMART resources are a must to explore! You can access the SMART education solutions website at www.smarttech. com/edredirect, business solutions at www.smarttech.com/ freestorm, and the SMART Exchange™ website at http://exchange. smarttech.com. I list a number of additional resources in Appendix A.

Projectors: Getting your message out there

You know you have an interactive whiteboard with a projector if there's a space-age-looking arm, called a *boom,* sticking out over the screen (see the figure). Alternatively, your organization may have purchased a projector separately, and the projector sits on a table in front of the interactive whiteboard.

As far as the functionality of the projector, it doesn't matter what kind or model your organization has — the interactive whiteboard still functions the same way.

If you need more information on SMART's interactive whiteboard systems and projectors, go to www.smarttech.com/kb/160464, which helps you identify your system. This document also links you with user's guides and more information. If you're responsible for looking after your organization's interactive whiteboard, read the user's guide for your project, because it explains how to take care of it.

Comparing the Different SMART Board Interactive Whiteboard Series

Many different interactive whiteboard models and systems are available. In the next few sections, I give you enough information for you to identify which interactive whiteboard you have and understand how it works. Be warned, though: If you brag too much about your new skills, you'll be identified as the team's expert and your colleagues will be coming to you for help!

Do you have an interactive whiteboard or an interactive display?

One of the first things you need to figure out is whether you have an *interactive whiteboard* or an *interactive display* (sometimes also called an *interactive flat panel*). The best way to figure it out is to look at the huge display and ask, "Does it look like a traditional whiteboard, or does it look more like a television set?" If it looks more like a whiteboard, you have an interactive whiteboard. If it looks more like a television set, it's an interactive display.

Another way you can tell is whether the system uses a projector. If it does use a projector, then it's definitely an interactive whiteboard. This book focuses on the interactive whiteboard, but fortunately, if you have an interactive display, you're not out of luck — much of the functionality is identical.

Do you have a 600 series or an 800 series?

If you've determined that what you have is an interactive whiteboard (see the preceding section), the next step is to figure out which series you have. It's not too difficult — there are only two main types: the 600 series (which is still the most widely used) and the newer 800 series.

Although some older models are still around, in this book I focus solely on the 600 and 800 series.

The simplest way to tell the difference between the two series is to look closely at the Pen Tray. If it's a 600 series, it'll have four pen slots (see Figure 1-2); if it's an 800 series, it'll have two pen slots (see Figure 1-3).

Figure 1-2:
The 600 series Pen Tray.

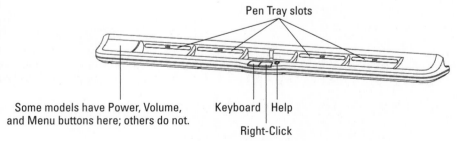

Pen Tray slots

Some models have Power, Volume, and Menu buttons here; others do not.

Keyboard | Help

Right-Click

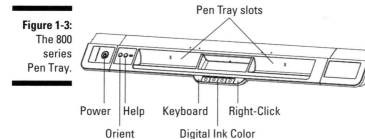

Pen Tray slots

Figure 1-3:
The 800
series
Pen Tray.

Power | Help | Keyboard | Right-Click

Orient | Digital Ink Color

While you're studying your Pen Tray so closely, notice that the Pen Trays on the 600 and 800 series also have different buttons. On the 600 series, there are the following buttons:

- ✔ Keyboard
- ✔ Right-Click
- ✔ Help
- ✔ Power (on some models)
- ✔ Volume (on some models)
- ✔ Menu (on some models)

On the 800 series, there are the following buttons:

- ✔ Power
- ✔ Orient
- ✔ Help
- ✔ Keyboard
- ✔ Digital Ink Color
- ✔ Right-Click

There's one more way you can tell the difference between the 600 series and 800 series: Take a look around the edge of the interactive surface. If you see shiny, reflective material between the whiteboard and its frame, then you have an 800 series. The 600 series has no gap between the whiteboard area and its frame.

Of course, none of this will be necessary if your interactive whiteboard has a sticker telling you what series it is.

Analog resistive versus DViT® technology

If you're itching to find out more technical detail about how the 600 series and 800 series differ, read on, but I'm warning you: I wouldn't boast this knowledge in a team meeting, unless you want to put everyone to sleep.

The main difference between the 600 series and the 800 series is that they use different methods to translate your touch into computer commands.

The 600 series uses analog resistive technology. Put simply, the interactive whiteboard surface is made up of two thin layers, with a narrow air gap between them. When you touch the surface, you close the gap between the layers and the system tracks the location of your touch by "reading" where the gap is closed (see the figure).

The 800 series uses DViT (short for Digital Vision Touch). This technology uses tiny digital cameras hidden in the frame of the whiteboard area to track the location of your finger or pen on the surface. How cool is that?

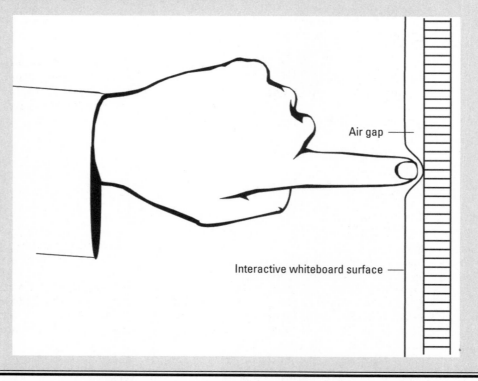

Air gap —

Interactive whiteboard surface —

Introducing the Interactive Whiteboard Tools

There are a number of different types of navigation tools and menus that enable you to interact with the interactive whiteboard and the software. All these tools have one thing in common: They give you quick access to work with the interactive whiteboard effectively and efficiently. In this section, I give you an overview of the tools, explain their functionality, and show you what they look like.

The Floating Tools toolbar

Part of SMART Board Tools, the Floating Tools toolbar (shown in Figure 1-4) is fully customizable. By default, it appears on the left edge of your screen (when SMART Product Drivers are installed). You can move it to other areas of your screen if you want.

To access the Floating Tools toolbar on a PC, choose Start⇨All Programs⇨ SMART Technologies⇨SMART Board Tools. To access the Floating Tools toolbar on a Mac, right-click the SMART Board icon in the Dock and select Open Floating Tools to launch the toolbar. Or click the SMART Board icon and select Show Floating Tools.

For much more on the Floating Tools toolbar, turn to Chapter 3.

SMART Tools

SMART Tools (see Figure 1-5) are additional administration, presentation, and collaboration tools and utilities. Magnifier, Spotlight, and Orientation are just a few of the SMART Tools.

To access the SMART Tools on a PC, choose Start⇨All Programs⇨SMART Technologies⇨SMART Tools. To access them on a Mac, Control-click the SMART Board icon in the Dock. The SMART Tools menu appears.

For more on the SMART Tools, turn to Chapter 4.

Figure 1-4:
The Floating
Tools
toolbar.

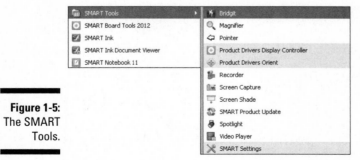

Figure 1-5:
The SMART
Tools.

SMART Notebook Tools

The main software program you use with most interactive whiteboards is called SMART Notebook. There are various plug-ins, such as Math Tools and 3D Tools, which are referred to as SMART Notebook Tools.

To access the SMART Notebook Tools, tap the Notebook icon on your desktop or in the Floating Tools toolbar.

For more on the SMART Notebook Tools, turn to Chapters 5 and 6.

SMART Ink toolbar

The SMART Ink toolbar (see Figure 1-6) appears on all windows and allows you to mark up any screen in digital ink. (For more on SMART Ink and Ink Aware, see Chapter 5.)

The SMART Ink toolbar appears on all open windows when SMART Ink is turned on.

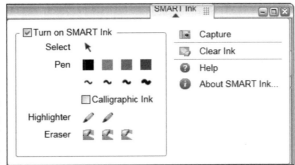

Figure 1-6:
The SMART
Ink toolbar.

SMART Aware toolbar

The SMART Aware toolbar (see Figure 1-7) appears in Microsoft Office and other software that is Ink Aware. These tools enable you to insert notes, text, or images using digital ink. (For more on SMART Ink and Ink Aware, see Chapter 5.)

The SMART Aware toolbar opens with the application. It can be anchored to the software menu bar or allowed to float.

Figure 1-7:
The SMART
Aware
toolbar.

Chapter 2

Setting Up Your SMART Board Interactive Whiteboard

*I*f you have an interactive whiteboard at work that has been set up, with all the software downloaded and registered and everything in working order, you can skip the first few sections of this chapter and get a cup of coffee. While you're at it, stroll down to the IT department and thank them for making a great piece of hardware available to you.

On the other hand, if you're responsible for setting up your interactive whiteboard yourself, you'll want to start this chapter at the very beginning. Here, I walk you through connecting your interactive whiteboard to your computer, guide you through installing the software, make a few suggestions on how to maintain your interactive whiteboard, and even provide a few troubleshooting tips.

The last sections of this chapter offer some ideas on how you can use your interactive whiteboard and suggest where to begin.

Installing the interactive whiteboard

In this chapter, I assume that you had help taking the interactive whiteboard out of the packaging — it's a two-person job — and that someone has helped you put it up, install it, and secure it according to the manufacturer's instructions. The interactive whiteboard can be free-standing on wheels or mounted to the wall; your organization will determine which option is preferable based on the organization's needs, but if the interactive whiteboard will stay in one room, wall mounting is the better option, in terms of stability, safety, and security.

If you're reading this standing in front of boxes, bewildered, put down this book and go find someone to help you — and bring the manufacturer's instructions. Because there are so many different models of interactive whiteboards, projectors, and stands, and various modes of installation, it's beyond the scope of this book to help you with these preliminary steps.

If you find yourself struggling with the instructions that arrived with your equipment, SMART Technologies has a wealth of information online. Go to www.smarttech.com/support, and browse the list of products or search the knowledge base for installation instructions and guides. If you get stuck, contact technical support (www.smarttech.com/contactsupport). Finally, Appendix A provides resources where you can turn for assistance.

Connecting Your Hardware

In this section, I focus on helping you connect the interactive whiteboard to your computer. You have two options: You can connect with a USB cable or with a wireless Bluetooth connection.

Using a USB cable

Your interactive whiteboard came with a high-power USB 2.0 high-speed interface and works with USB 2.0– and USB 1.1–compliant interfaces. The interactive whiteboard has a USB cable that hangs from the corner (called the *flying lead cable*). The flying lead cable is quite useful because if your interactive whiteboard is attached to a wall, you don't have to move it to get to the cable — you can easily hide the cable behind the board in the box attached (see Figure 2-1).

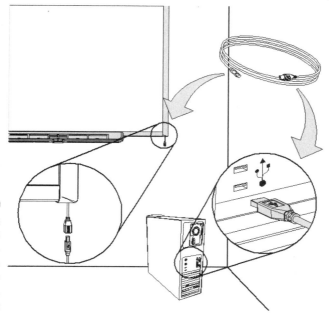

Figure 2-1:
The USB
connec-
tion to the
interactive
whiteboard.

To connect the interactive whiteboard to your computer, find the USB cable that came with the interactive whiteboard and follow these steps:

1. **Connect one of the ends of the USB cable to the connector hanging from the interactive whiteboard's bottom-right corner.**

2. **Connect the other end of the USB cable to a USB slot on your computer.**

3. **Turn on your computer to start your interactive whiteboard.**

   You may need to log on to your computer, and wait for the computer to completely start. You should recognize the default start screen.

   The Ready light on the interactive whiteboard turns red and then flashes green, meaning that the controller is receiving power from the USB connection and is operating in HID (Human Interface Device) mouse mode.

If the drivers are not installed on your computer, a Found New Hardware wizard will launch, helping you find the drivers for the USB HID. If your computer can't find the USB drivers, you'll have to install them on your computer (see "Finding Help If You Get Stuck," later in this chapter).

Don't use just any old USB cable you have lying around to connect your computer to your interactive whiteboard — some old USB cables could damage your interactive whiteboard. Always use the USB cable that came with your product. If you don't have the USB cable that came with the interactive whiteboard, make sure the cable you have has the USB logo and a USB-compliant interface.

After connecting the interactive whiteboard to your computer or laptop, you'll need to install the SMART Product Drivers. Just follows these steps:

1. **Turn on your projector so that you can see your computer screen on the interactive whiteboard.**

   For some interactive whiteboard systems, the projector turns on automatically.

2. **Insert the SMART Product Drivers CD into your computer's CD drive.**

   The installation screen appears.

3. **Follow the instructions on the installation screen.**

   If you're on a PC, the SMART Board icon appears in the Windows notification area; if you're on a Mac, the icon appears in the Dock.

   The Floating Tools toolbar should open automatically. If it doesn't open and you're on a PC, click the Start icon on your desktop and choose All Programs⇨SMART Technologies⇨SMART Board Tools; if you're on a Mac, Control-click the SMART Board icon in the Dock and select Show Floating Tools.

   Note: This process may vary slightly depending on your software version and operating system.

   In the right-hand corner on the interactive whiteboard, the Ready light should have turned from flashing green to solid green. This means that the SMART Product Drivers are communicating with the interactive whiteboard.

Now you're ready to start using the interactive whiteboard!

Going wireless with Bluetooth

If you don't want to use a USB cable to connect your interactive whiteboard to your computer, you can use a wireless Bluetooth connection. Bluetooth allows you greater mobility to work from anywhere in the room (within range of the wireless connector) without being tied down by cables.

You can purchase a Wireless Bluetooth Connection kit made by SMART Technologies; this kit enables you to connect the whiteboard to its external power supply and to your computer. *Note:* The Bluetooth option isn't available for the Dual Touch SMART Board SBD600 series.

The SMART Technologies Wireless Bluetooth Connection kit contains the following:

🗸 A Bluetooth-to-USB expansion module (which connects to the controller module)

🗸 A Bluetooth-to-USB converter (which connects to your computer)

Only use the power supply included with the Wireless Bluetooth Connection kit. According to the manufacturer, other power supplies could damage the equipment and/or can create a safety hazard. You can read more about this in the manufacturer's manual.

The Bluetooth-to-USB converter cannot be used as a general USB-to-Bluetooth adapter. Resist the temptation to try it with your handheld devices — it won't work.

Connecting your interactive whiteboard to your computer isn't complicated, but before you begin the process, do the following:

🗸 **Make sure your interactive whiteboard is fitted with the Wireless Bluetooth Connection expansion module, as shown in Figures 2-2 and 2-3.**

Figure 2-2:
The WC6 Wireless Bluetooth Connection expansion module (for 600 series interactive whiteboards).

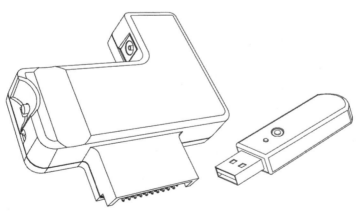

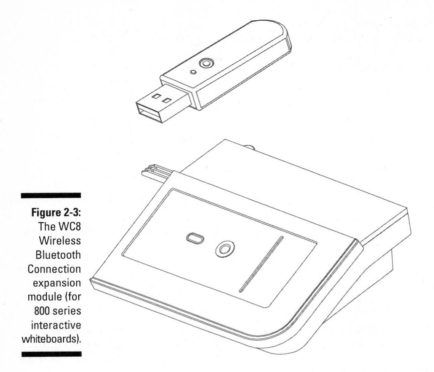

Figure 2-3:
The WC8
Wireless
Bluetooth
Connection
expansion
module (for
800 series
interactive
whiteboards).

✔ **Make sure that your computer works properly with your interactive whiteboard when you use the USB cable connector.** When you confirm that the computer and interactive whiteboard are communicating by means of the USB interface, you're ready to set up the wireless Bluetooth connection. If your computer isn't connecting to the interactive whiteboard, check to make sure that you have the correct controller firmware installed on your interactive whiteboard.

Now you're ready to set up the wireless Bluetooth connection. Install your Wireless Bluetooth Connection expansion module on your interactive whiteboard following the manufacturer's instructions.

You'll know that the interactive whiteboard is communicating with the USB interface for the Wireless Bluetooth Connection expansion module because the expansion module's light flashes green continuously.

If the expansion module's LED flashes green 14 times, and then turns red for a few seconds before repeating the sequence, the module isn't communicating with the Bluetooth-to-USB converter. Turn to Appendix B to troubleshoot.

Configuring Your Computer Settings

After all your hardware is connected, I recommend that you configure a number of computer settings that will ensure the best possible performance by your interactive whiteboard. Most of these changes can be found in the Control Panel on a PC or in System Preferences on a Mac:

- ✔ **Power settings:** Change your computer's power settings so that the monitor is turned off after one hour if there is no use and the system is put in standby mode after two hours if there is no use (see Figure 2-4). You don't want the computer to shut down during a class or meeting. You can do the same for the projector, but you'll need to follow the manufacturer's instructions; projectors vary.

- ✔ **Resolution settings:** You may need to match the resolution on your computer to the resolution on the projector if your interactive whiteboard screen shimmers or appears distorted.

  Start by checking the default resolution on the projector. You can find the resolution-setting instructions for the projector on the menu of the projector and in the projector's instructions.

  Next, go to the Control Panel (PC) or System Preferences (Mac) and adjust your monitor's resolution. Set the initial refresh rate at 60 Hz and adjust up until you find the ideal setting. You may need to adjust both to get the optimal setting.

Figure 2-4:
The Power Schemes tab of the Power Options Properties portion of the Windows Control Panel.

Downloading the Software

If your school or company has set up the interactive whiteboards, the software you need will be installed on the computer attached to the whiteboard. All you'll need to do is begin using it. You can use the Internet to access your documents if they're stored on a web-accessible server, or you can connect a USB thumb drive to your computer (or directly to some interactive whiteboards — note that not all the interactive whiteboards have USB ports) to access your work.

If you're setting up the interactive whiteboard yourself, you'll need to install the software using the CD that came with your product. It's a relatively simple process, just like installing any new software: You insert the CD into your CD-ROM drive and follow the instructions on the screen.

If your interactive whiteboard didn't come with a software CD, you may have to download the software from SMART's website (www.smarttech.com/downloads).

You can use most SMART software, including SMART Notebook software and SMART Meeting Pro software, without the interactive whiteboard. This means that you can work on your presentations at home, without being connected to the whiteboard through your work network. Don't forget that you first need to download the software on your laptop or home computer (see Chapter 5).

When you install the software to work with your interactive whiteboard, you'll also install a program called Ink Aware or SMART Ink, depending on the version you're installing. Ink Aware has been designed to work with a suite of office applications such as Microsoft Office (which includes Word, Excel, and PowerPoint) and SMART Ink works with everything — literally. Using Ink Aware or SMART Ink and your own files is a good way to start exploring the capabilities of the interactive whiteboard.

SMART Ink is enabled by default. To enable Ink Aware, follow these steps:

1. **Click the SMART Board icon in the Windows notification area and select Control Panel (Windows) or right-click the SMART Board icon in the Dock and right-click Control Panel (Mac).**

    The Control Panel window, also known as the SMART Settings screen (shown in Figure 2-5), appears.

2. **Click Configure SMART Tools.**

3. **Click Ink Aware Program Settings.**

    You can enable or disable Ink Aware for any of the software programs listed in the window.

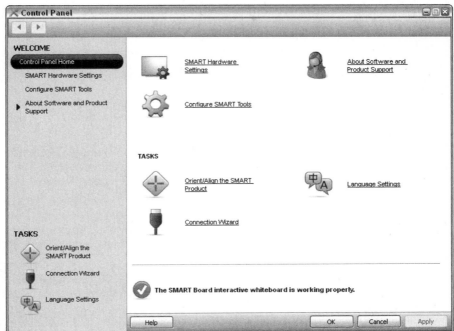

Figure 2-5:
The SMART
Notebook
Control
Panel.

4. **Make sure any programs you want to use Ink Aware with are selected.**

5. **Click OK to return to the Control Panel, click Apply, and then close the Control Panel.**

Now you're ready to experiment!

Discovering Do's and Don'ts

Each product comes with a number of precautionary warnings you should pay attention to. Usually, they're common-sense measures, like "Don't let students climb the interactive whiteboard." I won't list all the manufacturer's precautionary measures here, but you should always read and follow warnings of this nature.

However, I do want to draw your attention to a number of items the manufacturer points out in the documentation. If you don't have access to the manual or if you haven't received any training, I recommend that you take a few minutes to read the following do's and don'ts before you start using your interactive whiteboard:

✔ **Don't look directly into the light beam, and advise your audience not to do the same.** Face the interactive whiteboard straight on when you write over a projected image. When you finish, step to the side before you face your audience. Advise your audience to do the same.

✔ **Don't touch the projector, and advise your audience not to touch it either.** The projector can get very hot. You may see a speck on the board and assume it's dust on the projector, and before you know it, your fingers are on the hot surface. Use a dust cloth to clean it to manufacturer's specifications.

✔ **Only use the USB or serial interface that's recognized by the operating system and not being used by another application.** Use only the USB cables provided or recommended by the manufacturer.

✔ **Place all the pens and the eraser securely in the Pen Tray if you plan to use your finger on the interactive screen.** If you lose a pen, just place another object in the Pen Tray slot; otherwise, your interactive board will sense the missing pen and assume you're using it to write with on the interactive whiteboard.

✔ **Turn off your projector (or set it to Light Off mode) so you can view the streaks more easily as you clean the board.**

✔ **Use the interactive whiteboard as a regular whiteboard if you need more writing space in the classroom.** It's a myth that you can't write on the surface.

✔ **Don't use low-odor dry-erase markers (such as the Sanford Expo 2) on your interactive whiteboard.** They're tough to remove. Instead, use the standard, strong smelling dry-erase markers. Be sure to read the warning sign on the markers — they usually tell you to use them in ventilated areas.

✔ **Follow these tips when cleaning the surface of your interactive whiteboard:**

  • Disconnect or lock your computer before you clean your interactive whiteboard. Otherwise, you may find yourself scrambling the desktop icons or activating one of the applications when you wipe over them.

  • Erase dry ink as soon as possible. The longer you leave it on, the more effort it will take to clean it.

  • Remove dry-erase dust with a damp cloth before you start using a cleaner.

  • Use household glass cleaner to remove dry-erase markers. You can use them daily if necessary.

- Don't spray cleaner directly onto the writing surface. Spray it into a cloth and then wipe the screen.

- Don't allow cleaner to drip or flow anywhere into the Pen Tray slots or the cracks between the frames and the writing surface. You can easily forget when you're in a hurry between presentations or classes.

- Don't let your younger students clean the board. Kids get carried away with cleaning fluids, especially spray cleaners.

 If you're having a hard time removing any marks on the interactive whiteboard, find the smelliest whiteboard marker, write over the area, and then wipe with a soft cloth. The high-odor dry-erase markers contain solvents that will remove the ink.

Finding Help If You Get Stuck

If you have no luck connecting to your interactive whiteboard because Windows wasn't able to find the drivers, don't give up! Try inserting your installation software CD in your CD drive, and let the wizard walk you through installing the drivers. Make sure you install all the drivers because the default installation settings don't always include them. Then try again to install the USB HID. When you click Finish, you should see the Ready light turn red and then flash green, informing you that the controller is receiving power from the USB connection.

If you still aren't getting a connection, find the manual that came with the interactive whiteboard and make sure everything is set up correctly. You can also contact SMART Technologies technical support (see Appendix A).

 If you find that the pointer isn't aligned with your finger or pen, you need to orient your interactive whiteboard. Turn to Chapter 3 to find out all about orientation.

If your Ink Aware menus aren't appearing, turn to Appendix B to troubleshoot.

Chapter 3

Configuring Your SMART Board Interactive Whiteboard and Components

*N*ow that your interactive whiteboard is set up, you're ready to start using it. In this chapter, I show you how to orient your interactive whiteboard and where to locate the interactive tools and menu items. I also show you how to configure your interactive tools and how to customize and move the Floating Tools toolbar.

Note: This chapter assumes that your interactive whiteboard is connected and you know how to turn it on. If this isn't the case, turn to Chapter 2.

Your Interactive Whiteboard

One of the first things you need to know is how to synchronize your touch accurately with the interactive whiteboard. This is important because you need the cursor to appear where your finger or pen is positioned. SMART refers to this process as *orientation*. All this entails is aligning the projected image with the working area on the interactive whiteboard.

Orienting your interactive whiteboard

Before you can use your interactive whiteboard to deliver a fantastic presentation, you need to orient it to make sure your cursor appears where you're pressing.

I recommend that you check with both your finger and the pen. You may find that your finger is aligned and the pen may be slightly off point. If this happens, no need to panic — putting it right is quite simple.

When orientation is needed

You'll need to orient your interactive whiteboard in the following situations:

- **During initial setup:** You'll need to orient the interactive whiteboard before you can use it to activate and control applications.

- **If the interactive whiteboard or the projector is moved:** Often, even repositioning the projector may require you to go through the orientation process again.

- **If the cursor doesn't appear where you're pressing:** You want the cursor to appear where you press with your finger or pen. If it doesn't, you need to orient the interactive whiteboard.

- **If the interactive whiteboard is connected to a different computer:** Anytime you move your interactive whiteboard to a different computer, you need to reorient it.

How to orient your interactive whiteboard

To orient your 600 series interactive whiteboard, follow these steps:

1. **Go to the Pen Tray and find the Keyboard button and the Right-Click button (see Figure 3-1).**

2. **Press and hold the two buttons simultaneously until the Orientation screen (shown in Figure 3-2) appears.**

3. **Pick up one of the pens from the Pen Tray.**

4. **Firmly press the pen on the diamond-shaped graphic in the upper-left corner (refer to Figure 3-2).**

5. **When you reach the center of the target, release your pen from the surface of the interactive whiteboard.**

   When you release your touch, the orientation point registers and jumps to the next target. You'll know which target is next because the dot will change to the red cross (refer to the top-left corner of Figure 3-2).

6. **Repeat steps 4 and 5 for each target point on the screen.**

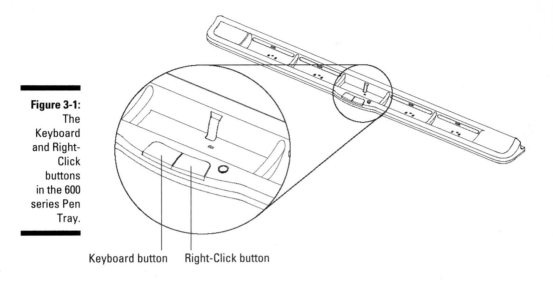

Figure 3-1:
The Keyboard and Right-Click buttons in the 600 series Pen Tray.

Keyboard button   Right-Click button

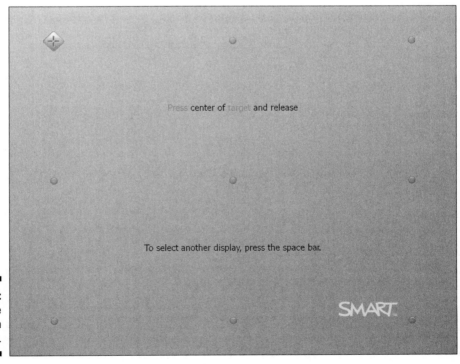

Press center of target and release

To select another display, press the space bar.

SMART

Figure 3-2:
The Orientation screen.

To orient your 800 series interactive whiteboard, follow these steps:

1. **Find the Orientation button on the Pen Tray (see Figure 3-3) and press that button.**

   The Orientation screen appears (refer to Figure 3-2).

2. **Pick up one of the pens from the Pen Tray.**

3. **Firmly press the pen on the diamond-shaped graphic in the upper-left corner.**

4. **Lift the pen from the screen at a 90-degree angle.**

   When you remove the tip, the next orientation point is highlighted.

5. **Repeat steps 3 and 4 for all the orientation points.**

   The Orientation screen closes when the process is complete.

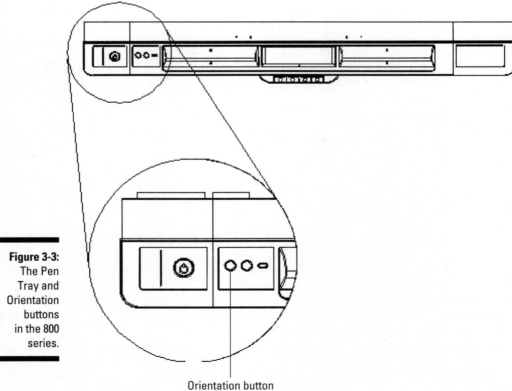

Figure 3-3:
The Pen
Tray and
Orientation
buttons
in the 800
series.

Orientation button

You can use your finger and follow the same process to orient your interactive whiteboard, but the pen is more accurate, allowing you to touch the target with more precision.

Changing the orientation settings

After orienting your interactive whiteboard, you may find that specific applications require a higher degree of precision. You can increase the orientation detail to a finer point by changing the orientation settings.

To change the orientation settings on your interactive whiteboard, follow these steps:

1. **Click the SMART Board icon in the Windows notification area and select Control Panel (Windows) or right-click the SMART Board icon in the Dock and right-click Control Panel (Mac).**

   The Control Panel window, also known as the SMART Settings screen (shown in Figure 3-4), appears.

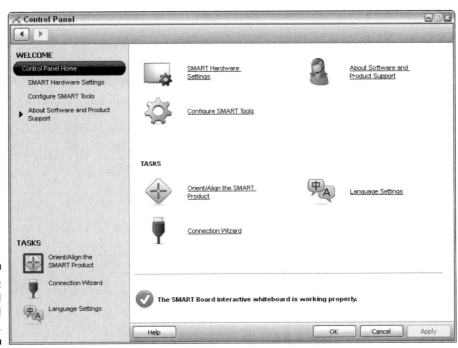

Figure 3-4: The Control Panel window.

2. **Click the SMART Hardware Settings button (refer to Figure 3-4).**

   The SMART Board options appear.

3. **From the drop-down menu, select Orientation/Alignment Settings (see Figure 3-5).**

4. **Select the Fine (20 Points) radio button (see Figure 3-6), and click Apply.**

5. **Click the Orient/Align the SMART Product button (see Figure 3-7) to begin the orientation process.**

Testing basic functionality

I know you're itching to dive in and start using your interactive whiteboard, but before you dive in, make sure that everything is working correctly.

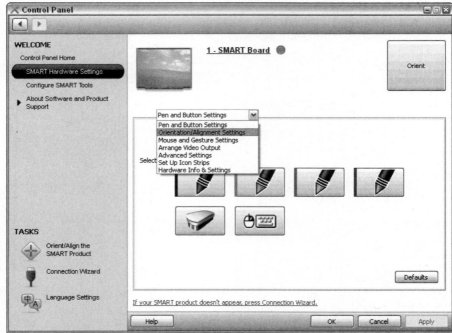

Figure 3-5:
Select
Orientation/
Alignment
Settings
from the
drop-down
menu.

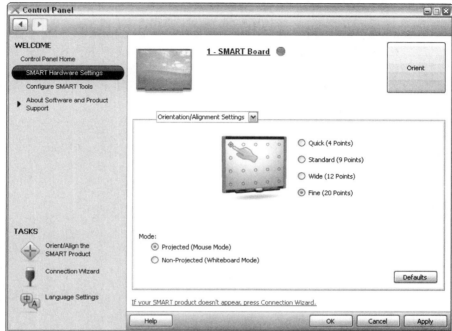

Figure 3-6: Select the Fine (20 Points) radio button.

Click here or here to begin the orientation.

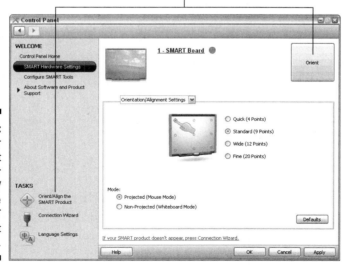

Figure 3-7: Click either the Orient button or the Orient/ Align the SMART Product button.

To run a quick check, follow these few steps:

1. **Using your finger, double-press the web browser icon (for example, Internet Explorer, Safari, or Firefox) on the desktop to open a web page.**

2. **Press the Keyboard button on the SMART Pen Tray (see Figure 3-8).**

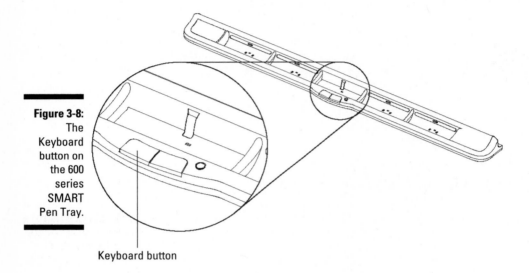

Figure 3-8:
The Keyboard button on the 600 series SMART Pen Tray.

Keyboard button

3. **Press once inside your web browser's address bar (see Figure 3-9) to select the URL.**

Press here to select web address.

Figure 3-9:
The web browser address bar.

IANA — Example domains - Windows Internet Explorer

http://www.iana.org/domains/example/

File   Edit   View   Favorites   Tools   Help   Convert   ▾   Select

4. **Using the on-screen keyboard (see Figure 3-10), type** www.google.com.

5. **Press Enter.**

Figure 3-10:
The on-screen keyboard.

When you're using the on-screen keyboard, note that each key is a single point-of-contact tool. Touch-typing or keystroke combinations, like you may use on your iPhone or tablet, aren't possible with the interactive whiteboard keyboard.

By going through these few steps, you'll be able to see if your orientation settings are enabling you to interact with the interactive whiteboard correctly.

Your Interactive Whiteboard Tools

Most of your interaction with your interactive whiteboard will involve using a number of tools with the display screen. You can use the basic tool set or the tools in preinstalled SMART Notebook software, which I cover in Part II. For the sake of simplicity, and so I don't have to cover this set of tools when I tell you all about SMART Notebook, I introduce the tool set in this section.

It may help to think of your interactive whiteboard the same way you think of your mouse and keyboard. Your mouse and keyboard are necessary devices that enable you to control applications on your computer; the interactive whiteboard is a huge computer screen that you interact with in various ways.

In this section, I cover the SMART Tools menu and the functions those tools control. Knowing where to find the tools and understanding the basics about how they work is probably one of the most important aspects of using the interactive whiteboard. The best way to do this is to start playing with the tools.

The toolbars and menus

The SMART Tools menu gives you instant access to all the utilities that enable you to operate the interactive whiteboard. To access the SMART Tools menu, do the following:

✔ **On a PC:** Click the SMART Board icon in the Windows notification area. The SMART Tools menu appears to the right of the notification area (see Figure 3-11).

✔ **On a Mac:** Click the SMART Board icon in the Dock. The SMART Tools menu appears.

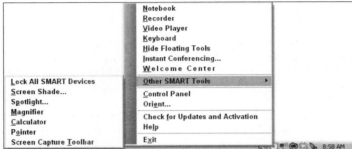

Figure 3-11:
The SMART
Tools
menu for
Windows.

If you don't see the interactive whiteboard icon in your Windows notification area or Dock, do the following:

✔ **On a PC:** Choose Start⇨All Programs⇨SMART Technologies⇨SMART Board Tools. The SMART Board icon will appear in the Windows notification area.

✔ **On a Mac:** In the Finder, navigate to Applications/SMART Product Drivers/SMART Board Tools. The SMART Board icon will appear in the Dock. Right-click the Dock icon and choose Options⇨Keep in Dock if you'd like the icon to remain there.

Using SMART Tools

As you can see from the SMART Tools menu (refer to Figure 3-11), you have a number of options:

✔ **Notebook:** See Part II of this book for more information on SMART Notebook software.

✔ **Recorder:** Enables you to record anything that takes place on your interactive whiteboard, such as training, workflow processes, or a guest speaker's presentation. You can use a microphone to add audio, control recording quality, and set the video format. Then you can share your recordings.

✔ **Video Player:** Enables you to play video files stored on your computer or view camera, VHS, CD-ROM, or DVD content. Allows you to draw or write during the presentation and capture a single video frame right into your SMART Notebook file.

✔ **Keyboard:** Enables you to type and edit text in any application right on the interactive whiteboard using the on-screen keyboard (refer to Figure 3-10).

✔ **Show/Hide Floating Tools:** Shows or hides the Floating Tools toolbar, which gives you quick access to frequently used tools (see the next section).

✔ **Instant Conferencing:** Allows you to create or join a conference without any need for third-party conferencing. You just need to use Bridgit conferencing software (see Chapter 13).

✔ **Welcome Center:** Enables you to access commonly used functions, recently accessed files, and more. Also includes a direct link to SMART Technologies online. (*Note:* This tool doesn't appear in some versions.)

✔ **Other SMART Tools:** If you select Other SMART Tools, you have the following options:

   • **Lock All SMART Devices:** Enables you to freeze or lock all SMART products in your classroom — particularly handy if you want to get your audience's attention.

   • **Screen Shade:** If you want to add suspense, use the Screen Shade to slowly reveal information. The Screen Shade can be moved up and down or right and left.

   • **Spotlight:** If you want your audience to focus on a particular area of the screen, use the Spotlight. All other material will be dulled, except where you place the Spotlight.

   • **Magnifier:** Magnifies small areas. When you select the Magnifier, two windows appear: The smaller window is the Magnifier, and the larger window displays the magnified object.

   • **Calculator:** Enables you to directly access a calculator.

   • **Pointer:** Allows you to point out important information.

   • **Screen Capture:** Allows you to capture the full screen or a selected area of the desktop. The image is automatically saved in your SMART Notebook file. *Note:* On Macs, Screen Capture is listed farther down the menu.

   • **Control Panel/SMART Settings:** Gives you access to a variety of SMART Board settings and hardware/software-related settings. Here you can adjust your interactive whiteboard settings, orient your interactive whiteboard, personalize the Pen Tray button settings, connect to a new interactive whiteboard, check for software upgrades, access the Help Center, manage Ink Aware applications, access the language settings, and manage wireless connections.

- **Orient:** Launches the Orientation screen (see "Changing the orientation settings," earlier in this chapter).

- **Check for Updates and Activation:** Launches SMART Product Update, which allows you to easily find and install new versions of SMART software.

- **Help:** Launches the SMART software online Help system.

The touch sensitivity of your interactive whiteboard enables you to operate each of these tools with your finger.

The Floating Tools Toolbar

The Floating Tools toolbar deserves its own special section because it's so handy, versatile, and useful that once you begin using it, you won't know how you ever lived without it. Even though most of the utilities are also available through the SMART Notebook menus, you'll find yourself using the Floating Tools toolbar more frequently as you transition from a novice to an expert interactive whiteboard user.

The Floating Tools toolbar should always appear on your screen when you turn on your interactive whiteboard. If you don't see the full toolbar, you should at least see the tab (see Figure 3-12).

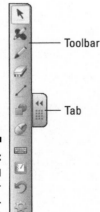

Toolbar

Tab

Figure 3-12:
The Floating
Tools tool-
bar and tab.

If you don't see either the Floating Tools toolbar or the tab on the screen, you can activate it by selecting it from the SMART Tools menu (see the "Using SMART Tools" section, earlier).

If you don't like the tools that appear on the Floating Tools toolbar, you can customize the toolbar to meet your needs. You can change the available tools, dock it to the sides of the interactive whiteboard, and move it around. By default, the Floating Tools toolbar is placed on the left side in the middle of the screen.

To customize and move the Floating Tools toolbar, follow these steps:

1. **On the Floating Tools toolbar, press the Customize button (it looks like a gear).**

   The Customize Floating Tools dialog box (shown in Figure 3-13) appears.

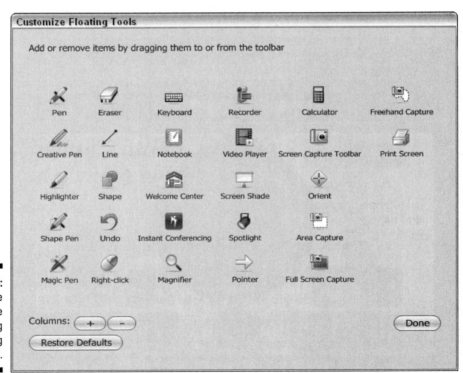

Figure 3-13: The Customize Floating Tools dialog box.

Here's what each of the tools does:

- **Pen:** Enables you to write or draw using digital ink. You can select the color by clicking it again.

- **Eraser:** Enables you to erase digital ink.

  You don't have to use the eraser. You can select the eraser by clicking on it, leave the actual eraser in its slot, use your finger to circle the area you want to erase, and then click in the middle, and everything disappears like magic.

- **Keyboard:** Launches the touch-activated on-screen keyboard.

- **Recorder:** Launches SMART Recorder, enabling you to record actions on the screen.

- **Calculator:** Opens an on-screen calculator.

- **Freehand Capture:** Lets you take a screen capture of any shape and size you want.

- **Creative Pen:** Lets you draw in a variety of funky patterns, colors, and designs.

- **Line:** Enables you to draw a line. You can also change the style of the line.

- **Notebook:** Launches SMART Notebook software.

- **Video Player:** Opens SMART Video Player.

- **Screen Capture Toolbar:** Opens the Screen Capture toolbar, enabling you to have more control over and options with your screenshots.

- **Print Screen:** Lets you print the screen.

- **Highlighter:** Enables you to highlight an area on the screen with luminous ink. You can select the color by pressing it again.

- **Shape:** Enables you to draw a formed shape, select the shape, and edit the shape.

- **Welcome Center:** Opens the SMART Notebook Welcome Center, which provides access to more tools and options.

- **Screen Shade:** Lets you reveal and conceal information on the screen.

- **Orient:** Launches the Orientation screen.

- **Shape Pen:** Recognizes shapes you're drawing and makes them perfect.

- **Undo:** Reverses your previous action.

- **Instant Conferencing:** Starts Bridgit conferencing software (see Chapter 14).

- **Spotlight:** Focuses attention on a circular area of the screen and conceals the rest.

- **Area Capture:** Takes a screen capture of a rectangular area.

- **Magic Pen:** Lets you magnify windows, write in fading ink, and do lots of other awesome stuff.

- **Right-click:** Makes your following press on the interactive whiteboard a right-click.

- **Magnifier:** Lets you expand a particular area of the screen when you draw a square around it.

- **Pointer:** Lets you draw attention to specific things on the screen.

- **Full Screen Capture:** Takes a full-screen screenshot.

2. **To add a button to the toolbar, press the icon in the Customize Floating Tools dialog box and drag the icon to the Floating Tools toolbar.**

    You can add more than one Pen, Magic Pen, Shape Pen, or Highlighter icon to the toolbar and then customize each icon with different properties (for example, multiple Pen icons with different digital ink styles).

3. **To remove a button from the toolbar, press the icon in the Floating Tools toolbar and drag it outside the toolbar.**

4. **To rearrange the buttons on the toolbar, press any icon on the toolbar and drag it to a new position on the toolbar.**

5. **To add a column, press the + button; to remove a column, press the – button.**

    The Floating Tools toolbar removes the column that's farthest to the right. It also removes the icons you've added to that column.

6. **When you're done customizing the Floating Tools toolbar, press Done.**

If you're sharing the interactive whiteboard with co-workers, you may want to return the toolbar to its default setting when you're done using it, so that you don't confuse your colleagues. To restore the Floating Tools toolbar to the default settings, on the Floating Tools toolbar, press Restore Defaults in the Customize Floating Tools dialog box, and then press Done.

Most of the tools have side menus allowing them to be customized. For example, if you press the side menu of the Pen icon, a Properties dialog box appears (see Figure 3-14), enabling you to change the fill effects and line styles for the tool. You can save the setting by pressing the Save Tool Properties button at the bottom of the dialog box, but be careful: If you press the Save

Tool Properties button, the saved setting will become the default. So, for example, if you choose to use a really thick pen in an obnoxious color for effect, you're better off *not* saving it — just use it as you need to for this particular task.

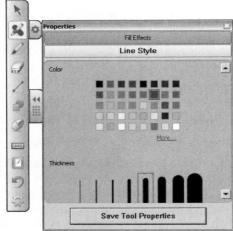

Figure 3-14:
The
Properties
dialog box.

Chapter 4

Performing Basic Tasks with Your SMART Board Interactive Whiteboard

. . . .

In This Chapter

▶ Drawing and writing directly on your interactive whiteboard

▶ Using Microsoft Office software with the interactive whiteboard

▶ Using finger and hand gestures

. . . .

*I*n this chapter, I assume that you know the capabilities of your interactive whiteboard and that you have access to one that is assembled, with the software installed and your computer connected to the Internet. This chapter asks you to roll up your sleeves and get ready for some serious hands-on practice. By the end of this chapter, you'll have gained enough interest and confidence to begin using the interactive whiteboard in your classroom or meetings, and you won't be satisfied until you experiment and discover all the functionalities and capabilities.

This chapter also shows you how to use your finger as a mouse and write on the interactive whiteboard, edit text, work with your Microsoft Office applications, add to your Office documents using SMART Ink or Ink Aware software, and access other resources.

Interacting with Your Interactive Whiteboard

After your hardware is connected and you have all the required software, you can begin playing with your new interactive whiteboard. As you begin using the interactive whiteboard, you'll be amazed by all the tools and functionalities bundled to create fantastic presentations and collaborate with others anywhere in the world. You'll also see how simple and intuitive the tools can be. Read on, and I show you how to use them.

As soon as you start your computer that's connected to the interactive whiteboard, the interactive whiteboard becomes touch sensitive, and you can start using your finger instead of the mouse. You can press anywhere on the interactive surface to interact with objects or menus — just as you do with a mouse click. For example, if you want to open a web browser such as Internet Explorer or Firefox, press the icon twice, rapidly, to launch the application. And if you need to activate a drop-down list, just press the arrow or title in the menu.

If you're not convinced of how easy it is to use, I'll walk you through a little exercise so I can prove it to you. Try this:

1. **Press the SMART Board icon in the Windows notification area (Windows) or in the Dock (Mac).**

   A menu appears.

2. **Press Notebook.**

   SMART Notebook software opens. (I cover the software extensively in Part II of this book.)

3. **Using your finger, tap the Pen icon on the toolbar, and write something in the white workspace.**

4. **When you're finished, tap the Select tool on the toolbar, and then tap anywhere on the text.**

   You see a selection box around the text, with a drop-down arrow in the top-right corner (see Figure 4-1).

5. **Just to show off handwriting recognition, press the drop-down arrow and then press Recognize.**

   Your text is converted to typed text.

6. **Choose File⇨Save to save your text.**

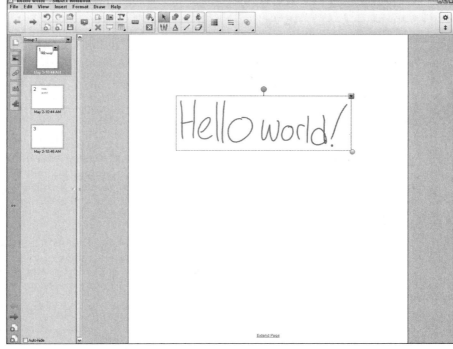

Figure 4-1:
Selected
text on the
interactive
whiteboard
is now an
object that
can be
edited.

You can use the pens from the Pen Tray to write in digital ink or the on-screen keyboard to type text directly into the file. If you want to use the keyboard, you can select the keyboard from the same menu you selected Notebook from, or press the Keyboard button on the SMART Pen Tray.

You can use the pens and eraser to write or erase digital ink on the interactive whiteboard. On a 600 series interactive whiteboard, the Pen Tray recognizes the color of the ink when you remove the pen. The color of the pen last lifted from the tray will be the one that's displayed. For example, if you're holding onto your pen and you pick up the eraser, the sensor sends a message that the ink will be erased when the board is pressed with the tool. On an 800 series Pen Tray, you push a button to pick your ink color, and the last button pressed is the color you'll get. The 800 series also automatically recognizes whether you're using a pen, finger, or eraser.

Introducing Ink Aware Applications

There are two main digital ink applications on SMART Board interactive whiteboards: SMART Ink and Ink Aware. SMART Ink is pretty new — it came out in 2012 — so if you have SMART software earlier than that, you're probably going to use Ink Aware. (See the next section for more info on SMART Ink.)

You're probably very familiar with using Microsoft Office applications, like Word, Excel, and PowerPoint. Here's some great news: SMART Technologies created Ink Aware, a feature that enables SMART Board interactive whiteboards to be integrated with a number of applications. So, when you write or draw on your interactive whiteboard in digital ink, your notes become embedded in the particular software file, such as Excel or Word, instead of being just an external note created on top of the files.

Microsoft Office applications interact very well with SMART software. You edit Office files using your finger, whiteboard pens, and drawing tools. The cool thing about this is that you can save the file, and your notes and drawing will be there the next time you need the file with your presentation.

Now that you understand this important application, you need some hands-on practice. Pick the Office application that you use most frequently for lessons or presentations, and jump to one of the following sections.

To see which software is Ink Aware on your computer, press the SMART Board icon and select Control Panel, press Configure SMART Tools, and then press Ink Aware Program Settings.

Microsoft Word

From the interactive whiteboard, go to one of your Word files or open a new document in Word. As soon as Word opens, you'll see that three new buttons appear — either integrated with the Word toolbar (see Figure 4-2) or on a separate floating toolbar located at the top under the main Word horizontal menu (see Figure 4-3). If one of the toolbars doesn't appear when you launch Word, press View⇨Toolbars⇨SMART Aware Toolbar.

SMART Aware toolbar

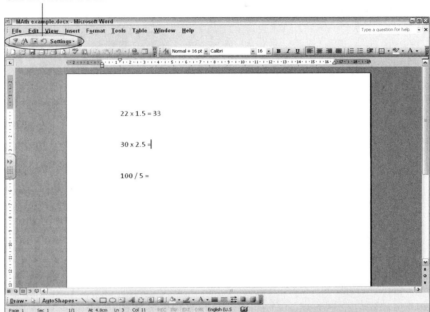

Figures 4-2:
The integrated SMART Aware toolbar in Microsoft Word.

SMART Aware toolbar

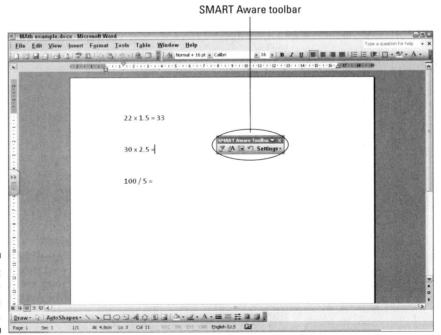

Figure 4-3:
The separate floating toolbar.

Try the following activity to get a feel for how simple and neat this software is. No doubt, you'll find many different ways of using it to meet your learning or presentation goals.

1. **Open a blank document in Word.**

2. **Using the keyboard, type a couple math problems.**

   Make sure you leave space between them so that you can work out the answer.

   If you already have a worksheet, use that instead.

3. **Place some incorrect answers after the equal sign.**

4. **Pretending that you're in front of your class, pick up one of the pens from the Pen Tray.**

5. **In the space below the problem, work out, step by step, the correct answer, writing on the display with the pen in digital ink.**

6. **Put the pen back in the tray.**

7. **Press the Insert as Image button to add the answer to the Word file.**

   Figure 4-4 shows the answer written out and the Insert as Image button circled.

Insert as Image button

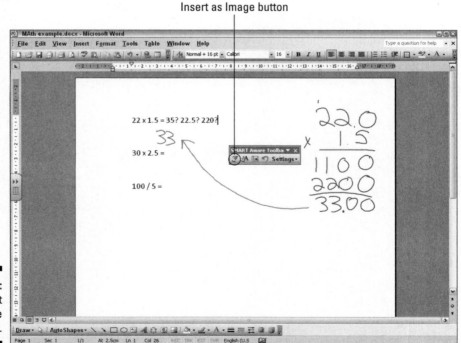

Figure 4-4:
The Insert as Image button.

If you want to insert text into the document, follow these steps:

1. **Open a Word document, touch the interactive whiteboard where you want to make a change or add a new word.**

   The cursor appears.

2. **Pick up the pen from the Pen Tray, and write the correct word on the interactive whiteboard.**

3. **Press the Insert as Text button (see Figure 4-5).**

   The handwritten text converts to typed text, right where you wanted it to appear (assuming you placed the cursor in the correct place).

You can do the same types of things in many other applications.

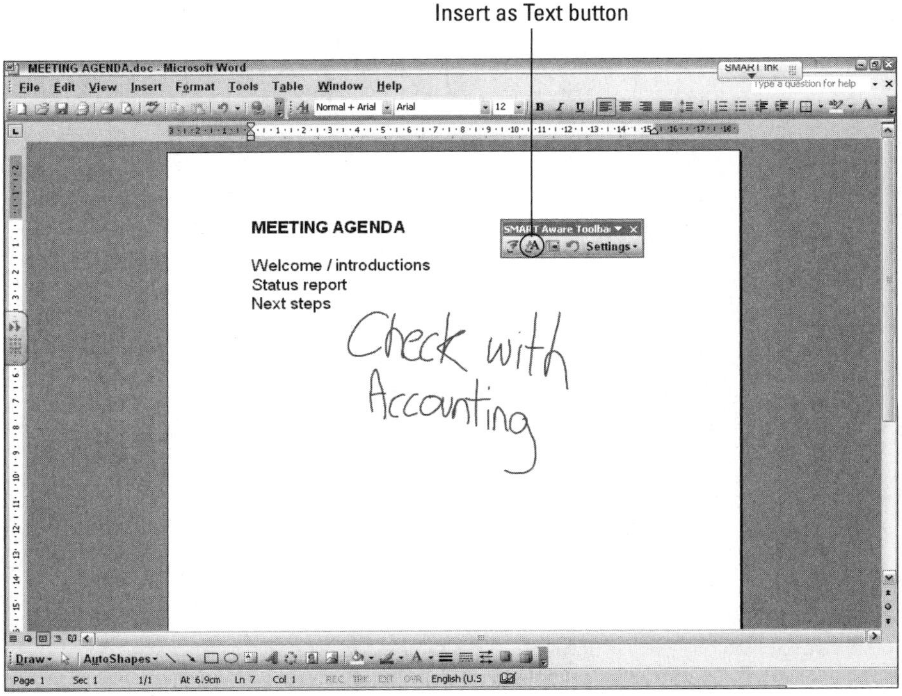

Insert as Text button

Figure 4-5:
The Insert
as Text
button.

Microsoft Excel

As with Word documents, Excel spreadsheets can be written over using a pen tool, and then the text or image can be added to the file. To get started with Ink Aware applications, open an Excel spreadsheet.

Your interactive whiteboard is like a huge computer screen. You open one of your files on the interactive whiteboard just as you would on your computer, except your finger is the mouse.

After you have the Excel file open on your interactive whiteboard, follow these steps:

1. **Take a pen from the Pen Tray and, on the interactive whiteboard, write "Meeting notes" (see Figure 4-6).**

2. **Place the pen back in the Pen Tray, and press once on *Meeting notes* to delete the note.**

Figure 4-6:
Entering
data using
Excel and
Ink Aware.

3. **Press the cell again, take the pen from the Pen Tray, and write somewhere on the board, "Action items."**

4. **Press the Insert as Text button on the Ink Aware tool menu, shown in Figure 4-7.**

Insert as Text button

The note appears in the cell, as typed text, in the color of the chosen pen (see Figure 4-8).

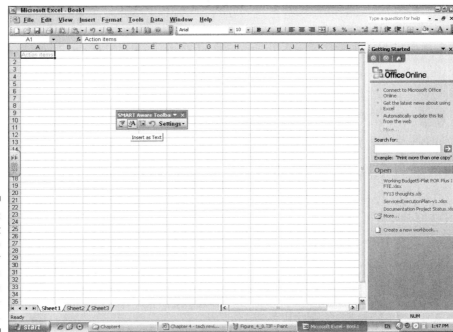

You can have Ink Aware automatically insert your written notes as an image as soon as you write them, save your notes as an image when you save the file, or clear your settings.

Microsoft PowerPoint

PowerPoint works similarly to Excel (see the preceding section). Your mark-ups can be saved either in the presentation itself or in SMART Notebook software. The only difference is that, in PowerPoint, your Ink Aware options appear on the Slideshow toolbar that you use to control your slides (see Figure 4-9). The toolbar appears automatically when you first open PowerPoint or a PowerPoint presentation.

Figure 4-9: The Slideshow toolbar.

If you have SMART Ink on your computer, this toolbar looks and behaves differently.

The best way to see how the Slideshow toolbar works is to open a slideshow and press the buttons on the Slideshow toolbar.

The center of the toolbar is a button with a down arrow (refer to Figure 4-9). This button opens the Command menu, which you'll need when working with your slideshow. The drop-down menu includes a number of important options:

- ✓ **Save Ink Notes:** Captures the image on the slide and saves it in SMART Notebook software

- ✓ **Insert as Image:** Saves your notes as an image in your PowerPoint presentation

- ✓ **Clear Drawing:** Deletes your notes from the page

- ✓ **Add Blank Slide:** Adds a new slide to your PowerPoint presentation

- ✓ **PowerPoint Commands:** Opens the PowerPoint Commands submenu

- ✓ **Settings:** Opens the Settings submenu

- ✓ **SMART Floating Tools:** Opens the Floating Tools toolbar

- ✓ **End Shows:** Ends the slideshow

Introducing SMART Ink

SMART Ink is a new and very different approach to using digital ink on an interactive whiteboard. The biggest change from Ink Aware programs is that it doesn't matter what software you're using — the SMART Ink features are available regardless of whether the program is Ink Aware. SMART Ink is included with SMART Notebook version 11 and SMART Meeting Pro version 3 (more about those programs later).

With SMART Ink, whenever you start a program on your computer, a SMART Ink toolbar appears in the title bar of the program screen. It has a drop-down arrow that opens a small menu of basic, intuitive features like ink colors, highlighter tools, and erasers. It also has a Capture button that takes a snap-shot of your screen and opens it in SMART Notebook software.

To find out about SMART Ink, the best thing to do is play! Open any program — say, your web browser — and look for the SMART Ink toolbar. Click the drop-down arrow and pick an ink color. With either your finger or a Pen Tray pen, do a little scribble on the website you're viewing. Then pick a different color and do another squiggle. Now click the Select icon from the drop-down menu and resize your browser window. Check out how the ink stays where you put it. Try dragging one of your squiggles to a different spot. Then move the window again. Last, select Capture from the drop-down menu and check out how the screenshot appears in SMART Notebook software.

There's lots to learn with SMART Ink. Check out www.smarttech.com/support and pick your operating system from the SMART Ink drop-down list for help. For training, check www.smarttech.com/trainingcenter for awesome videos and downloads.

Experimenting with SMART Tools

In Chapter 1, I explain the toolbar located on the left side of your interactive whiteboard, the SMART Notebook tools, and the difference between the various SMART tools. The SMART Tools menu (shown in Figure 4-10) gives you access to the tools. Although I explain each tool in more detail later in this book, the interactive whiteboard is so simple to use and in many ways so intuitive that I want you to go ahead and try a few tricks.

Make sure you have access to the Floating Tools toolbar. If you can't see it, go to the SMART Board menu in the Windows notification area or Mac Dock, and select Show Floating Tools. It should appear on the left side of your screen. Then follow these steps:

1. **Using your finger, press the Pen.**

2. **Start writing on the board with your finger, as shown in Figure 4-11.**

3. **Pick up the eraser from the tray and wipe it clean.**

4. **Now pick up one of the pens, and write all over the board.**

5. **With your finger, tap the eraser, and then draw a large circle around the scribbles.**

6. **Tap your finger in the middle, and watch everything disappear — like magic.**

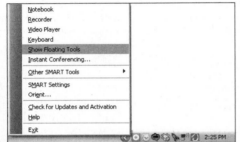

Figure 4-10:
The SMART Tools menu.

Figure 4-11:
Writing on your interactive whiteboard.

If you require more precision than you can get with your finger, pick up one of the pens and use it instead of your finger. If you want to use different ink color, remove the pen from the Pen Tray with the color you want (600 series) or press the button with the color you want on the Pen Tray (800 series). You can write over images and applications. Doing so won't change the original file.

If you want, you can save what you've written using screen capture. For example, if you had an organization chart, and you started to take notes and reassign roles, you could capture your changes without altering your original document.

To erase your notes, you have two options:

✔ You can pick up the eraser, choose the thickness from the Floating Tools toolbar eraser button, and move it over your writing on the interactive whiteboard.

✔ You can draw a circle around the area, tap inside the circle, and watch everything disappear. If you need to erase a large area, this method is the quickest. *Note:* You also can use the eraser to draw this circle, but it saves you time not having to pick it from the tray if you can use your finger.

When you use your finger on the interactive whiteboard, you need to leave the pens in the Pen Tray.

A number of the SMART Board interactive whiteboards have a feature called touch recognition, which can tell whether you're using a pen or your hand, and even whether you want to erase or write in digital ink! If you use your finger, it'll assume you want to click. If you select a Pen tool on the Floating Tools toolbar but leave the pen in the Pen Tray, it'll assume you want to use your finger to write digital ink. And if you use the palm of your hand instead of your finger, it'll assume you want to erase. All this without having to pick up anything from the Pen Tray!

You can easily figure out if your interactive whiteboard has touch recognition and turn it on by following these steps:

1. **Press the SMART Board icon in the Windows notification area (Windows) or in the Dock (Mac).**

   A menu appears.

2. **Press Control Panel (SMART Settings).**

   The Control Panel window appears.

3. **Press SMART Hardware Settings.**

4. **Select Mouse and Gesture Settings from the drop-down list (see Figure 4-12).**

Mouse and Gesture Settings option

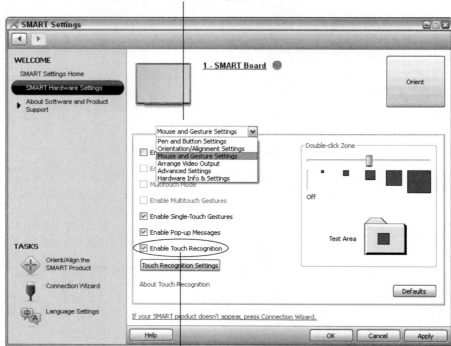

Enable Touch Recognition option

Figure 4-12:
The Control
Panel with
Gesture
settings
highlighted.

5. **Select the Enable Touch Recognition check box.**

   If that option is grayed out or doesn't appear, your interactive white-board doesn't have touch recognition.

Now you're ready to experiment. Try writing with your fingers and erasing with your hands. Have fun! And just think — no need to wash your hands because they're full of ink or chalk. Remember those days?

Part II

Creating Lessons and Presentations with SMART Notebook Collaborative Learning Software

The 5th Wave   By Rich Tennant

"If only their ideas were as smart as the board they're presenting them on."

In this part . . .

The fun truly begins here, because this part is where you find out how to use and become an expert with SMART Notebook software, the product that enables your interactive whiteboard to come to life. Spend some time reading through these chapters. Allow yourself time to explore, ponder, and create.

Chapter 5 walks you through installing the software and adjusting the settings. Chapters 6 and 7 show you how to work with and organize files and pages. When you know where things are and understand how everything is organized, the rest falls into place. In Chapter 8, I show you how to work with all kinds of cool objects and add links, sound, and animation to the objects. Chapter 9 is all about using your own content so that you don't need to rewrite or rebuilt anything new. In Chapters 10 and 11, you find out how to use content from SMART resources or create new content and share it with other interactive whiteboard users around the world. I push you to stretch your knowledge and imagination and introduce skills that will help you add another dimension to your presentations or lessons.

Chapter 5

Getting Acquainted with SMART Notebook Software

In This Chapter

▶ Getting SMART Notebook software on your computer

▶ Taking a tour of SMART Notebook software

▶ Writing using Ink Aware and non–Ink Aware programs

SMART Notebook is collaborative software that enables you to create incredible lessons or presentations for your audience. It's written to work with the touch screen, adding another dimension to the capabilities of the interactive whiteboard. Earlier in this book, I explain how your interactive whiteboard is an extension of your computer. By adding SMART Notebook software to the mix, you have at your disposal various `.notebook` files, each containing accessories and applications to which you can add geometric shapes, graphics, text, and pictures. You also can add content compatible with Adobe Flash, and add to the files and manipulate your presentation to create exactly what you want and need.

In this chapter, I show you how to download and install SMART Notebook software. Then I guide you through the various menus and tools that will empower you to dive into the rest of the chapters in this part and create really cool interactive presentations. Finally, I show you how to write using Ink Aware and non–Ink Aware programs.

Installing SMART Notebook Software

SMART Notebook software usually is installed when you start using your interactive whiteboard. If SMART Notebook software wasn't installed when your interactive whiteboard was set up, you'll need to install the software yourself. I provide installation instructions for the three operating systems in the following sections.

If you don't have the installation disc that came with your product, you can download SMART Notebook software online:

1. **Go to** www.smarttech.com/downloads.

2. **From the Choose a Version drop-down list under SMART Notebook Collaborative Learning Software, select the version for your operating system (see Figure 5-1).**

Figure 5-1:
The Choose a Version drop-down list.

The version number may have changed, but all that matters is that you choose the version for your operating system at the top of the drop-down list.

You're taken to a page that provides more information about specific software bundled with the download, shown in Figure 5-2.

3. **Click the Download button.**

You're taken to a page where you have to indicate whether you have a product key or whether you're just wanting to download the 30-day free trial of the software.

4. **Select the appropriate radio button, fill out the corresponding form, and click Start Download.**

5. **Save the file to a temporary location.**

You can use SMART Notebook software without the interactive whiteboard to prepare your presentation at home. All you have to do is download the software onto your home computer. You have a 30-day free trial period; after 30 days, you'll need to enter the license key for the product your organization purchased.

Figure 5-2:
More information about software bundled with the download.

SMART Notebook software can be installed on computers running Windows, Mac OS X, or Linux. The `.notebook` files you create with the software can be opened on other operating systems, as long as SMART Notebook software is installed.

Before you can install SMART Notebook software, you need to get a hold of a product key. To get the key follow these steps:

1. **Go to** 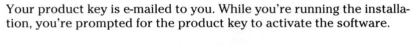 `www.smarttech.com/NB10ProductKey`.

2. **Enter your SMART product's serial number and your e-mail address and click Submit.**

3. **Fill in the information on the form.**

4. **Download and run the installation.**

   Your product key is e-mailed to you. While you're running the installation, you're prompted for the product key to activate the software.

You must activate the software before the 30-day free trial runs out.

Windows

To install SMART Notebook software, follow these steps:

1. **Insert the DVD into your computer or double-click the installation file you downloaded from the SMART Technologies website.**

   The Education Software Installer dialog box appears (see Figure 5-3).

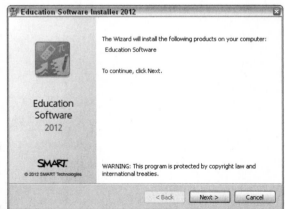

Figure 5-3: The installation wizard.

If the dialog box doesn't appear, using Windows Explorer search for \ **CDBrowser.exe**.

2. **Click the Install button.**

   The installation wizard launches.

3. **Follow the steps in the wizard, clicking Next until you finish the process.**

Mac

To install SMART Notebook software, follow these steps:

1. **Insert the DVD into your computer or double-click the installation file you downloaded from the SMART Technologies website.**

   The Education Software Installer dialog box appears.

2. **Follow the steps in the wizard, clicking Continue until you finish the process.**

Linux

You have three different options to install SMART Notebook software on a Linux operating system:

- ✔ Autopackage
- ✔ Debian packages
- ✔ RPM packages

The processes slightly differ, so I recommend that you download the manual to guide you through the processes. For more information, go to www. smarttech.com/kb/135949.

The Autopackage system is what you'll be most likely using unless you're running the software on a network. SMART Notebook uses the Autopackage system, for which you need a root password. Go to www.autopackage.org/howtoinstall.html to get more information.

Knowing Where to Begin

To start using SMART Notebook software, just double-click the SMART Notebook icon on the desktop. You also can access the software from the Start menu (on a PC) or from the Dock (on a Mac), or you can launch it from the Floating Tools toolbar.

If this is the first time you've used the software, a tutorial opens. After the initial launch, a blank file opens when you launch the software, enabling you to create a new file or open an existing file.

Before you start opening files and playing with the software, I recommend that you first familiarize yourself with four basic sections of the application:

- Page area
- Tabs
- Menu
- Toolbar

Page area

The page area is your main workbench where you can display content from a selected page, create new content, and work with objects. Every time you open SMART Notebook, a single empty page will open for you to start working with. Figure 5-4 shows the main work area, the toolbar with the default page opened, and the sidebar, which lists your pages and allows you to sort them.

Try using the blank page to post a welcome message and use it as an interactive activity to engage everyone. For example:

> Welcome, everyone. Please walk up to the board, sign your name, and tell me what you want out of this session.

Figure 5-5 shows what this may look like.

To create a new slide, click the + (insert) icon in the toolbar.

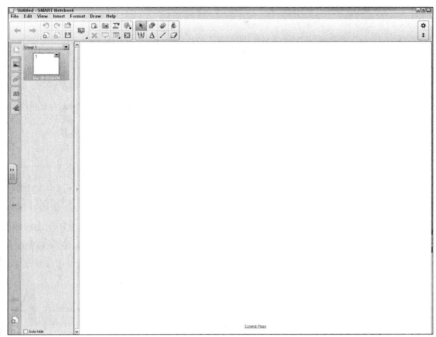

Figure 5-4:
The main
work area
with menus.

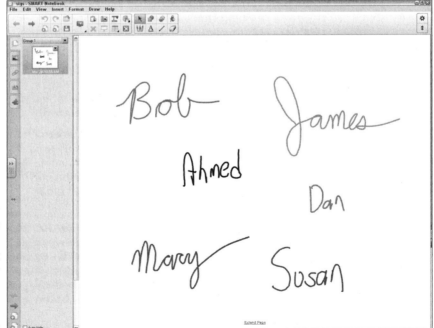

Figure 5-5:
Interact
with your
audience in
this simple
activity.

Tabs

On the left side of the main page area, to the left of the pages column, are several tabs (the exact number depends on what options you selected to install). Each tab has a unique functionality related to the pages and files you create.

If your default settings have been changed, you may see the tabs on the right side of your screen.

Page Sorter tab

Similar to the functionality of PowerPoint, the Page Sorter tab lists all the pages in each file as small document icons. As you make changes to each page, SMART Notebook instantly updates the pages. To open the Page Sorter, click the tab that looks like a stack of paper.

You can customize the Page Sorter tab — for example, you can

- ✔ **Move it from one side to the other.** The default position is left side of the screen. To move it, click the Move Sidebar double-headed arrow button.
- ✔ **Resize it by clicking the same arrows again.**
- ✔ **Hide it by selecting the Auto Hide check box on the bottom of the column.** To display it again, click the Page Sorter tab.

There are a number of things you can do with the Page Sorter, such as:

- ✔ Display pages
- ✔ Create pages
- ✔ Clone pages
- ✔ Clear pages
- ✔ Delete pages
- ✔ Rename pages
- ✔ Rearrange pages
- ✔ Move objects from one page to another
- ✔ Group pages

Use the drop-down arrow next to each page (see Figure 5-6) to display the various options.

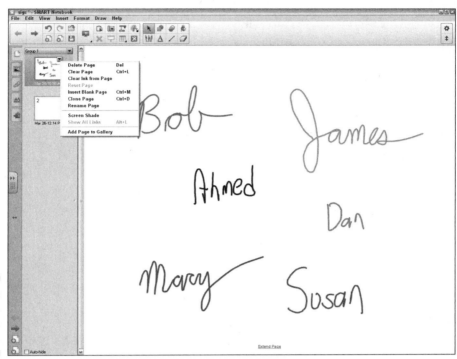

Figure 5-6:
The drop-
down menu
for a page.

Gallery tab

SMART Notebook software is bundled with similar content to clip art. The
Gallery tab includes clip art, backgrounds, multimedia content, game and
lesson files, and templates, as well as creative pages available for use in presentations and classroom lessons. The Gallery tab also enables you to access
online resources.

To open the Gallery tab, click the tab next to the Gallery icon, which looks
like a painting. Notice that the sidebar is divided into two sections. The top
section lists four distinct folders, enabling you to organize and search your
resources (see Figure 5-7). Notice the plus sign next to each of the four categories. Clicking the plus sign opens the next subsection. You can open the
subcategories in the top level by clicking another plus sign or by opening
them in the lower half of the sidebar. You'll use the lower half of the sidebar
to add specific content from the Gallery to your slides (see Figure 5-8).

Figure 5-7:
The Gallery
tab opened.

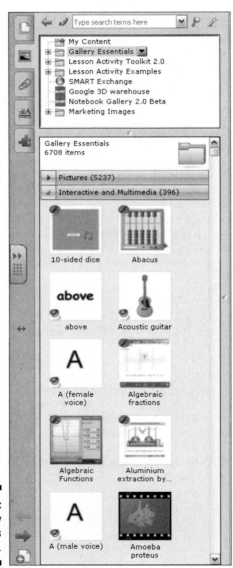

Figure 5-8:
The Gallery
categories
opened.

In general, the four Gallery categories include the following (these categories vary slightly in SMART Notebook versions 10 and 11):

- ✔ **My Content:** A place for you to store all the info you create. This content is specific to your computer and what you add to the default Gallery.

   Make sure to back up this folder at the end of the school year so you don't lose the content.

- ✔ **Gallery Essentials:** A variety of content for you to use with your presentations.

- ✔ **Gallery Sampler:** A sample of the Gallery installed with the default application. If you don't see the Gallery Essentials category, contact your IT department and ask them to install the rest of the Gallery.

- ✔ **Lesson Activity Toolkit:** A cool set of tools. SMART Technologies boasts that there are over 714 different tools to help you create interactive presentations and lessons. These templates are easy to edit, save, and add to your files. Each activity includes an edit button and a question mark that walks you through how to build the activity.

Let's use one of the activities from the Lesson Activity Toolkit so you can see how simple it is. Follow these steps:

1. **Open SMART Notebook.**

2. **Click the Gallery icon in the sidebar menu.**

3. **Click Lesson Activity Toolkit and then click Activities (see Figure 5-9).**

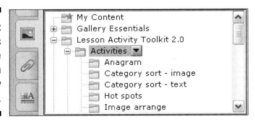

Figure 5-9:
Activities
under the
Lesson
Activity
Toolkit.

4. **Click Multiple Choice.**

   You should see a set of questions in the lower section when you select Interactive and Multimedia (see Figure 5-10).

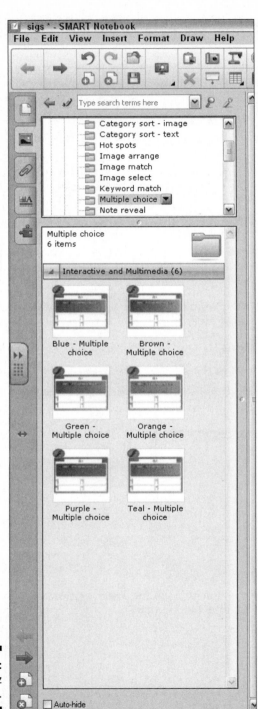

Figure 5-10:
Your quiz
choices.

5. Double-click one of the questions (I selected the blue option).

It appears in the main viewing area.

6. Click Edit, add your own questions, select the answer from the menu (see Figure 5-11), and click OK.

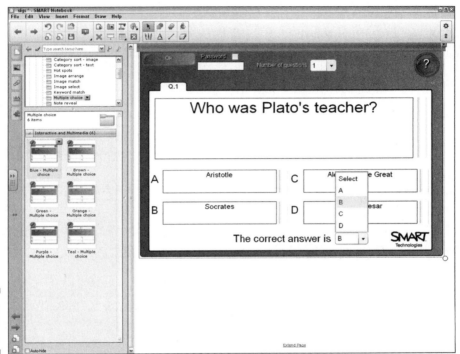

Figure 5-11:
A completed
quiz.

7. Check to make sure you have the right answer.

Figure 5-12 shows that I selected the wrong answer, and SMART Notebook tells me the correct answer.

When you select a category, the lower half of the sidebar displays subfolders of the types of files located in the subcategories:

✔ Pictures

✔ Interactive and Multimedia

✔ Notebook Files and Pages

✔ Background themes

✔ 3D objects

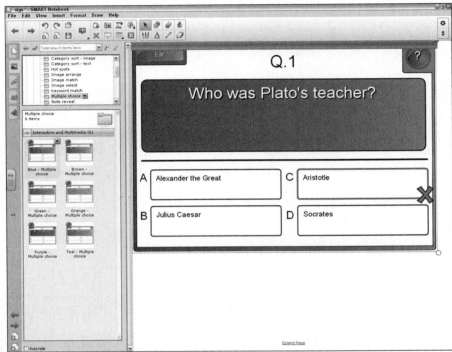

Figure 5-12:
The wrong
answer.

A number tells you how many files are located in the folder. For example, in Figure 5-8, you see "Pictures (5237)" and under it, "Interactive and Multimedia (396)." Note that this subcategory is opened and you see the various files you can add to your presentation.

You can manipulate the Gallery tab, making it convenient for you to work with the various resources. Move it from one side of the window to the other by clicking Move Sidebar, resize the width by dragging the border left or right, or hide it when you aren't using it by selecting the Auto-hide check box. (You can display it again by clicking the Gallery icon.)

Adding info to your slide

Knowing what's available for you to use from the Gallery tab and how to find the information is just the first step in being able to create great activities. Now you need to know how to add information from the Gallery to your slides. You have two options:

- You can double-click the content.

- You can drag and drop the content into the opened slide (Notebook page).

Each file can be saved as a SMART Notebook file or in another format (such as a PDF). I discuss SMART Notebook files in Chapter 6 and 7 and objects in much more detail in Chapter 8.

I know what you're thinking: You want a concrete example of the activities I keep talking about. Here's an example, using my own personal nemesis, time. A fun way that you can teach students about time is by displaying a digital clock and asking them to manipulate an analog clock to move the hands to display the time. You can then ask students to play a time game on the board and set up a game to see who beats the clock. Go to `www.netrover.com/~kingskid/clock/clock7hour.html` to play this game. While students are taking turns playing the game, bring up Google Earth (`http://earth.google.com`) and zoom in on Greenwich, London, United Kingdom; find the museum; and explain the concept of Greenwich mean time. If you prepare in advance, find a school with a SMART Board interactive whiteboard in another part of the world (perhaps Greenwich, London), and use the conferencing functionality to combine your lesson with a class in England!

As you can see, you can accomplish a lot with the software and hardware. SMART Technologies provides you with extensive resources to help you create incredible activities. Why spend hours reinventing the wheel when you have resources free to use at your fingertips? I talk more about finding and using content from SMART Gallery and the SMART Exchange website in Chapters 9 and 10.

Attachment tab

You can attach copies of files, shortcuts to files, and links to web pages using the Attachment tab (see Figure 5-13). This feature makes it easier for you to access a variety of resources while you're presenting. The attachment can be represented as small sliding tabs, appearing in color or as links.

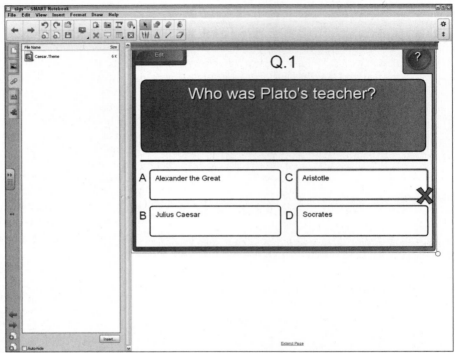

Figure 5-13:
The
Attachment
tab.

To attach a file or link, follow these steps:

1. **Click the Attachment tab (the icon that looks like a paper clip).**

2. **Click the Insert button at the bottom of the column.**

   A menu opens with three options:

   • Insert Copy of File

   • Insert Hyperlink

   • Insert Shortcut to File

3. **Browse to or type the location of the file or hyperlink you want to attach, select the file, and click Open or OK.**

As with the other tabs, the Attachment tab can be moved to either side of the screen by clicking Move Sidebar. You can hide it by selecting the Auto-hide check box. (You can display it again by clicking the Attachment tab.)

Properties tab

The Properties tab (shown in Figure 5-14) has two main functions:

- ✔ **Format Object:** The options available are dependent on what you select. For example, if you select a shape, you may have only fill effect options. Generally, you'll be able to change line styles, fill effects, and text styles, in addition to enabling digital ink, transparencies, and animation of objects. I show examples and discuss this in more detail in Chapter 8.

- ✔ **Page Recording:** Enables you to add recordings to your current page. For example, you can show a graph on a page and record your voice explaining what the graph represents.

You can move the Properties tab from one side of the SMART Notebook software window to the other. You can hide the Properties tab when you aren't using it by selecting the Auto-hide check box, and resize the Properties tab by dragging the border or clicking and dragging the sidebar to move it left or right.

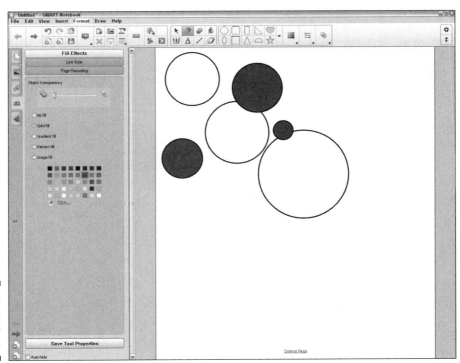

Figure 5-14:
The Properties tab.

Menu

Located at the top of the opened SMART Notebook screen, you'll see the menu with standard commands that enable you to work with all kinds of files. The menu items include File, Edit, View, Insert, Format, Draw, and Help — all standard and recognizable menu items used in most software applications.

Toolbar

The tools located at the top right, under the menu, provide you with numerous options to interact with the software. You can use these tools to get creative and bring your interactive pages to life.

You can customize the SMART Notebook toolbar to make it easier to access the buttons you use the most. If you need to add or remove toolbar buttons or reorder any of them, follow these few steps:

1. **Place your cursor anywhere on the SMART Notebook software toolbar and right-click.**

   The Customize Toolbar dialog box (shown in Figure 5-15) appears.

   Note that the tools and the toolbar itself look different in SMART Notebook versions 10 and 11. Also, if you chose to install additional plug-ins or accessories for SMART Notebook software, you may have additional or different tools than the ones shown in Figure 5-15.

2. **If you want to add a button to the toolbar, select the icon and drag it to the toolbar.**

3. **If you want to remove a button from the toolbar, select the icon and drag it to the Customize Toolbar dialog box.**

4. **You can reorganize the toolbar by clicking an icon and dragging it to a new position on the toolbar.**

5. **When you're finished, click Done.**

   You can restore the default buttons by clicking Restore Default Toolbar.

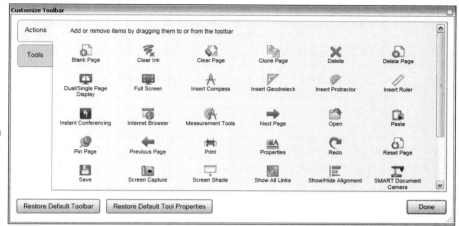

Figure 5-15:
The
Customize
Toolbar
dialog box.

Writing and Drawing in Ink Aware Programs versus Non–Ink Aware Programs

You likely have numerous documents created in programs such as Word, Excel, and PowerPoint. To be able to bring these documents to life, you don't need SMART Notebook software. SMART Technologies developed Ink Aware and SMART Ink software for that. One of these programs will be available to you, depending on which version of SMART software you install.

Ink Aware programs recognize industry-standard applications such as those in Microsoft Office and display a small toolbar. When you write or draw on the interactive board displaying the file (for example, an Excel spreadsheet), it becomes a component of the file instead of just an external annotation over the file. (I explain how to use Ink Aware in Chapter 2.)

SMART Ink software lets you write over any screen, regardless of whether the program is Ink Aware. You can mark up anything you see on your display using digital ink.

When you use software that's Ink Aware, you can insert anything you draw or write on the screen as part of the file instead of writing or drawing *over* the file.

Non-Aware applications create content or objects using the interactive white-board software and save it in SMART Notebook files or as PDFs.

Your interactive whiteboard and SMART Ink software enable you to add text or ink notes into non-Aware applications. For example, you can create a writing activity by showing your students a badly written blog by linking to it; then you can ask your students to underline the grammatical errors in this blog. You can save the marked-up blog in a file and ask your students to rewrite it. You can make it more fun by setting up a quiz in SMART Notebook software using the sentences from the bad blog and the corrected blog. The SMART Notebook Gallery has many games and quizzes you can easily edit to create topic-based activities.

Go ahead and try this simple activity. (This procedure is a little different depending on what version of software you have. If things look a little different than described here, check out the Help system for the software for more detailed instructions.)

1. **Open the website you want to annotate.**

2. **Select a colored pen from the Pen Tray and write, underline, circle, or use whatever annotation method you usually use to write on the inter-active whiteboard.**

3. **From the SMART Ink drop-down menu on the toolbar, select Capture (see Figure 5-16).**

   A screen capture with your notes appears in SMART Notebook or SMART Meeting Pro software with your notes. You can save it as a PDF or as a .notebook file.

If you touch the interactive whiteboard after writing on it and then place the pen back in the Pen Tray, the annotations you made will disappear. If this happens, open the Floating Tools toolbar and click the Restore Annotation button.

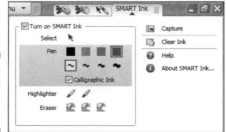

Figure 5-16: The SMART Ink drop-down menu.

Chapter 6

Creating and Working with SMART Notebook Files

• •

In This Chapter

▶ Seeing what a SMART Notebook file is

▶ Creating, opening, saving, printing, exporting, and attaching files

• •

*I*n Chapter 5, you discover the basics of SMART Notebook software. In this chapter, you start creating your presentations and lessons by seeing how to create files and make them work for you. I start by outlining the differences between files, groups, and pages — tricky concepts for people new to SMART Notebook software. Then I fill you in on all the basics important to working efficiently and effectively with the software.

Educators and SMART Technologies have done a lot of work to make your life easier by creating lessons, graphical components, and game templates that get you started.

Note: SMART Notebook software has different versions that are similar but have slightly different features and functions. The most common versions are 10 and 11. If your screen doesn't look exactly like the images in this chapter, you may have a different version. Usually, the screen elements are the same, just in different places — poke around the screens and the Help system (choose Help⇨Contents) for more information.

Exploring SMART Notebook Files

A SMART Notebook file, which has a .notebook file extension, is similar to other files you're used to working with, such as Microsoft PowerPoint, Microsoft Publisher, and OpenDocs files. Each .notebook file is comprised of a series of pages and can be saved in a number of different formats and exported.

However, the difference between the applications you're familiar with and .notebook files is that within each file, you can create groups of related pages with different objects and properties, adding a dimension to your pages unique to this software. These groups of pages are known as — drumroll, please — *groups*. Groups are useful if you have many pages in your file. (Chapter 7 covers grouping pages in greater detail.)

Other powerful features of .notebook files, and good reasons for using them, are the following:

- You can save and print .notebook files as you can in any other software.
- You can use templates and import .notebook files ready to use with your class or business.
- You can save the files as PDF, HTML, or graphic files.
- You can use .notebook files on computers running Mac OS X and Linux, as well as Windows. SMART Notebook software is cross-platform.

Poking around the SMART Notebook window

Open SMART Notebook software by double-clicking the SMART Notebook icon on your desktop or on the Floating Tools toolbar. If you click the New Page icon (it looks like a page with a green plus sign) on the toolbar at the top of the screen, a new page appears under the default open page.

The toolbar at the top of the screen and the tabs on the left side of the Page Sorter are the main gadgets and devices for you to work with. They allow you to manipulate and bring life to your pages. (If you aren't familiar with these tools, turn to Chapter 5.)

Figure 6-1 shows the basic workspace. Everything I cover in this chapter is related to this workspace.

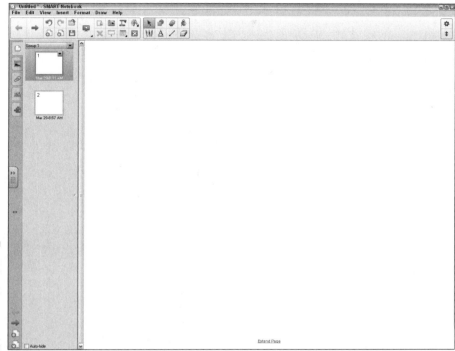

Figure 6-1:
SMART
Notebook
software
open, with
two pages.

The Page Sorter

The Page Sorter is a vertical column on the side of the screen that enables you to display your new pages and groups. Each page is represented by a thumbnail image. The current page you're working on is displayed with a rectangle in a different color (usually blue) around the page, as well as a drop-down menu with extra functionality for that page. By default, the Page Sorter appears on the left side (refer to Figure 6-1).

If you don't see the Page Sorter when you open the software, choose View⇨ Page Sorter or click the Page Sorter tab on the far left side of the screen.

You can use the Page Sorter to

- ✔ Display all the pages you're working with
- ✔ Jump from page to page
- ✔ Rearrange your pages

✔ Access attachments

✔ Move all kinds of objects between pages

✔ Clone pages

I describe each of these functionalities in more detail in Chapter 7.

Working with SMART Notebook Files

Now that you know what a SMART Notebook file looks like, you need to know how to work with files. In this section, I walk you through opening, saving, exporting, and printing files, as well as attaching files to e-mail messages.

Creating a new SMART Notebook file

To create a new SMART Notebook file, choose File⇨New. A .notebook file will open with a first page.

Opening an existing SMART Notebook file

If you want to open an existing .notebook file, follow these steps:

1. **Choose File⇨Open.**

   The Open dialog box appears.

2. **Select the file you want to open, and click the Open button.**

   The file opens.

Saving a SMART Notebook file

To save a file, follow these steps:

1. **Choose File⇨Save or File⇨Save As.**

   The Save or Save As dialog box (shown in Figure 6-2) appears.

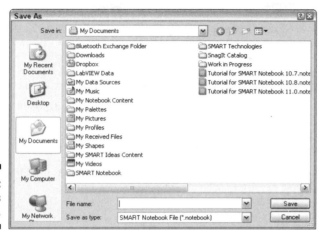

Figure 6-2:
The Save As
dialog box.

2. Give your file a name and click OK.

Note that the file will be saved in your default directory, as a `.notebook`
file. If you want to save the file in a different directory or on another
drive, just locate that directory or drive and save the file there.

You can set up SMART Notebook software to save a file automatically, after
you start interacting with a new or different page or after a specific period of
time. This feature can be very useful if you're on a network computer and your
network has a tendency to shut down, or if you're working on a computer that
isn't stable. To set up SMART Notebook software to save a file automatically,
follow these steps:

1. Choose File⇨Timed Saves.

The Timed Save Wizard dialog box (shown in Figure 6-3) appears.

Figure 6-3:
The Timed
Save Wizard
dialog box.

2. **Select the Every Time I Move to a Different Page radio button, or select how often you would like your file to be saved (1 minute, 5 minutes, 15 minutes, or 30 minutes).**

3. **Click Next.**

   Now you get to choose which file type you want your file saved as.

4. **Select the file type by selecting one of the radio buttons: Web Page, PDF, Time Stamped PDFs, Image Files, PowerPoint, or Notebook Document (see Figure 6-4).**

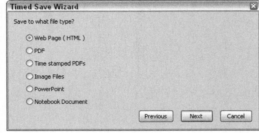

Figure 6-4:
Select the file type you want your file automatically saved to.

5. **Click Next.**

   The Save As dialog box appears, enabling you to save your file automatically in a specified folder.

6. **Find the folder where you want to save the new file.**

7. **Give your file a name and click Save.**

   The file is automatically saved.

To cancel automatic file saving, follow these steps:

1. **Choose File⇨Timed Saves.**

   The Timed Save Wizard dialog box (refer to Figure 6-3) appears.

2. **Select the Do Not Save the Document Automatically radio button.**

3. **Click Next.**

   The Timed Save Wizard dialog box closes.

Exporting SMART Notebook files

You can export SMART Notebook files to a variety of formats, covered in this section. Although you may lose some of a file's interactive capabilities if you export it as, say, a PDF, exporting as a PDF will enable you to open the file on any computer, regardless of whether it has SMART Notebook software installed.

If you include pictures, for best results export the file as HTML or PDF. SMART Notebook files that use gradient, pattern, and image effects may appear without the pattern, but a solid fill may or may not appear correct. Experiment or don't use gradients or patterns if you know you'll need to export the file.

Exporting as a PDF file

To export as a PDF, follow these steps:

1. **Choose File⇨Export⇨PDF.**

   The Export PDF dialog box (shown in Figure 6-5) appears.

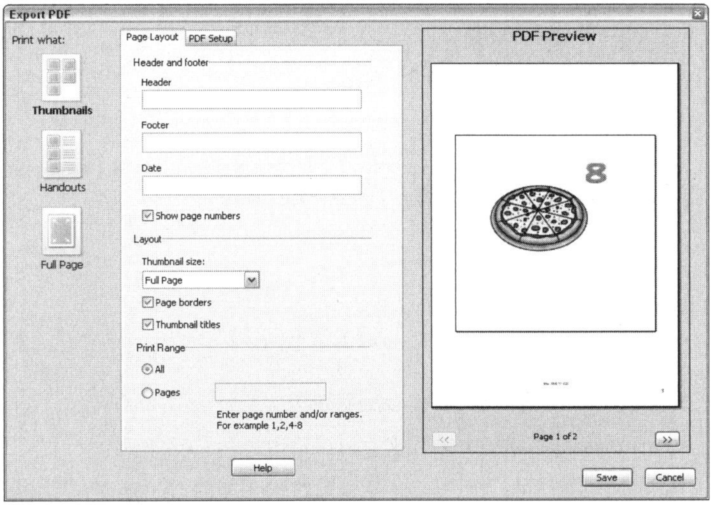

Figure 6-5:
The Export PDF dialog box.

2. **On the Page Layout tab, select Thumbnails, Handouts, or Full Page.**

3. **On the Page Layout tab, set any other options you want.**

   In the Header and Footer section of the tab, you can add the header text in the Header field, the footer text in the Footer field, and the current date in the Date field. If you want to show page numbers in the PDF, select the Show Page Numbers check box.

In the Layout section of the tab, if you chose Thumbnails or Handouts in Step 2, you see a Thumbnail Size drop-down menu where you can select the size of the thumbnails you want. If you want borders around each thumbnail, select the Page Borders check box. If you want a title under each thumbnail, select the Thumbnail Titles check box.

In the Print Range section of the tab, select the All radio button to include all pages or select the Pages radio button and enter the page numbers you want to export (for example, 3, 4, 8–10).

4. **When you're done setting the options on the Page Layout tab, click Save.**

    The Print as PDF dialog box appears.

5. **Find the folder you want to export the file to.**

6. **Type the name of the file in the File field.**

7. **Click Save.**

Exporting as an HTML file

To export as an HTML file, follow these steps:

1. **Choose File⇨Export⇨Web Page.**

    The Save As dialog box appears.

2. **Click the Browse button, select the folder you want to export the file to, and type a name in the Filename field.**

3. **Click Save.**

Exporting as a picture file

To export as a picture file, follow these steps:

1. **Choose File⇨Export⇨Image Files.**

    The Export Image Files dialog box appears.

2. **Click the Browse button and select the folder you want to export the file to.**

3. **In the Image Type drop-down list, select the picture format.**

4. **In the Size drop-down list, select the picture size.**

5. **Click OK.**

Exporting as a CFF file

If you're working with other programs and they support the interactive whiteboard Common File Format (CFF), you can export a CFF file from that program and then import that CFF file into SMART Notebook software, and vice versa. A number of cool games and education files are saved in the CFF format, and CFF files can be used cross-platform.

To save a file to CFF, follow these steps:

1. **Choose File➪Export➪CFF.**

   The CFF Files dialog box appears.

2. **Click the Browse button, select the folder you want to export the file to, and type a name in the Filename field.**

3. **Click Save.**

You can also import CFF files.

Exporting as a PowerPoint file

To export as a PowerPoint file, follow these steps:

1. **Choose File➪Export➪PowerPoint.**

   The PowerPoint Files dialog box appears.

2. **Click the Browse button, select the folder you want to export the file to, and type a name in the Filename field.**

3. **Click Save.**

You can import PowerPoint files, too (see Chapter 9).

Exporting files automatically

SMART Notebook software allows you to export .notebook files to a variety of formats, including HTML files and PDFs, automatically. You can set the exporting to occur after you display a different page or after a specified number of minutes.

SMART Notebook software doesn't include attachments, so if you use pictures in your file, export as a web page or PDF.

To export a file automatically as a web page or PDF, follow these steps:

1. **Choose File⇨Timed Saves.**

   The Timed Save Wizard dialog box (refer to Figure 6-3) appears.

2. **Select the Every Time I Move to a Different Page radio button, or select how often you would like your file to be exported (1 minute, 5 minutes, 15 minutes, or 30 minutes).**

3. **Click Next.**

   Now you get to choose which file type you want your file exported as.

4. **Select the file type by selecting either Web Page or PDF (refer to Figure 6-4).**

5. **Click Next.**

   The Save As dialog box appears, enabling you to save your file automatically in a specified folder. The file will be automatically exported to that folder as you specified.

The default file format for SMART Notebook versions 10 and 11 is .notebook; for versions 8, 9.0, and 9.1, the file format is .xbk. If you're working with older interactive whiteboard software, or taking your format to another location and you don't know what version they have, you may want to save it in both formats and/or as a PDF. The .xbk format doesn't support some of the objects and properties in SMART Notebook 10.

Printing files

You can print a whole .notebook file or select a specific page in a .notebook file to print. You can print the pages as thumbnails, handouts, or full pages.

To print a .notebook file:

1. **Choose File⇨Print.**

   The Print dialog box (shown in Figure 6-6) appears.

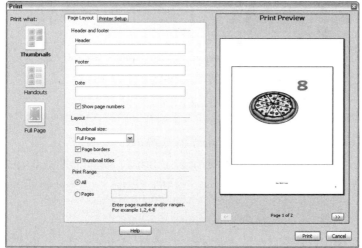

Figure 6-6:
The Print
dialog box.

2. **On the Page Layout tab, select Thumbnails, Handouts, or Full Page.**

3. **On the Page Layout tab, set any other options you want.**

   In the Header and Footer section of the tab, you can add header text in the Header field, footer text in the Footer field, and the current date in the Date field. If you want to show page numbers on your printout, select the Show Page Numbers check box.

   In the Layout section of the tab, if you chose Thumbnails or Handouts in Step 2, you see a Thumbnail Size drop-down menu where you can select the size of the thumbnails you want. If you want borders around the thumbnails, select the Page Borders check box. If you want a title under each thumbnail, select the Thumbnail Titles check box.

   In the Print Range section of the tab, select the All radio button to include all pages or select the Pages radio button and enter the page numbers you want to print (for example, 3, 4, 8–10).

4. **Select the Printer Setup tab.**

5. **Choose the print setting, printer, and the number of copies.**

6. **Click Print.**

Attaching files to e-mail messages

You can send your `.notebook` file (or a version of it — for example, a PDF) by attaching it to an e-mail message. I often send myself files if I'm working from a remote computer and want to make sure I have the file ready to use at my fingertips.

To attach a `.notebook` file to an e-mail message, follow these steps:

1. **Choose File⇨Send To⇨Mail Recipient.**

   Your default mail program opens with a new e-mail message.

   If the file hasn't been saved, SMART Notebook software saves it for you as a temporary file called `Untitled.notebook`.

   The file is attached to the e-mail message.

2. **Type the address of the person you're sending the message to and a subject line and message (if you want), and then send the message.**

To attach the file as a PDF, follow these steps:

1. **Choose File⇨ Send To⇨Mail Recipient (As PDF).**

   Your default mail program opens with a new e-mail message.

   If the file hasn't been saved, SMART Notebook software saves it for you as a temporary file called `Untitled.pdf`.

   The file is attached to the e-mail message.

2. **Type the address of the person you're sending the message to and a subject line and message (if you want), and then send the message.**

Pay attention to the file size before you send your message. If you used a lot of pictures in your file, the file size could be huge. You can reduce picture sizes to reduce the overall file size (see Chapter 8).

Chapter 7

Creating and Working with SMART Notebook Pages

In This Chapter

▶ Finding out how to create and clone pages

▶ Rearranging pages, grouping pages, and more

▶ Fine-tuning your pages to meet your needs

SMART Notebook pages make up the files discussed in the previous chapter. They are the core, the powerhouse, of your lessons and presentations. A SMART Notebook page is like a page in a PowerPoint presentation or a Word document, except it has extensive flexibility to make your audience active participants in your presentations and lessons.

You can organize each new page in the Page Sorter, create new pages, clone existing pages, and delete pages. You have full editing capabilities and more, for all basic tasks. This chapter shows you the ins and outs, giving you skills that will enable you to prepare exceptional lessons and presentations. When you begin using SMART Notebook software and realize the extensibility it adds to your presenting and learning goals, you'll never go back to presenting without an interactive whiteboard and SMART Notebook software at your side. As one of my colleagues said, when he started using the interactive whiteboard in his business classes, "There's no going back."

Note: Various versions of SMART Notebook software are available. The most common versions are 10 and 11. They have very similar functions and tools, but the buttons and icons are in slightly different places — although it's usually pretty easy to find them. If the instructions in this chapter (which are based on version 11) seem a bit off, you may have version 10. I'm sure you'll be able to figure it out, but if you need help, choose Help⇨Contents in SMART Notebook software to find out more about your version.

Creating, Displaying, and Cloning SMART Notebook Pages

To create a new SMART Notebook file, open SMART Notebook software; a new blank page opens by default. If you've already created a file, open the file by choosing File➪Open.

In the following sections, I show you how to create pages, display pages, and clone pages.

Creating pages

When you first open the software, a new blank page appears by default. If you want to add a new, blank page to a file, you have a couple options. One of the easiest ways is to click the Add Page icon on the toolbar (the icon looks like a page with a green plus sign). The new page appears as a thumbnail below the current page (see Figure 7-1).

The other way to create a new page is to use the Page Sorter. To insert a page using the Page Sorter, follow these steps:

1. **Make sure the Page Sorter is visible (you should see it on the side of the screen).**

   If the Page Sorter isn't appearing, click the Page Sorter tab on the left side of the screen, and the Page Sorter appears on the left with a default page.

2. **Click the thumbnail of the page after which you want the new page to appear.**

   The new page appears *after* the page you selected.

3. **Click the thumbnail's menu arrow, and select Insert Blank Page (see Figure 7-2).**

   The new blank page appears.

Page Sorter tab

New Page icon

New Page thumbnail

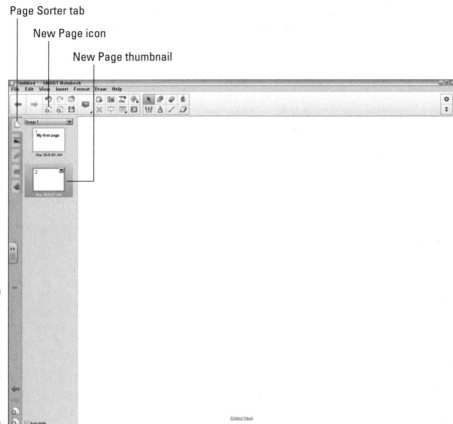

Figure 7-1:
The New
Page icon,
the Page
Sorter tab,
and the new
page
thumbnail.

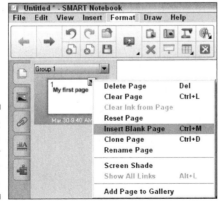

Figure 7-2:
Using the
Page Sorter
to create a
new page.

When you get comfortable adding and editing new pages, you can use the keyboard shortcut to create a new page. Instead of using the drop-down arrow in the Page Sorter, just make sure the thumbnail is selected and then press Ctrl+M; the new page appears.

Displaying and zooming in and out of pages

SMART Notebook software gives you options to resize the pages, move from page to page, and zoom in and out of a page.

Resizing pages

You can display your page in Full Screen view and it expands, filling the whole screen. Note that everything else on the screen disappears if you use the Full Screen mode. You also can use a dual-page display, enlarge the screen from 50 percent to 300 percent, or change the length and/or width of the page.

To resize a page, click the View Screens button to the left of the red X on the toolbar, located at the top of the page (see Figure 7-3). A drop-down menu appears, displaying resizing options. If you choose the Full Screen option, a small, full-screen toolbar appears, enabling you to move from page to page, return to the default screen size, access a menu with more editing options, and select a SMART Pen.

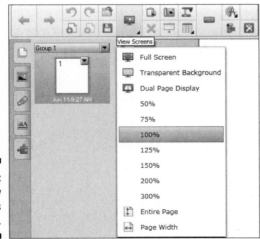

Figure 7-3:
The View
Screens
button.

Moving between pages

Select the page you want by clicking on it. (You know the page has been selected because a border appears around it.) To display the next page, click the Next Page icon (a big left-pointing arrow) or, if you're using your interactive whiteboard, simply swipe your finger across from right to left to move forward and from left to right to return to previous pages.

Zooming in and out of pages

You can zoom in and out by selecting Zoom from the View menu item and then the magnification level (see Figure 7-4 where I zoomed 150 percent on the map of Russia). If you want to use the interactive whiteboard's entire page, select Entire Page and it fits your display. This feature is most impressive when you're playing with Google Earth or showing a video.

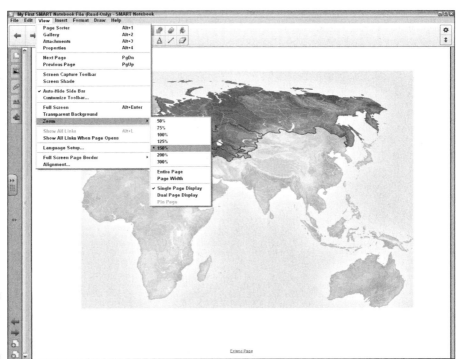

Figure 7-4:
Zooming in
on a page.

 An even easier way to zoom in on a page is to use multi-touch gestures to zoom in and out. Just position your fingers on the interactive whiteboard page, and drag your two fingers in opposite directions to zoom in (see Figure 7-5, top) and toward each other to zoom out (see Figure 7-5, bottom).

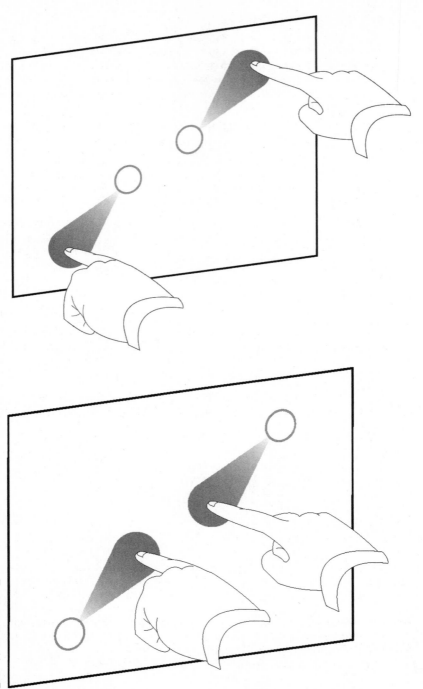

Figure 7-5:
Using
gestures
to zoom in
(top) and out
(bottom).

Cloning pages

If you create a nice layout that you want to use with every page, and you just want to change the text, instead of re-creating the page, you can duplicate it. This is called cloning, and it saves you lots of time.

If you clone pages that contain media such as video, sound, or links or attachments, you clone only the content — you have to add the media separately.

To clone a page follow these steps:

1. **If you can't see the Page Sorter, click the Page Sorter tab.**

2. **Select the thumbnail of the page you want to clone by clicking it.**

    You'll know it's selected because a border appears around the thumbnail, and the drop-down arrow on the page appears.

3. **Click the thumbnail's drop-down arrow.**

    The drop-down menu appears.

4. **Select Clone Page.**

    The new page appears under the cloned page.

You can clone as many individual pages as you want.

Working with SMART Notebook Pages

In this section, I fill you in on more techniques that enable you to work with your pages. An abundance of tools is bundled with SMART Notebook software. If you understand how to put these tools to work for you, you'll be able to work more efficiently and effectively.

Rearranging pages

When you've finished creating a number of pages and you're working on preparing your class or presentation, you may need to rearrange the order of the file. It's a simple four-step process:

1. **When you open SMART Notebook, click the Page Sorter tab if the Page Sorter isn't already visible.**

    You also can find the Page Sorter by choosing View⇨Page Sorter or pressing Alt+1.

2. **Click the thumbnail of the page you want to move.**

   A blue border appears around the thumbnail and a drop-down arrow appears on the thumbnail.

3. **Drag the thumbnail down (or up) to where you want it to be in the sequence of the Page Sorter.**

   Notice in Figure 7-6 that as you're dragging the thumbnail, a blue line appears where you intend to position the new page.

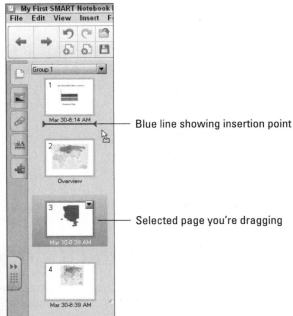

Blue line showing insertion point

Selected page you're dragging

Figure 7-6:
Rearranging
pages.

4. **Release the thumbnail.**

   Your page will be placed in the new position.

Grouping pages

Grouping pages in a file is very useful if you have a lot of pages and you jump around in your presentation or lesson. Grouping allows you to get to a specific group and page quickly.

Creating a group

Creating a group is easy:

1. **When you open SMART Notebook, click the Page Sorter tab if the Page Sorter isn't already visible.**

2. **Press the first group's menu arrow, and then select Edit Page Groups.**

   If this is your first group, it's displayed above the first thumbnail (see Figure 7-7).

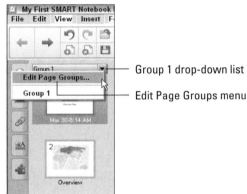

Group 1 drop-down list

Edit Page Groups menu

Figure 7-7:
Edit Page
Groups.

Notice that, by default, all your pages are displayed (see Figure 7-8). The groups appear as blue bars, and pages appear as thumbnails.

Renaming a group

To rename a group, follow these steps:

1. **Click the blue bar, click the drop-down arrow, and select Rename Group (see Figure 7-9).**

   The blue bar becomes editable.

2. **Type the name of the group.**

Figure 7-8:
A group
with pages.

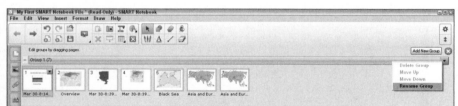

Figure 7-9:
Adding a
name to
your group.

Creating another group

To create another group:

1. **On the right side, above the first group blue bar, press the Add New Group button.**

   A new blue bar group appears with a default page, as shown in Figure 7-10.

2. **Rename the group as described in the preceding section.**

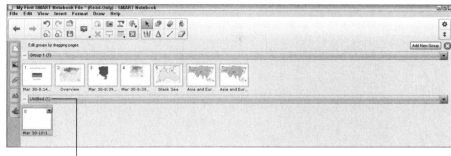

Figure 7-10:
A new
group.

New group appears

Working with groups

When you have more than one group, you can move pages between groups and within groups:

- ✓ **To move pages from group to group:** Select the thumbnail, and drag it below or above the blue line, depending on where you want to move it.

- ✓ **To reorder pages in a group:** Select the thumbnail, and drag it to where you want to position it in the group. You'll see the blue line as when you were moving the thumbnails in the Page Sorter.

- ✓ **To rearrange the order of groups:** Select the blue bar of the group you want to move, and drag it above or below the group. You also can change the order by selecting the group's drop-down menu and selecting Move Up or Move Down (see Figure 7-11).

New group moved up

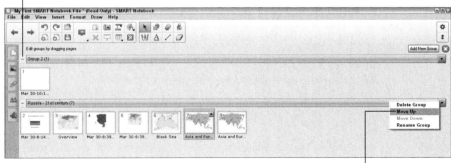

Figure 7-11:
Rearranging
the order of
groups.

Move up menu

All pages are numbered sequentially in the file. If you delete a page, SMART Notebook software rearranges the pages. The page numbering continues sequentially, even if they're located in different groups. For example, if Group 1 contains pages 1 through 12, Group 2 will start with page 13.

You can jump to different groups by using the drop-down arrow on the Page Sorter group label. The drop-down arrow displays the groups and the name of the first page in the group. This allows you to jump quickly to various groups and pages when you're giving your presentation or delivering a lesson or lecture.

Deleting a group

If you want to delete a group, move all the pages into a new group. When a group is empty, SMART Notebook software automatically deletes the group and keeps its pages, moving all its pages to different groups.

To delete a group and all its pages, click the drop-down arrow on the group bar and select Delete Group. All pages within the group are deleted.

Renaming pages

As soon as you create a page, SMART Notebook software automatically gives it a default name using the date and time you created it. It takes only seconds to rename each page, and trust me, those names will be useful when you're accessing the pages during your presentation or organizing it — especially if your files contain a large number of pages.

To rename a page, follow these steps:

1. **When you open SMART Notebook, click the Page Sorter tab if the Page Sorter isn't already visible.**

2. **Double-click the page's name.**

   A small white box appears with the date.

3. **Enter the new name for the page in the field.**

4. **Click anywhere (for example, on the main page area or Page Sorter).**

   The name on the page is changed.

Recording pages

You can record your actions on the current page. This feature is similar to the recording capabilities in PowerPoint. Using the page recording utility in SMART Tools allows you to record only to the current page.

This tool is slightly different from the SMART Recorder, which allows you to record your voice as well as the whole interactive whiteboard screen or any portion of the screen. I discuss the SMART Recorder in Chapter 12.

To record a page, follow these steps:

1. **Select the Properties tab (the icon looks like a color palette with some text and lines).**

2. **Click Page Recording (see Figure 7-12).**

3. **Click the Start Recording button.**

   Notice that the button is replaced with the Stop Recording button, and a red circle appears on the top-left corner of the page you're recording over (see Figure 7-13).

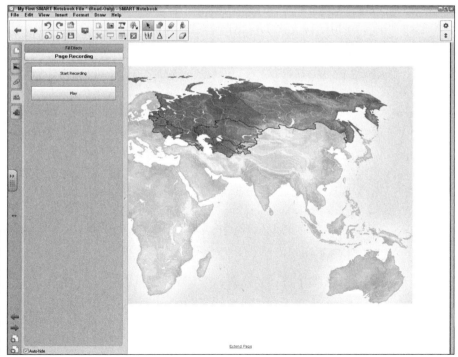

Figure 7-12:
The Page Recording sidebar with the Properties tab opened.

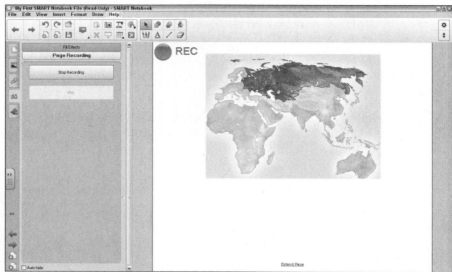

Figure 7-13:
Recording
enabled on
the page.

4. **Record onto the page, and then click the Stop Recording button.**

   Notice that the buttons switch back to Start Recording and Play.

   To play a page recording, display the page, and if the recording was success-
   ful, a playback toolbar will be displayed on the page, as shown in Figure 7-14.
   Press Play. You have access to the standard Playback toolbar: Play, Pause,
   Rewind, Forward, and Stop.

Figure 7-14:
The
Playback
toolbar.

If you want to remove your recording, just click Close on the toolbar.

Deleting pages

You can easily delete a page from the file you're working with, and you won't
need to start over and re-create a whole new file. Here are your two options:

✔ **The Delete Page button:** Select the page you want to delete and press the Delete Page button, which looks like a page with a red X on it.

✔ **The Page Sorter:** Select the thumbnail of the page you want to delete, and click the drop-down arrow. From the drop-down menu, select Delete Page.

If you feel uncomfortable deleting pages, you can just clear all the page's objects and start over (see the next section).

Clearing pages

You can remove all the content from your pages without deleting them by deleting specific objects from the page or clearing everything.

You won't be able to clear a locked object without unlocking it first. I discuss how to unlock objects in Chapter 8.

To clear all objects from the page, follow these steps:

1. **Display the page you intend to clear.**

2. **Choose Edit⇨Clear Page.**

   You also can select the page menu by right-clicking on the page, as shown in Figure 7-15, or, from the Page Sorter, select the page drop-down arrow and select Clear Page.

Figure 7-15:
The drop-down menu from which you can select Clear Page.

This option isn't available if there are no objects on the page.

To clear all digital ink objects from the page, select the page and choose Edit⇨Clear Ink from Page. You also can right-click the page and use the Page Sorter to clear the ink from the pages.

If there is no digital ink on the page, the option is disabled and grayed out.

Customizing Pages

To create more interesting and captivating pages you have lots of editing tools at your disposal. By default, when you create a new page, it appears in boring white. In this section, I show you how to make the pages more interesting, professional looking, or just plain fun.

Keep in mind your presentation goals when you're creating your page. The possibilities are endless, but using too much razzmatazz can be counterproductive.

Working with page backgrounds and themes

SMART Notebook allows you to customize your pages using various colors, patterns, pictures, or themes. Themes allow you to define a specific custom background for your pages in a .notebook file.

There are two ways you can apply and define the way the background appears in your pages: the Properties tab and the Gallery tab.

Using the Properties tab

The Properties tab enables you to add solid colors, gradients combining two colors, patterns, or pictures. Follow these steps to apply a background:

1. **Choose Format⇨Background.**

   The Properties tab opens showing Fill Effects options (see Figure 7-16). You also can access this tab by selecting a page and clicking the Properties tab (the icon looks like a color palette with some text and lines).

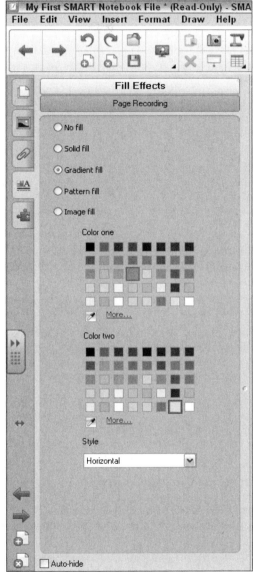

Figure 7-16:
The Fill
Effects
tab with
Gradient Fill
selected.

2. **Select a fill style.**

You have a number of options:

   • **No Fill:** Leaves it as is.

- **Solid Fill:** You can decide which colors in the palette you like — you have 40 colors to choose from. You also can click More and click the color in the dialog box. Or click the eyedropper and select a color on the page.

- **Gradient Fill:** Follow the same procedure as you did for Solid Fill, except you're choosing two colors.

- **Pattern Fill:** Use the up and down arrows on the top and bottom of the Pattern menu to select the pattern you like. A blue box appears around the pattern. Select the foreground and background colors as well.

- **Image Fill:** Click Browse and the Insert Image File dialog box appears. Browse and select the image you want as a background, and then click Open. *Note:* If the image is too large, you'll get a warning message. You will need to reduce the image size and then try to insert it.

To remove a background from a page, choose Format⇨Background. The Properties tab opens showing the Fill Effects options. Select No Fill, and the background is removed from your page.

Using the Gallery tab

The Gallery tab gives you some more flexibility than the Properties tab. I cover the Gallery tab in greater detail in Chapters 9 and 10, but here I show you how to set the theme. Using the Gallery tab, you can set a background or theme for a page, every page in a group, or all the pages in a file.

To set a background or theme, follow these steps:

1. **Select the Gallery tab on the left side of the screen (the tab icon looks like a painting).**

2. **If you've already created backgrounds and themes, select My Content in the Gallery's category list (the upper pane of the Gallery) to view your own backgrounds and themes. If you haven't created your own backgrounds and themes, click Gallery Essentials or Gallery Sampler, which contain lots of options that came with your installation.**

3. **Click Backgrounds and Themes (in the lower pane of the Gallery tab).**

   You see thumbnails of a number of different backgrounds and themes.

4. **Click the thumbnail of the theme you want to apply.**

5. **Select the thumbnail's drop-down arrow and select Insert in Notebook (see Figure 7-17).**

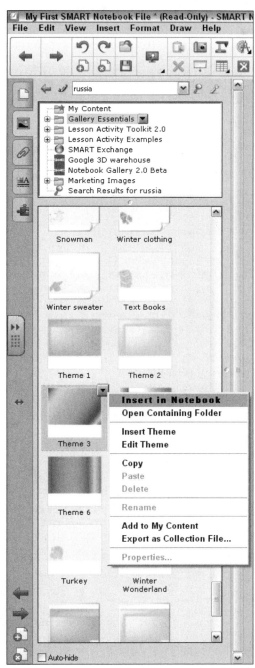

Figure 7-17:
Select
Insert in
Notebook.

6. **In the Insert Theme dialog box, select whether you want to insert the theme on all pages, all pages of the current group, or the current page only (see Figure 7-18).**

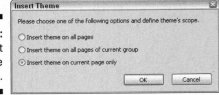

7. **Click OK.**

The theme appears on the pages you selected.

To remove a background or theme, right-click the theme image on your page itself in the main work area. (Don't right-click an object or ink you've added.) Select Delete Theme.

You can create your own themes, add them to your Gallery, and apply them to a page, group, or every page in the file. To create your own theme, follow these steps:

1. **Choose Format⇨Themes⇨Create Theme.**

A blank new theme appears on the page.

2. **In the Theme name field, type the name of your theme.**

3. **Select the Theme Text Style box on the page, and use the options on the Properties tab to format how you want default text for this theme to appear.**

4. **Set the background as you did for the page earlier in this chapter.**

5. **Decide whether you want to add and modify objects on the theme.**

See Chapter 8 for more information.

6. **Click Save in the lower-right corner of the page.**

This theme will now be saved in the My Content category on the Gallery (see Figure 7-19).

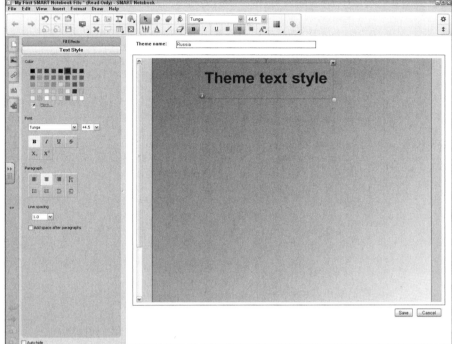

Figure 7-19:
The
background
theme I
chose from
the My
Content file
located in
the Gallery.

To create a theme based on a page, you also can follow these steps:

1. **Choose Format⇨Theme⇨Create Theme from Page.**

2. **In the Theme Name field at the top, type a name for the theme.**

3. **Press Save.**

   The theme will now be saved in the `.notebook` directory and available in the My Content category.

Displaying student page borders

Your students may have access to the SMART Notebook Student Edition (SE) software, if your school or organization installed it on student computers.

SMART Notebook SE is specially designed for students and is part of SMART's larger group of education software known as SMART Classroom Suite™ interactive learning software. It isn't covered in detail in this book, but you can find lots more information online at www.smarttech.com.

SMART Notebook SE is useful because each student has files accessible on his or her computer, and you see students' computers as small thumbnail icons on yours. Students can interact with games, answer questions, or take quizzes and tests. For your own management, it's useful to be able to display a student page border, which may be different from your own pages, especially if you're using a larger laptop, and your students are using smaller laptops or tablets. You can use the Student Page Borders feature to make sure that what you display on the interactive whiteboard looks good on their smaller screens. This is very important, especially if questions or answers on your display don't show up on their computers.

Note: This is most useful if you're using SMART Response™ software as part of SMART Classroom Suite interactive learning software.

To display a student border, follow these steps:

1. **Choose View⇨Alignment.**

   The Alignment dialog box appears.

2. **Click the Student Page Border tab.**

   If you don't have the SMART Classroom Suite installed, you won't have this tab.

3. **Click the Show a Border around the Area That Will Be Visible in SMART Notebook SE during an Assessment check box.**

4. **Click the Preset Value and from the drop-down list select a screen resolution.**

   Alternatively, select Custom Value and add the width and height of the screens your students will be using in the boxes.

5. **Click OK.**

   A colored border appears on the page around the area your students will be viewing on their computers. This border is different from your borders.

Chapter 8

Creating and Working with Objects

In This Chapter

▶ Creating objects

▶ Working with objects

*I*n this chapter, I dive into the nitty-gritty details of SMART Notebook software by explaining all there is to know about objects. An *object* is every element (the core interactive feature on a page) that you create with the `.notebook` tools or import into your pages. In essence, it's what you bring into your lesson or presentation. Objects are your foundation for being able to create interactive pages.

In the second part of this chapter, I explain how SMART Notebook software allows you to bring life to your objects. I show you how to rotate, resize, animate, group, link to the web, and add sound.

Creating Basic Objects with SMART Notebook Software

In this section, I cover all the basic objects available to you and explain how you interact with them.

Writing or drawing objects on a page

Digital ink is a type of object that enables you or your audience to add free-hand text to your SMART Notebook pages. You can use digital ink to add content to your `.notebook` files or use it in your class or presentations to engage others to participate (for instance, for a brainstorming session or as an icebreaker). Digital ink software includes a number of different ink types (see Table 8-1).

Table 8-1	Digital Ink Pens and What They Can Do	
Digital Ink Pen	*What It Looks Like*	*What It Can Do*
Pen		Draw or write anything on your .notebook pages. You can use different colors and styles. Useful for adding notes or creating slides in a presentation. You can even set up digital ink to fade.
Calligraphic Pen		Teachers have found this pen useful for teaching handwriting. Add fancy text to presentations or use it as a signature.
Crayon		The Crayon is useful with younger children or if you and your audience want to have fun when annotating .notebook pages. Useful for brainstorming session — each group or person gets a color.
Highlighter		I use the Highlighter more than the other digital ink pen options. When you import or link to articles and want to highlight something on your slides, use this pen type.
Creative Pen		The Creative Pen lets you add colorful and original elements to your presentation. In addition to being able to draw in spray paint, rainbows, gold stars, happy faces, and more, you can define your own styles using images you upload. It's a fun way to engage your audience in a collaboration or presentation.
Magic Pen		This pen has loads of cool stuff like fading ink, a spotlight window, and a magnification window. A powerful presentation tool.
Shape Recognition Pen		This pen figures out what shape you're drawing and makes it perfect.

The Pen tool

To use the Pen tool, follow these steps

1. **Open SMART Notebook by clicking the SMART Board icon on your desktop and selecting Notebook or by clicking the Notebook icon on the Floating Tools toolbar.**

2. **Open an existing .notebook file or use the default page displayed when you first open the software.**

3. **Click the pen on the toolbar at the top of the page (see Figure 8-1).**

   A small submenu appears.

Figure 8-1:
The Pen
icon in the
toolbar.

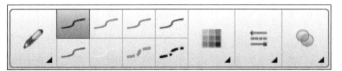

4. **Select the line style you need (see Figure 8-2), and write or draw the digital ink on your page.**

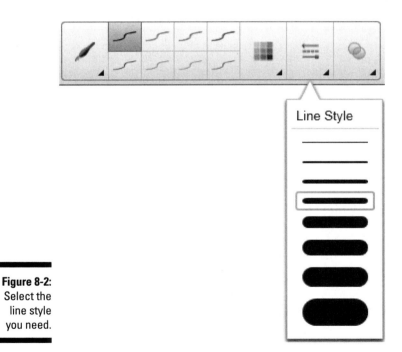

Line Style

Figure 8-2:
Select the
line style
you need.

You can change the line properties by clicking the tool to reveal more options on the toolbar (see Figure 8-3).

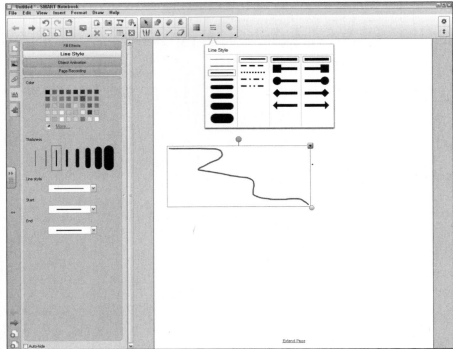

Figure 8-3:
The
Properties
window for
the Pen tool.

Chapter 7 discusses all the tools and menu bars. Refer to this chapter to help you navigate the SMART Notebook page.

The Creative Pen

To customize a Creative Pen using a picture, follow these steps:

1. **Click Pens, click the Pen Type drop-down arrow, and select Creative Pen.**

2. **Select a line style.**

3. **In the Properties tab, select Line Style.**

4. **Select Use a Custom Stamp Image.**

5. **If you want to use an object or picture that's on the page, click Select Object and choose your objects. If you want to use a picture file on your computer, click Browse, select the image, and click OK.**

6. **Go to your page and write.**

7. **Click Use Default Pattern to go back to using the line type.**

Note: If you're using version 10.8 of SMART Notebook software, you can't customize your styles using pictures or objects.

Fading digital ink

You can have fun with all the pens, but I have the most fun with fading. You can set up this tool so that after you write something on your `.notebook` page, the text fades. The timing is up to you.

I've used the fading pen as an icebreaker. In one of my presentations, I wrote a statement related to my presentation and asked the audience to remember it. Then I used the fading pen to put up a diagram and a series of key statements. After adding about nine different objects, I asked members of the audience to write them down. I gave a simple prize to the person who was able to recall the most items. The audience participated in the activity and was intrigued by how the pens disappeared. It had a "wow" effect, but more important, I was able to grab everyone's attention and engage them in a collaborative activity related to the presentation.

To make your digital ink fade, select your pen type and line type and then the Properties tab, and follow these steps:

1. **Click Fill Effects.**

2. **Select Enable Ink to Fade after You Write It.**

3. **Select the time between writing/drawing to fading from the Fade Time drop-down list.**

4. **Write or draw on your page and watch the ink disappear.**

   If you plan to use this option with an activity, as described earlier, make sure you test the timing.

Note: If you're using version 10.8 of SMART Notebook software, you can't control the timing of the fading pen.

Erasing digital ink

If you aren't happy with what you've written, there are a couple ways to erase them using the Eraser tool. (You also can use the physical eraser from the Pen Tray.) To erase digital ink, follow these steps:

1. **Click the Eraser icon in the Tools menu.**

2. **Select the eraser type.**

   You have a choice among three different widths.

   The cursor changes to an eraser, allowing you to move it on the page to erase the ink.

As on the interactive whiteboard, if you have a lot of text, you can use your eraser and draw a large circle around the text, and then tap it in the center, and the ink disappears. You can use your finger to do the same.

You won't be able to use the Eraser tool to erase other objects, such as shapes, lines, text, and pictures. You have to use the Delete function from the selected object's drop-down list.

Creating or drawing shapes and lines on a page

You can create all kinds of shapes using the Pen tool, but if you want precision (or you have terrible handwriting as I do!), use the Shapes tool to create perfect shapes such as circles, triangles, and rectangles. Figure 8-4 shows you all the shapes you can use in your .notebook pages.

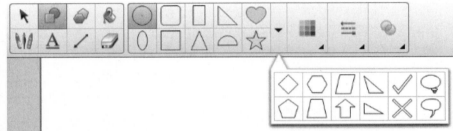

Figure 8-4:
Your shape
options.

In addition to being able to add the shapes, you can customize each shape — for example, by changing the outline color, fill color, thickness, and patterns. You also can work with the other objects to make your lesson or presentation livelier.

Creating shapes

Shapes are very easy to add to your pages:

1. **Press Shapes and then select a shape from the options that appear on the right.**

2. **If desired, use the drop-down menus on the toolbar to change the line style and thickness, color, and transparency.**

3. **Create a shape by pressing where you want to place the shape and drag the pen or your finger until the shape is the size you require.**

   Hold down the Shift key when you draw the shape to keep the proportions the same as you resize it.

More options are available on the Properties tab to further customize your shapes. Click Fill Effects and click one of the four radio buttons to select the fill effect you need. You also can select the transparency from the Fill Effects tool list if you want the figure to be transparent.

TIP

By right-clicking on the shape, or pressing the drop-down arrow, you can access a menu that enables you to manipulate that particular shape. The Properties functionality is listed at the bottom of this drop-down menu.

In addition to standard shapes, you can add regular polygons with 3 to 15 sides. You'll need to access the Regular Polygons tool to do this. If the tool isn't available on the toolbar, right-click on the toolbar, and the Customize Toolbar window appears. Find the Regular Polygons icon on the Tools tab, and drag it to the toolbar. Then follow the previous steps — the process is the same as for creating shapes.

Another way to create a shape is by using the Shape Recognition Pen tool. This tool is great when you're brainstorming because you don't have to stop and change the tool to draw a circle, oval, square, rectangle, triangle, or arc. To use the Shape Recognition Pen tool, follow these steps:

1. **Click Pens on the toolbar.**

2. **Select the Shape Recognition Pen tool from the Pen Types menu.**

   Now when you draw a square, triangle, circle, oval, or other shape, it will be recognized and replaced with a perfect shape (see Figure 8-5).

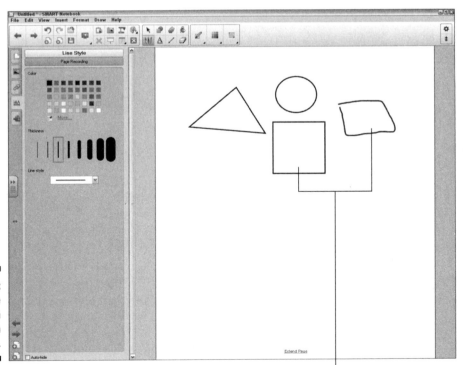

Figure 8-5:
The Shape Recognition Pen tool in action.

Shapes you draw freehand become perfect with the Shape Recognition pen.

Creating straight lines and arcs

If you need to draw straight lines or arcs, there's a specific tool for that job. For instance, if you're creating a flow chart and you need to connect the shapes, you can select the Line tool and then customize it using the edit properties.

To add a line or an arc to your .notebook page, follow these steps:

1. **Click the Line tool on the toolbar.**

2. **From the menu that appears, choose the line or arc.**

3. **Add the line to your page by pressing where you want it to start and then dragging it to the end.**

4. **To change the style, select the line or arc, use the options on the side menu of the toolbar or on the Properties tab to further customize the line style, color, transparency, and more.**

Anytime you use the Properties functionality for shapes, lines, or pens, you can save the line style and fill effects by clicking the Save Tool Properties button located at the bottom of the Properties column.

Creating text

SMART Notebook software enables you to add text anywhere in your .notebook page. You have a number of different options for adding text:

- ✔ Type the text using the on-screen keyboard.
- ✔ Type the text using the keyboard connected to your computer.
- ✔ Write the text using digital ink (covered earlier in this chapter), and then use the Recognition feature to convert it to typed text.

Typing text using the on-screen keyboard

To use the on-screen keyboard, follow these steps:

1. **Select the keyboard icon from the Floating Tools toolbar.**

    You can also select it by clicking the Keyboard button located on the Pen Tray. A keyboard appears on your screen.

2. **In SMART Notebook software, click the Text icon located on the toolbar (with the letter A), and then click on the page where you want the typed text to go.**

    The text field appears with basic editing capabilities (see Figure 8-6).

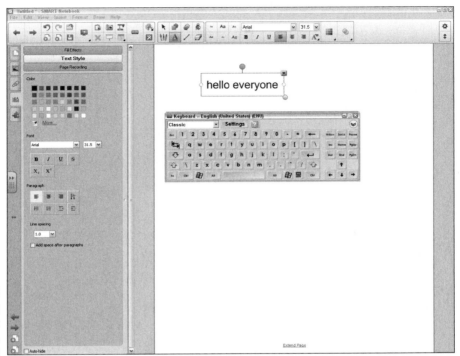

Figure 8-6:
The text
editing box.

3. **Press buttons on the on-screen keyboard to type into the text box and use the editing features to format it.**

   You also can use the Properties tab for formatting your text.

4. **When you finish, just click anywhere on your .notebook page.**

   The text box disappears, leaving the text on the page.

Converting handwriting to text

If you prefer to handwrite while you present or deliver your lessons, SMART Notebook supports handwriting and text recognition. This function enables you to convert handwritten text to typed text. Here's how:

1. **Select the Pen tool and write on your .notebook page.**

2. **Click the Select icon (the arrow in the menu bar).**

3. **Click the word you wrote.**

   A select box appears, with a down arrow in the top-right corner.

Mathematical notation

When you're using the text editing box, remember that you can insert mathematical symbols. The mathematical symbols are located second from the right, denoted by the square root symbol (in version 10.8) or on the Text Options drop-down menu (in version 11).

Mathematical symbols can be inserted anywhere in your text. Notice that these are symbols only — the software isn't capable of carrying out any mathematical calculations.

Click here to access the Insert Symbols screen.

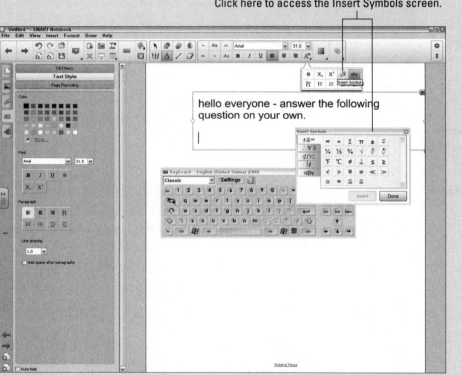

4. **Click the arrow and a drop-down menu is displayed.**

   At the top of the menu you see "Recognize <your word>."

5. **Select this option in the menu and it appears on the .note-book page.**

   You can edit the word by clicking it using the Select tool and the Properties menu. You have full editing capabilities to change the text style and color.

You need to write quite neatly, and horizontally, in order for the recognition software to match the word. If you try it a few times, you'll get the hang of it!

In addition to text recognition, a number of other functions and capabilities are located in the drop-down list. You can

- ✔ Recognize handwriting
- ✔ Recognize languages
- ✔ Recognize shapes or tables (if that's the object you added to your page)
- ✔ Clone, cut, copy, paste, and delete
- ✔ Check spelling
- ✔ Lock, group, flip, and order the objects
- ✔ Add functionality such as links, sound, and animation

Adding tables to your pages

You can add tables to your `.notebook` pages in SMART Notebook software. The cool part is the ability to add any object into the table cells.

The table function has all the usual features you'd expect. You can

- ✔ Move the table
- ✔ Change the text properties
- ✔ Resize columns, rows, and the whole table
- ✔ Insert or delete rows, columns, and cells
- ✔ Split or merge cells
- ✔ Add and remove a cell shade
- ✔ Delete the table

In the following sections, I show you how to add a table into your `.notebook` pages and then explain some of the editing capabilities.

How to add a table

You have two options for adding a table to your pages: You can create the table using SMART Notebook software, or you can copy and paste the table from another program. If you're skilled at creating tables, I recommend the first option.

Creating a table

To create a table, follow these steps:

1. **Click the Table button (the grid button on the toolbar).**

   A small table grid appears below the menu (see Figure 8-7).

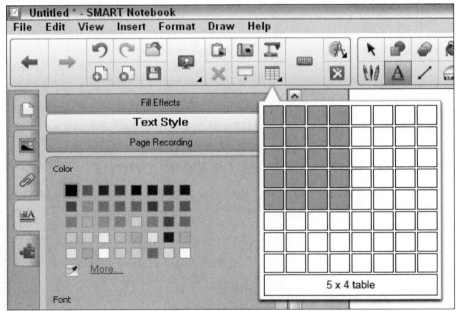

Figure 8-7:
Adding a
table to your
.note-
book page.

2. **Move your cursor across and down, selecting how many rows and columns you need.**

3. **Click the mouse or mouse pad.**

   The table appears on your .notebook page.

You also can draw the table on your page similar to how you draw geometric shapes, and SMART Notebook recognition software will recognize it as a table. This feature is really useful when you're presenting or brainstorming, and you want to save the pages in a neater format. To draw a table, follow these steps:

1. **From the Toolbar menu, tap or click the Pens tool (it's located next to the Select tool).**

   Make sure not to select the highlighter line style.

2. **On your .notebook page, draw the table.**

   Try to make the lines as straight as possible, connecting all the corners, so that the software can recognize the drawing as a table.

3. **When you finish, click the Select tool (the arrow located to the right of the Table button).**

4. **Select the table on your page by drawing around it with the Select tool.**

   When you're finished, you see a box around the table with a drop-down arrow.

5. **Click the drop-down arrow.**

   A drop-down menu appears (see Figure 8-8).

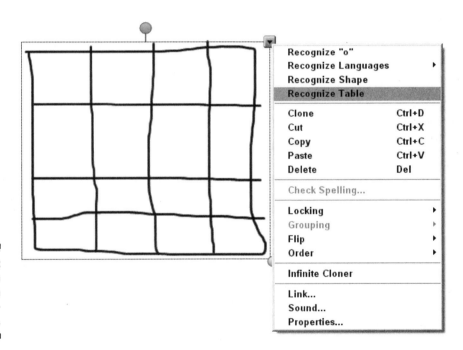

Figure 8-8:
A drawn table with the drop-down menu.

6. **Tap Recognize Table.**

   SMART Notebook software recognizes the object as a table and replaces the drawn table (see Figure 8-9).

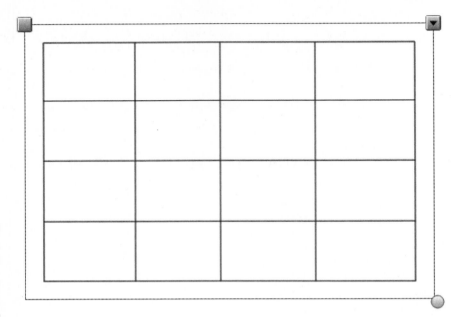

Figure 8-9:
The drawn
table rec-
ognized and
replaced.

Copying and pasting a table from another application

You can insert tables from other applications, such as Word and Excel. To copy and paste a table from another application, follow these steps:

1. **Open the document that has the table you want to import to your .notebook page.**

2. **Select the table and choose Edit⇨Copy (or press Ctrl+C/⌘+C).**

3. **Open your .notebook page, and click the page to put the cursor where you want the table to go.**

4. **Choose Edit⇨Paste (or press Ctrl+V/⌘+V)**

   The table appears in your .notebook page (see Figure 8-10).

Note that the formatting may be slightly different from the way it appeared in the other software. No worries, though: You can format the table by opening the Properties tab.

You also can copy a table you created in the .notebook page and paste it into other applications.

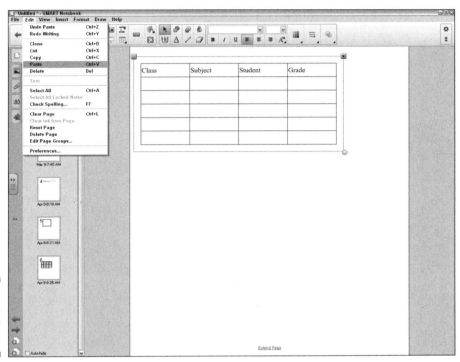

Figure 8-10:
Adding a
table to your
page.

What you can do with tables

You can do a number of cool things with tables:

TIP

✔ **Inserting objects into a cell:** You can insert any object into a cell by selecting the object and dragging it into the cell. You can remove the object by doing the reverse or by selecting the object and selecting Delete from the drop-down list.

If you want to add several objects to a cell, you need to group the objects. I discuss grouping objects later in this chapter.

✔ **Manipulating the table, columns, rows, and cells:** You can change the formatting of the cells, columns, and rows, as well as move the table. Use the Select tool to resize columns or rows. Use the Properties tab (or click the drop-down arrow in the table) to format the cells, line, and text style.

✔ **Resizing the table, columns, and cells:** Using the Select tool, click the border of the table. You see a horizontal or vertical arrow pointing both directions. This arrow enables you to resize the table or individual rows or columns.

  ✔ **Splitting or merging the cell:** Select the cell with the Select tool. Click inside the cell and right-click. From the drop-down menu that appears, select Split or Merge Cells.

  ✔ **Deleting a table:** Select the table. A select box appears around the whole table object. As with the other objects, click the drop-down arrow located in the top-right corner, and choose Delete.

Working with Objects

Now that you understand how to create various objects and add them in your lessons or presentation, you need to be able to work with the objects. SMART Notebook software has a number of capabilities allowing you to be very creative with objects. In this section, I fill you in.

Selecting objects

When you add an object to your .notebook page, you have to select it before you can work with the object. SMART Notebook software allows you to select one object or multiple objects.

Selecting one object

To select one object, follow these steps:

1. **Click the Select tool in the toolbar.**

2. **Click the object you want to select.**

   You see a rectangle around the object (see Figure 8-11).

   The selected rectangle has three capabilities enabling you to manipulate the object:

   • The green dot at the top of the selected rectangle allows you to rotate the object.

   • The gray dot at the bottom-right corner of the rectangle allows you to resize the object.

   • The drop-down arrow at the top-right corner of the rectangle displays the drop-down menu (see Figure 8-12).

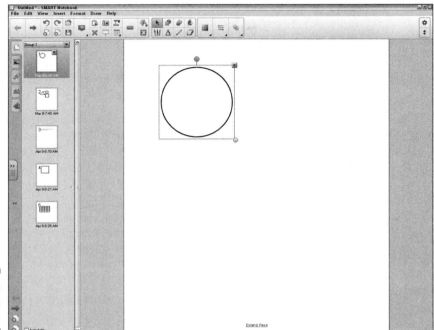

Figure 8-11:
Selecting an object.

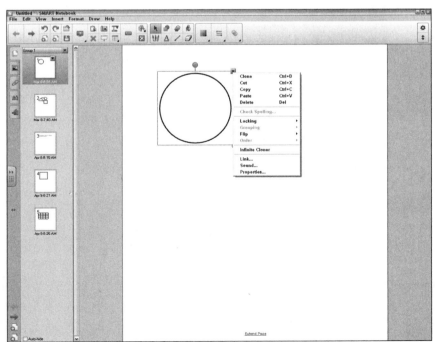

Figure 8-12:
The drop-down menu.

TIP

You also can access the drop-down menu on any selected object by right-clicking the object.

Selecting multiple objects

If you want to select multiple objects on your page, you can do any of the following:

✔ Click the Select arrow and drag your finger (or cursor) in a diagonal motion from the upper left to the lower right, drawing a selection rectangle around the objects you want to select.

✔ Hold down the Ctrl key and select the individual objects by tapping or clicking on them.

✔ To select all objects on a page, choose Edit➪Select All (or press Ctrl+A/⌘+A). All the objects will be selected and grouped, so that if you move one, all the other objects will be affected, too. In Figure 8-13, I selected all the objects and rotated them to the right; you can see that they all rotated at the same angle.

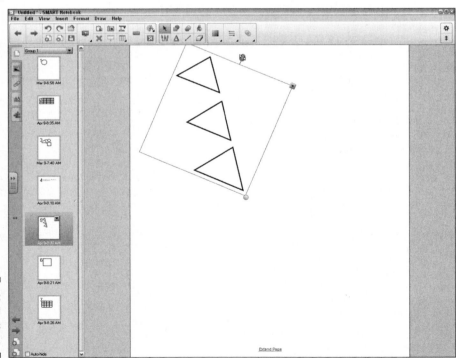

Figure 8-13:
Selected
objects
rotated.

Changing an object's properties

You can change an object's fill style, transparency, or lines style. The properties depend on the type of object you're using. For instance, if you're using the Pen object, you can change line styles. You can change an object's properties by selecting the Properties tab or choosing View⇨Properties.

You can change the properties of multiple objects at the same time by selecting and grouping them.

I discuss properties in greater detail in Chapter 7.

Moving objects

You have a number of different options for moving objects around your .notebook page or between pages. This is useful because it enables you to make more room on the page for another activity, cover text with an object shape, or order objects in a list (for example, asking your audience to order various objects into categories in a Venn diagram).

When you present, you want to engage your learners or participants. Asking your participants to move objects engages them in an activity that can be more fun and meaningful than just listening to your presentation.

Moving an object around a page

Moving an object is a very simple procedure:

1. **Select the object by tapping it with the Select tool.**

2. **Drag the object to a new position.**

   You can use your finger, use a mouse, or press the arrow keys. If you use the arrow keys, the object will move in tiny increments.

Moving an Adobe Flash Player–compatible file is slightly different. Just tap the colored bar located at the top of the compatible file and drag it to the new position on your page.

If your computer's operating system supports flicks, you can flick an object. Just quickly move your finger in the direction you want the object to flick. Flicking is useful if you're trying to make a point. For example, place a picture or an icon of a garbage can on one side of your page, place the object (words) you want to quickly "throw away" on the other side of the page, and flick the object into the garbage can.

Moving objects between pages

To move objects from one page to another, follow these steps:

1. **Make sure the Page Sorter is visible.**

   If you can't see it, tap the Page Sorter tab on the left side of the screen. The icon looks like a page with a corner bent over.

2. **Find the page you want to move the object to.**

   You may need to scroll to find the thumbnail.

3. **Select the object on the page you want to move.**

4. **Drag the object you want to move into the Page Sorter onto the page on which you want the object to appear.**

5. **Take your finger off the thumbnail.**

Aligning objects

If you have a number of objects on a page, you can reposition them to appear centered or aligned vertically or horizontally. The cool thing is that you can set objects to align automatically when you manipulate them on a page. There are guidelines in the software to help you with the procedure.

Follow these steps:

1. **Choose View⇨Alignment.**

   The Alignment dialog box appears (see Figure 8-14).

2. **Select an option.**

   Your options are as follows:

   - Show guides for active objects
   - Show vertical page center guide
   - Show horizontal page center guide
   - Snap objects to guides (This feature "grabs" the object when it's close to a guide and aligns it automatically.)

3. **To change the color of the guideline box, click the color bar and select a color from the palette.**

4. **Tap or click OK.**

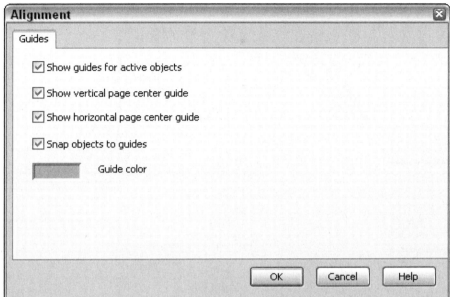

Stacking objects

Stacking objects, or putting one object on top of another, is a functionality you'll use frequently. For example, you might place text inside a chart, or you might cover content with an object and, as you present, use your finger to move the object over the hidden content.

Moving an object to the front

To stack objects, follow these steps:

1. **Tap the Select tool.**

2. **Tap or click the object you want to move to the front.**

3. **Tap or click the drop-down arrow.**

   The drop-down menu shown in Figure 8-15 appears.

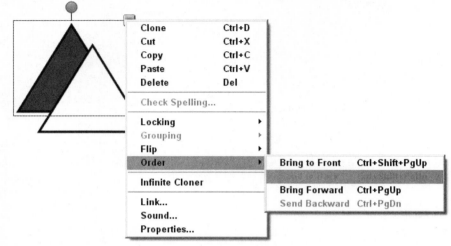

Figure 8-15:
Changing
the stack
order of
objects.

4. Select Order.

5. Tap Bring to Front if you have only two objects or Bring Forward if you have multiple objects stacked.

The object will move to the front.

Moving an object to the back

To move objects behind one another, follow these steps:

1. Tap the Select tool.

2. Tap or click the object you want to move to the front.

3. Tap or click the drop-down arrow.

The drop-down menu appears (refer to Figure 8-15).

4. Select Order.

5. Tap Send to Back if you have only two objects or Send Backward if you have multiple objects stacked.

Locking objects

You can lock objects so that they can't be resized, changed, moved, or rotated. You also can lock an object but enable movement. To lock an object, follow these steps:

1. **Tap the Select tool.**

2. **Tap the object you want to lock.**

   The selection rectangle appears with a drop-down arrow in the top-right corner.

3. **Tap the drop-down arrow and select Locking.**

   Notice that a submenu opens to the right. The options are as follows:

   - Unlock
   - Lock in Place (This option doesn't allow anyone to move the object.)
   - Allow Move (This option allows movement — for instance, repositioning on the page — but the object can't be rotated, resized, or otherwise modified.)
   - Allow Move and Rotate (This option allows full movement, but no other functionality is enabled.)

After you select one of the options, your object will be locked and cannot be manipulated until you unlock it.

To unlock an object, tap the Select tool, tap the object you want to unlock, and select the little padlock where the drop-down arrow was located.

Copying, cutting, pasting, and cloning objects

You can copy, cut, and paste objects in SMART Notebook software just as you can in Word, Excel, or PowerPoint. You also can clone (duplicate) an object.

Copying, cutting, and pasting an object

To cut or copy and paste an object, follow these steps:

1. **Tap the Select tool and click or tap the object.**

2. **From the drop-down menu, select Copy or Cut.**

3. **Go to the Page Sorter, and select the page where you want to paste the object or a position on the same .notebook page.**

   If you're pasting into another application, go to that file and put your cursor where you want the pasted object to go.

4. **Choose Edit⇨Paste (or press Ctrl+V/⌘+V).**

Cloning objects

If you spent a lot of time creating an object or a series of objects, you can easily clone that object. Cloning is faster than the copy/paste option, but you can clone only on your current page — you can't clone from one page to another.

To clone an object, follow these steps.

1. **Tap or click the Select tool.**
2. **Select the object you want to clone.**
3. **Tap or click the drop-down arrow and select Clone.**

   A duplicate object appears on the screen.

You can use the Infinite Cloner tool to replicate the object as many times as you want. This tool is useful if you want a quick succession of replicate objects on the page. To use the Infinite Cloner tool, follow these steps:

1. **Tap or click the Select tool.**
2. **Select the object you want to clone.**
3. **Tap or click the drop-down arrow and select Infinite Cloner.**
4. **Tap the object again.**

   Instead of the drop-down arrow, you see an infinity symbol (∞).

5. **Drag the object to a new position on the page.**

   The object is replicated.

6. **Keep doing this until you have enough clones displayed on your page.**
7. **When you're finished, tap or click on the infinity symbol and deselect the Infinite Cloner option.**

   The drop-down arrow reappears.

When you're cloning an object using the Infinite Cloner tool, it's easy to think that as you clone the first duplicate, you continue to clone from the new object, when in fact you have to go to the original each time to create the next clone. Just remember you can't clone from a clone.

Resizing objects

You can resize objects either by using the gray dot on the bottom-right side of the select rectangle or by using the scaling gesture. To resize an object, follow these steps:

1. **Make sure the object is selected.**

2. **Locate the gray dot and press and drag outward to make the object larger or drag inward to make it smaller.**

   When you're happy with the size, tap somewhere else on the page.

If you need to keep the height-to-width ratio, hold down the Shift key while you're dragging to resize the object.

You also can resize multiple objects on the same page. This is useful, for instance, if you have a large diagram with many separate objects. First, you need to group the objects; then you can resize them:

1. **Click or tap the Select tool.**

2. **If you want to group and resize all the objects on your page, choose Edit⇨Select All (or press Ctrl+A/⌘+A).**

   If you want to group and resize objects only within a certain area (but not everything on the page), use your finger to drag a selection rectangle around the objects by pressing in the top-left corner of the area and dragging diagonally to the bottom-right corner.

   You know the objects have been selected because the select rectangle with the drop-down arrow appears on all the objects.

3. **From one of the objects (it can be any one), click the drop-down arrow.**

   The drop-down menu appears.

4. **Select Grouping and then Group.**

   This groups every selected object on the page, enabling you to interact with all the objects at the same time. You can move, rotate, or resize all the objects at the same time when they're grouped.

5. **To resize, select the gray button, and drag outward to enlarge the object and inward to reduce the size.**

Don't forget to ungroup the objects before you begin working on your page again. To ungroup objects, choose the Select tool, click the group, click the group's drop-down arrow, and select Grouping and then Ungroup.

When you write or draw lines on your `.notebook` page, SMART Notebook software automatically combines lines into a single object. For example, when you write a word, the software creates one object from all the letters, so when you select the word it becomes one object and you can rotate it, add a link, and so on. If you want each letter to be a separate object, leave space between the letters, use a different pen for each letter, or place the pen back into the Pen Tray for a second. This is useful if you're moving letters around to correct spelling or stacking letters.

Using gestures to resize

SMART Notebook software also allows you to use gestures to resize objects. This is quicker than having to select the tools or pens. It's also quite impressive when you're using the interactive whiteboard and you start manipulating and interacting with a variety of objects using your fingers. It almost looks magical.

To resize objects, follow these steps:

1. **Tap the Select tool.**

2. **Tap the object to select it.**

3. **Using one finger from each hand, press the screen, on the outside of the object, and drag to the opposite ends of each object.**

4. **Applying the same pressure, move your fingers in opposite directions to enlarge the object. To make the object smaller, place your fingers on the inside of each object and drag your fingers toward each other.**

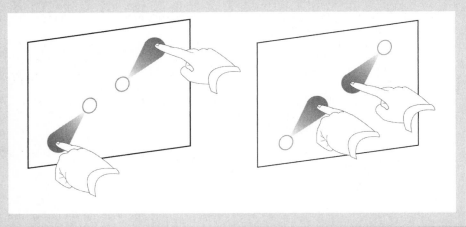

Rotating objects

You can rotate objects using the rotating handle. The rotating handle appears when you select the object — it's a green circle attached to a line. The steps for rotating an object are the same as for resizing an object — you just use the green circle instead of the gray dot.

If you need to rotate a number of objects together, follow the instructions for grouping objects in the preceding section, and then rotate them.

Flipping objects

You can flip objects, turning them over like a playing card. For example, you might flip shapes and move them together to create a picture.

You can download puzzles from the SMART Exchange website (`http://exchange.smarttech.com`) or other educational websites (see Appendix A).

Another fun icebreaker is to test your audience's recognition capabilities. Download faces of famous people and flip the faces upside down. Then ask your audience to see if they can recognize the faces. You'll surprise them with how difficult it is to recognize faces when they're upside down. You can further demonstrate your interactive whiteboard skills by handwriting the name of the famous person, use SMART Notebook software hand recognition to change the handwriting to typed text, and then insert a link related to the identified individual.

Flipping objects is a simple three-step process:

1. **Tap the Select tool and then tap the object.**

2. **Select the drop-down arrow.**

   A menu appears.

3. **Select Flip and then, from the submenu, select Up/Down or Left/Right.**

To flip multiple objects, choose Edit⇨Select All (or press Ctrl+A/⌘+A) instead of selecting just one object.

Adding links to objects

One of the most useful things you can do with objects is to link an object to a web page, to another page in the same file, or to a file on your computer. You also can link objects to an attachment, which acts as a shortcut to a file or a web page.

When you start linking objects to web pages or other pages, you'll see your interactive whiteboard come to life. For example, you can create circles, add presidents' faces to them, and then link each face to a sound file or a web page.

To add a link follow these steps:

1. **Select the object that you want to link.**

2. **Tap the drop-down arrow.**

   A menu appears.

3. **Select Link.**

   The Insert Link dialog box appears.

   You have a number of different options to add links:

- To add a web page link, copy and paste or type the web address into the text box.

- To link to a different page in the same file, tap Page in This File and a Select Page window appears with a list of all the pages in your current file.

- To link to another file on your computer, tap File on this Computer. Then, using the Browse text box, find the file on your computer, and select Copy of File so the file is attached to your .notebook file or select Shortcut to File and insert a shortcut on the page.

- To add a link to an attachment, tap Current Attachments. A text box appears. Select the attachment from the list.

4. Decide how you want to open the link.

You can open the link displaying an icon denoting a link near the object or by making the whole object active, enabling you to tap anywhere in the object to activate the link.

5. Tap OK.

If you select Corner Object, you see one of three tiny icons in the lower-left corner of your page:

- A little globe represents a link to a web page.

- A bent page represents a link to another page in the same file.

- A paper clip represents a link to another file on your computer.

To remove the link, select the object, click the drop-down arrow, select Link, and click Remove Link from the Insert Link dialog box.

Adding sounds to objects

Adding sound to your object makes your lessons and presentations more powerful. You can add a sound file to any type of object and activate the sound with an icon in the corner of the object or by pressing anywhere on the object.

Note: You can't attach a sound file to Adobe Flash Player–compatible objects.

SMART Notebook software supports only MP3 audio format. You can install encoders to support other sound file types. Chapter 12 covers audio formats.

Follow these steps to begin adding sound files to your objects:

1. **Press the Select tool, and select the object.**

2. **Tap the drop-down arrow, and select Sound.**

   The Insert Sound dialog box appears.

3. **Click Browse and find your sound file.**

4. **Press Open.**

5. **Select whether you want to display an icon to activate the sound or whether Notebook can enable the object to play the sound file if tapped.**

6. **Click Attach Sound.**

To remove a sound from the object, select the object, tap the drop-down arrow, and select Remove Sound.

Animating objects

You can animate your objects and use the functionality to support a variety of presentation or learning objectives. Follow these steps to animate your objects:

1. **Tap or click the Select tool.**

2. **Tap your object to select it.**

3. **Tap the drop-down arrow, and select Properties.**

   The Properties tab opens in the left column.

4. **Tap Object Animation.**

   The Animation dialog box appears with a number of options to bring your object to life. You have a number of different choices, each with several options. To see the options, click the drop-down arrow for each choice.

   - **Type:** Spin, None, Fade in, Fade out, Flip around axis, Fly in, Fly out, Shrink, and Grow

   - **Direction:** Clockwise, Counterclockwise (*Note:* Depending on the Type you chose, these options vary.)

   - **Speed:** Slow, Normal, Fast

   - **Occurs:** When the object is clicked, when the page is entered

   - **Repeats:** None, Once, Twice, Five times, Ten times, Until the object is clicked, Forever

Chapter 9

Using Your Own Content

*Y*ou can use your work stored outside SMART Notebook software in your SMART Notebook files. In this chapter, I show you how to reuse various types of documents and include them in your .notebook files, such as:

✔ Content from other applications (like PowerPoint or Word)

✔ Pictures, video, and sound files and Adobe Flash Player–compatible files

✔ Links to web pages

You can even save your favorite content in the Gallery. In this chapter, I show you how.

Adding Your Own Content from Other Applications

If you're anything like me, you have folders full of PowerPoint presentations, Excel spreadsheets, and Word documents. The good news is, when you start working with your interactive whiteboard, you're not starting over from scratch — you can import the content you've saved in other applications. After your content is imported, you can use the full functionality of the inter-active whiteboard and SMART Notebook software and prepare a presentation or lesson that will bring life to your old material.

There are a number of different ways you can bring your content into SMART Notebook. In this section, I show you the different ways you can reuse your old content.

Copying, cutting, and pasting content

The simplest and most familiar method for adding your content to a SMART Notebook file is to copy/cut and paste. Follow these steps:

1. **Open the file from which you want to copy content (for example, a Microsoft Word document).**

2. **Select the content you want to use, and choose Edit⇨Copy or Edit⇨Cut.**

3. **Open an existing SMART Notebook file or a new one.**

   If you're using an existing SMART Notebook file, use the Page Sorter to navigate to the place where you want to paste your content.

4. **Choose Edit⇨Paste.**

   The new content appears in your .notebook page.

Importing content using SMART Notebook Print Capture

If you're using SMART Notebook on the Windows XP operating system, you can install SMART Notebook Print Capture when you install the software for the first time. This functionality works similar to normal printer drivers, except the SMART Notebook driver captures and then outputs the image in a .notebook file instead of printing the content on paper. The cool part is that the whole page is captured as an object and placed on its own in a .notebook page with the original formatting saved.

Different programs have different levels of quality output when you print to SMART Notebook. Most files (such as Word documents and PDFs) work pretty well, but some fancier files may lose resolution in SMART Notebook.

To import using SMART Notebook Print Capture, follow these steps:

1. **Open the file you intend to import into your SMART Notebook file.**

2. **Choose File⇨Print.**

   The Print dialog box appears.

3. **From the drop-down list of printers, select SMART Notebook Print Capture.**

4. **If you want to import specific pages, select the Page Range radio button and enter the page range.**

5. **Press OK or Print.**

   Each page from the file appears on a new .notebook page.

This process may take several minutes. When the process is complete, you must unlock all the graphic objects if you want to make any changes — they're locked during the import process. (For more on unlocking objects, turn to Chapter 8.)

If you want to change the page orientation and the resolution during the print capture process, follow these steps:

1. **In the Print dialog box (see the preceding steps), press the Properties or Preferences icon.**

   The SMART Notebook Print Capture dialog box appears.

2. **Choose Portrait or Landscape.**

3. **Insert numbers in the Horizontal Resolution and Vertical Resolution fields to change the resolution on the .notebook page.**

   Make sure you use comparable values to the original so that the images aren't distorted. For example, if the original image is 100x200 pixels, and you want to enlarge it, make it 200x400 pixels.

   Remember: The higher the resolution, the larger the image will appear.

   Refer to Table 9-1 for the recommended resolutions.

4. **Press OK.**

Note: Depending on the program you're printing from, the preceding procedure may vary slightly.

Table 9-1	Recommended Resolutions
Screen Resolution	*Recommended Graphic Resolution*
1152x867	100x100
1024x768	90x90
800x600	60x60
640x480	50x50

Importing content using SMART Notebook Document Writer

If you're using Windows 7 or Vista, you installed SMART Notebook Document Writer with SMART Notebook. This program works just like SMART Notebook Print Capture, explained in the preceding section.

To import using SMART Notebook Document Writer, follow these steps:

1. **Open the file you intend to import into your SMART Notebook file.**

2. **Choose File⇨Print.**

   The Print dialog box appears.

3. **From the drop-down list of printers, select SMART Notebook Document Writer.**

   You can change the page orientation at this point (see the preceding section).

4. **If you want to import specific pages, select the Page Range radio button and enter the page range.**

5. **Click SMART Notebook Pages with Images if you want to import the files as pictures or SMART Notebook Pages with Editable Objects if you want to import the files as objects.**

6. **Press OK.**

   Each page from the file appears on a new .notebook page.

Importing PowerPoint files

Importing your PowerPoint files is easy. The only thing to keep in mind is that if you've used gradients, patterns, or other effects as backgrounds or fill in your PowerPoint pages, when you import them, there may be some deterioration in the .notebook files. For example, the text may not be clear, images may be distorted, or colors may be different. I suggest that you remove any special effects in your PowerPoint pages before you import them. Standard images, themes, and backgrounds are fine.

Follow these steps to import PowerPoint files:

1. **In your SMART Notebook software, choose File⇨Import.**

   The Open dialog box appears.

2. **Select All PowerPoint Files (*.ppt; *.pptx) from the drop-down list.**

3. **Select the PowerPoint file that you want to import.**

4. **Press Open.**

   The contents of the PowerPoint file are copied into the `.notebook` file.

Importing files from other software and interactive whiteboard programs

SMART Notebook allows you to import content from other programs such as Word, including other interactive whiteboard programs if they support the Interactive Whiteboard Common File Format (CFF). This is similar to saving documents in formats cross-platform like RTF, (`.rtf`), ASCII (`.txt`), or comma separated value (`.csv`). You can import and export using the CFF format.

To import CFF files into SMART Notebook, follow these steps:

1. **In SMART Notebook, choose File⇨Import.**

   The Open dialog box appears.

2. **From the Files of Type drop-down list, select All Common File Format Files (*iwb), as shown in Figure 9-1.**

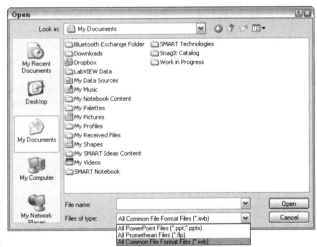

Figure 9-1: Importing files from an interactive whiteboard program.

3. **Browse to and select the file you want to import.**

4. **Press Open.**

   The file opens.

To import other files into SMART Notebook, follow these steps:

1. **In SMART Notebook, choose File⇨Open.**

   The Open dialog box appears.

2. **From the drop-down menu in the bottom-right corner, select All Files (*).**

3. **Select the file you want to open.**

4. **Press Open.**

If the file is not supported by SMART Notebook software, it will be added to an Attachment tab (see the next section), and you'll be able to open it using third-party software. Note that you need this third-party software on your computer in order to be able to open the attachment.

Using the Attachment Tab

The SMART Notebook Attachment tab is a neat utility that enables you to link to web pages and add shortcuts to files, as well as attach copies of files. In this section, I fill you in on how to use the Attachment tab to attach things to your SMART Notebook pages.

Attaching a link to a web page

Attaching web pages to your SMART Notebook workspace allows you to access the web pages quickly when you're presenting or teaching.

To attach a link to a web page, follow these steps:

1. **Select the Attachments tab (it looks like a paper clip).**

   The Attachment pane displays.

2. **Press the Insert button in the bottom-right corner.**

   The Insert menu (shown in Figure 9-2) appears.

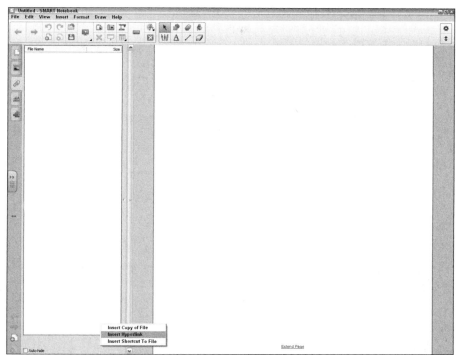

Figure 9-2:
The Insert
menu.

3. **Select Insert Hyperlink.**

   The Insert Hyperlink dialog box appears.

4. **Enter the web address in the Hyperlink box.**

5. **Type the name of the link in the Display Name box.**

   Use something that makes sense to you or that supports the goals of the presentation.

6. **Press OK.**

   The link appears on the Attachment tab (see Figure 9-3).

You can attach a web page to objects displayed in a SMART Notebook page (see Chapter 8).

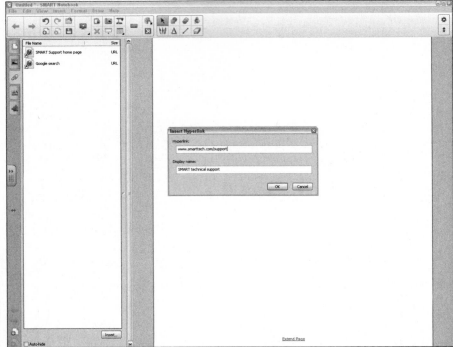

Figure 9-3:
A link added
to the
Attachment
tab.

Attaching a shortcut to a file

When you attach a shortcut to a file, you reduce the size of your .notebook file. Also, if you want to use a file that's a work in progress (for example, a report that changes from day to day), you'll always have the most recent version available.

The location of the file must be accessible on the computer you're using with your interactive whiteboard.

To attach a shortcut to a file, follow these steps:

1. **Select the Attachments tab (it looks like a paper clip).**

   The Attachment pane displays.

2. **Press the Insert button in the bottom-right corner.**

   The Insert menu appears (refer to Figure 9-2).

3. **Select Insert Shortcut to File.**

   The Insert Shortcut to File dialog box appears.

4. **Find and select the file you want to attach.**

5. **Press Open.**

   The shortcut appears on the Attachment tab.

Attaching a file

You may need to attach a whole file instead of just a link to it. Note that if you attach a large file, it may increase your `.notebook` file size. (SMART Notebook software can compress some files types efficiently, but not all of them.)

To attach a file to your SMART Notebook file, follow these steps:

1. **From the tabs on the right of the Page Sorter, select the Attachment tab (it looks like a paper clip).**

   The Attachment pane displays.

2. **Press the Insert button in the bottom-right corner.**

   The Insert menu appears (refer to Figure 9-2).

3. **Select Insert Copy of File.**

   The Insert Copy of File dialog box appears.

4. **Find and select the file you want to attach.**

5. **Press Open.**

   The file appears on the Attachment tab.

Inserting Pictures in Your SMART Notebook Pages

A picture is worth a thousand words, and that's more true than ever in today's rich media and interactive world. Too much small text on the computer or interactive whiteboard can be hard to read, so using a variety of media is an important part of making your presentations and lessons successful. SMART Notebook software allows you to insert pictures into your pages from a number of different resources. In this section, I walk you through your options.

Regardless of how you add a picture to your page, the picture is recognized as an object. You can move, resize, rotate, and add links to the picture, just as you can with any other object you create in SMART Notebook software (see Chapter 8).

One of the cool things you can do is create transparent areas in the picture that you can insert into the page. This feature is very useful if you want to remove the picture's background. You can use any color for the transparency. To create a transparent area, follow these steps:

1. **Select the picture (see Chapter 8).**

2. **Press the drop-down arrow that appears when the picture is selected.**

3. **Select Set Picture Transparency.**

   The Picture Transparency dialog box appears.

4. **Select the part of the picture that you want to be transparent.**

5. **Press OK.**

From files

You can insert a picture into a page saved in a number of different formats. SMART Notebook supports BMP, PNG, JPG, GIF, TIFF, and WMF files. To insert a picture into your `.notebook` page, follow these steps:

1. **Choose Insert⇨Picture File (see Figure 9-4).**

   The Insert Picture File dialog box appears.

2. **Find and select the picture you want to insert into your page.**

   To select more than one picture, hold down the Ctrl key and then select the pictures.

3. **Press Open.**

   The picture appears in the upper-left corner of the page.

If you select a large file, you may be prompted to optimize the image. The software just makes a lower-resolution copy of the image, and it usually looks just fine. If it doesn't look how you want it to, perform the procedure again but select Keep Resolution instead.

From a scanner

You can insert pictures from any scanner if it's connected to your computer.

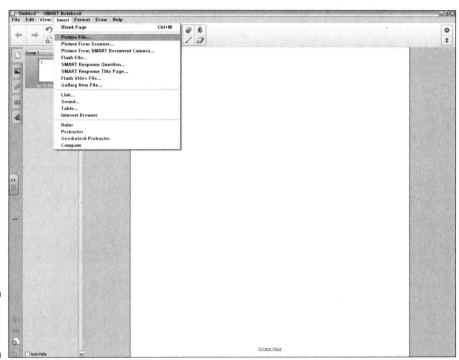

Figure 9-4:
Inserting a
picture.

Make sure that the scanner drivers and software are installed on your computer and working properly before you insert a picture from the scanner into SMART Notebook software.

To insert a picture from a scanner, follow these steps:

1. **Choose Insert⇨Picture from Scanner.**

   The Insert Picture from Scanner dialog box appears.

2. **Select the scanner from the Picture Source drop-down list.**

3. **Press Scan.**

4. **Follow the on-screen instructions for your scanner software.**

   The picture appears in the upper-left corner of the page.

From a SMART Document Camera™

If you have a SMART Document Camera connected to your computer, you can use it to add pictures into your presentation or lesson. Follow these steps:

1. **Choose Insert⇨Picture from SMART Document Camera.**

   The SMART Document Camera window appears.

2. **Follow the instructions in the SMART Document Camera Guide.**

Because there are so many different models, I can't get more specific than that. If you run into trouble, go to www.smarttech.com/support and browse to the SMART Document Camera page to find user's guides.

Inserting Multimedia Files into Your SMART Notebook Pages

You can insert a number of different types of multimedia files — including video files, sound files, and Adobe Flash Player–compatible files — into your .notebook pages.

You also can insert various media files from the Gallery tab (see the next section).

Similar to inserting pictures (see the previous section), when you insert a multimedia file into your SMART Notebook page, the media file becomes an object. You can move it, rotate it, resize it, and more (see Chapter 8).

All media files are inserted from the Insert menu. The steps are the same for all the various file types. Just choose Insert and then the type of file you want to insert. For the remainder of this section, I focus on Adobe Flash Player–compatible files.

When an Adobe Flash Player–compatible file is inserted into a page (or if the page already has the file inserted), the file plays as soon as it's opened. You can control playback of a file. If the file has buttons, you can press the interactive whiteboard to control the settings; if the file doesn't have buttons, use the file's menu arrows. Table 9-2 outlines the various Flash Player controls.

Table 9-2	Flash Player Controls
Function	*What to Do*
Play file	Press the file's menu arrow and select Flash⇨Play.
Play file from beginning	Press the file's menu arrow and select Flash⇨Rewind.
Advance file and pause playback	Press the file's menu arrow and select Flash⇨Step Forward.
Rewind file and pause playback	Press the file's menu arrow and select Flash⇨Step Back.
Play file continuously	Press the file's menu arrow and select Flash⇨Loop.
Stop playing file continuously	Press the file's menu arrow and select Flash⇨Loop again to clear the selection.

If you want to write on top of the Adobe Flash Player–compatible file using handwriting recognition, begin writing outside the file and then continue to write over the file. You need to do this in order for SMART Notebook software to be able to recognize the digital ink as a separate object.

You can't drag an Adobe Flash object from a web browser into a page as you can with other objects.

Adobe Flash files need to be self-extracting if you insert them into .notebook pages because they can't rely on other Flash Player files to be launched.

You can download Flash Player from http://get.adobe.com/ flashplayer. For best results, use Internet Explorer (Windows or Mac) or Safari (Mac) to install Adobe Flash Player. If you use another browser, Adobe Flash files may not work in SMART Notebook software.

To insert Adobe Flash Player–compatible files, follow these steps:

1. **Choose Insert⇨Flash File.**

   The Insert Flash File dialog box appears.

2. **Find and select the file you want to insert into your page.**

3. **Next to the File Name field, select Flash File (.*swf) from the drop-down list.**

4. **Press Open.**

   The Adobe Flash Player–compatible file appears in the upper-left corner of the page.

If you want to insert an Adobe Flash Player–compatible video file, follow the same procedure, except in Step 1 select Flash Video File and in Step 3 select Flash Video File (.*flv).

SMART Notebook software also supports Adobe Flash Player–compatible video files formats. You can identify this video format by the file extension .flv. SMART Notebook software supports other FLV and MP3 formats. If you have other formats, you need to convert the files to FLV and MP3 first.

Adding Your Content to the Gallery

The Gallery tab is an excellent utility with thousands of resources free for you to use in your lessons or presentations. You can browse and search the Gallery and, with a few presses and drags, add content to your pages. (I discuss the Gallery in much more detail in Chapter 10.)

Another cool functionality the Gallery has built in is something called the My Content folder, which is a holding space for all the content that you find yourself using over and over. So, instead of looking for it in the main Gallery, you can move it to your own folder. You can import content from other files or the Internet into your My Content folder. You also can share the file with your colleagues and enable them to contribute to it.

Adding an object to the Gallery

Follow these steps to add an object to your My Content folder in the Gallery:

1. **Press the Gallery tab, located on the left side of the Page Sorter (it looks like a framed picture).**

   The Gallery lists open with all the categories organized in the top half of the Page Sorter. The Gallery Essentials folder is selected by default. In the lower half, you see subfolders.

2. **Select the My Content folder.**

   If you have something in the folder, the subcategories open, as shown in Figure 9-5.

3. **Open the page with the object you want to place in your My Content folder, select the object, and drag it into your My Content folder (see Figure 9-6).**

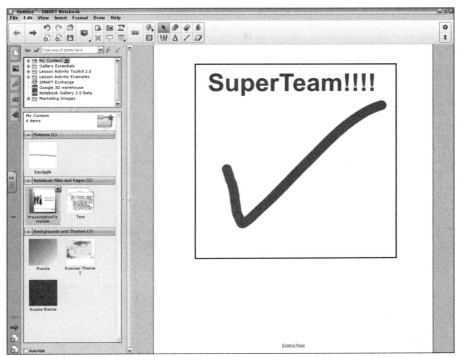

Figure 9-5:
The My
Content
directory in
the Gallery.

If you can't move the object, select it in your page and make sure that it isn't locked. If it is locked, unlock it (see Chapter 8).

Adding a page or file to the Gallery

When you create a page, and you find yourself using that page over and over, you may want to add it to the Gallery so that it's easily accessible when you're preparing presentations. You might do this with an introduction page or a page that serves as an icebreaker for group sessions.

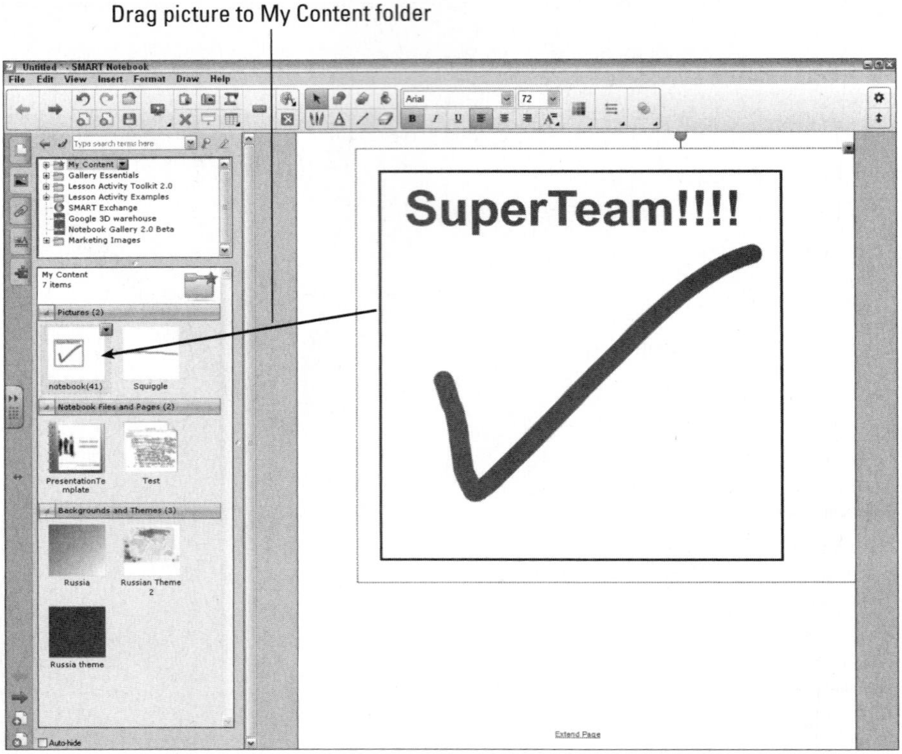

Drag picture to My Content folder

Figure 9-6:
Dragging
an object
into the My
Content
folder.

To add a page to the Gallery, follow these steps:

1. **Create or optimize for generic use the page that you want to save in the Gallery.**

2. **Choose File⇨Save Page as Gallery Item.**

   The Save Page As Gallery Item dialog box appears.

3. **Locate a place where you want to save the page.**

4. **Enter a name in the File Name box.**

5. **Press Save.**

6. **Press the Gallery tab.**

7. **Press My Content or one of the subcategories if you already have a few.**

8. **Press the drop-down arrow on My Content (or the subcategory) and select Add to My Content (see Figure 9-7).**

   The Add to My Content dialog box appears.

Figure 9-7:
Adding a
page to the
My Content
folder.

9. **Find and select your file.**

10. **Press Open.**

> Your file appears as a subfolder in My Contents. In the lower half of the sidebar, it's listed and displayed as a thumbnail image.

Depending on the size of the file or slowness of your network, this may take a few seconds.

To add a whole file to the Gallery, follow the same steps, starting with Step 6.

Organizing Your Content in the Gallery

When you find yourself adding more and more objects and pages to your My Content folder in the Gallery, you may think, "I really need to organize this so I can find things more easily." If you realize how useful the My Content folder can be, you'll start organizing your resources as soon as you start using it.

To create a subcategory, follow these steps:

1. **Select the Gallery tab.**

2. **From the Category section, select My Content or one of the subcategories.**

   A drop-down arrow appears in the corner.

3. **Press the drop-down arrow.**

   A menu appears.

4. **Select New Folder.**

   A new, untitled category appears (see Figure 9-8).

Figure 9-8:
A new folder in the My Content folder.

To rename the category, follow these steps:

1. **Select the untitled category.**

2. **Press the drop-down arrow and select Rename.**

3. **Type the name of the new Category and press Enter.**

After you create your categories and subcategories, you can drag objects and pages from one file to the other.

Chapter 10

Using Content from SMART Resources

In This Chapter

▶ Locating and using content in the Gallery

▶ Finding content in the Lesson Activity Toolkit

▶ Exploring content on the SMART Exchange website

A number of very useful tools are bundled into SMART Notebook software. SMART Technologies, the company that manufactures the interactive whiteboards, has over 20 years of experience supporting end-users, like you and me. You don't need to reinvent the wheel. Instead, you can use the tools at your disposal.

Here's a rundown of the free items that come with SMART Notebook software:

✔ **Gallery Essentials:** A fantastic resource of thousands of images, clip art, multimedia files, and more. It should be one of the first things you explore before you start creating your presentations or lessons. Each folder is organized into neat subcategories that are easy to explore by browsing or using the search tool.

✔ **Lesson Activity Toolkit:** This collection of tools and templates that you can customize and use to develop great interactive lessons and professional presentations is a must for every teacher and trainer. This toolbox includes word games, quizzes, various sorting activities, and many Adobe Flash Player–compatible files. This is a must to explore. I guarantee you'll create a wow effect with the tools and templates you find here.

✔ **SMART Exchange website:** If you can't find ideas or something you need for your presentation in one of the preceding two utilities, I guarantee you'll find it in this online resource. Here you find free content created by SMART Technologies developers, teachers, and presenters. SMART Exchange really adds another dimension to what the interactive whiteboard can do for you.

In this chapter, I fill you in on how to use each of these tools.

Finding and Using Content from the Gallery

The Gallery is part of SMART Notebook software. You can find the Gallery in the sidebar when you open SMART Notebook. If you don't see the Gallery icon, choose View⇨Gallery.

The Gallery is divided into two sections (see Figure 10-1):

- ✔ The top half is a list of categories and folders.
- ✔ The bottom half displays the contents of the selected category with expandable lists, giving you a number of options for selecting an item.

Gallery icon

Gallery

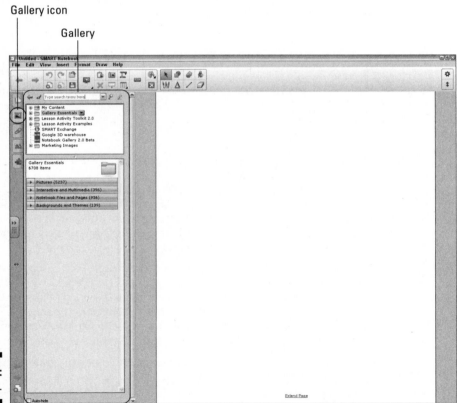

Figure 10-1:
The Gallery.

The Gallery is filled with content that's easy to locate, easy to add to your presentations, and easy to add your own favorite content. After using it for a while, you'll wonder how you ever lived without it.

I suggest that you first browse the Gallery to see what content is located in each category. Use the thumbnails to preview the content. Here's a list of the categories and some hints to help you find various images:

- ✔ **Pictures:** Pictures appear as small thumbnails.
- ✔ **Interactive and Multimedia:** Sound objects have a speaker icon in the corner; video objects have a single frame from a video in the corner; Adobe Flash Player–compatible files appear as an Adobe Flash icon or a thumbnail with a small Adobe Flash icon in the upper-left corner.
- ✔ **3D Objects:** Small 3D model thumbnails.
- ✔ **Background and Themes:** Backgrounds are displayed as binders and pages with a folder in the right corner; themes are displayed as thumbnails.

Browsing and searching the Gallery

Each of the categories can be searched by browsing — a good strategy to explore what's there and inspire your creative side. If you know exactly what you want, use the keyword search.

To browse the Gallery, follow these steps:

1. **Open SMART Notebook and press the Gallery icon (refer to Figure 10-1).**

2. **Press Gallery Essentials in the upper pane.**

   A list of categories (such as Arts, Geography, Mathematics, and so on) appears in the upper pane, and a list of the items in the folders appears in the lower pane.

3. **Press the plus sign (+).**

   The subcategories open. Selecting a folder displays its contents, arranged by type, in the lower pane. Click the arrows to view all items within a type list. To close a category, press the minus sign (–).

When you're ready to prepare presentations or lessons, you'll have an idea what you need or want to use to deliver your learning goals or message. That's when you would want to use the search utility. Follow these steps to search the Gallery:

1. **Open SMART Notebook and press the Gallery icon (refer to Figure 10-1).**

2. **Type a keyword into the Type Search Items Here box.**

3. **Press Enter or press the Search (magnifying glass) button.**

   All the content generated by your keyword will be displayed in the Gallery in the lower half of the sidebar.

Adding a Gallery item to your file

When you find the object you want to add to your lesson or presentation, follow these steps, press two times, in quick successions, on the thumbnail simulating a double-click. (You also can drag the object into the file.)

When the object appears in your page, you can work with it. There are slight differences in working with the different types of objects, which I cover extensively in Chapter 8. Here's a quick rundown:

- ✔ You can add objects such as pictures, Adobe Flash Player files, video files, and audio files to a currently opened page.

- ✔ Adding a background or theme replaces the current page's background (see Chapter 8 for more information).

- ✔ When you add a page from a `.notebook` file, SMART Notebook places it before the currently opened page; for instance, if you're experimenting with the default opened page and you want to insert a new one, it appears right above on the sidebar as a thumbnail. Press to open it.

- ✔ When you add a whole new file, SMART Notebook will insert all the pages from the file directly above the currently opened page, not before the first or last page for the particular file opened.

I cover adding content and working with objects and the Gallery in Chapters 8 and 9.

Finding and Using Content from the Lesson Activity Toolkit

The Lesson Activity Toolkit is a Gallery resource that includes a number of really nifty customizable tools and templates to design and develop professional-looking presentations. You also can create interactive lessons that will captivate and engage your audience. This resource is conveniently bundled in the Gallery, ready for you to use.

Customizing your tools

You can customize the tools in the Learning Activity Toolkit. Some objects and activities are trickier than others, including the Adobe Flash objects, so SMART Technologies built in some hints and Help files to help you when you first begin. Here are a few hints and tricks to get you going:

✔ Look for the Help button, which describes the object and gives you some hints on how to build and/or use the activity.

✔ If you need to customize a specific activity, press the Edit button.

✔ To add text to the Text field, you can type or drag text from a page you've already prepared or from another application.

✔ You'll likely be sharing your interactive whiteboard with other colleagues. To ensure that no one can edit your game (or accidentally mess it up during your class), you can password-protect it. Press the Password box and create a password.

✔ Many of the games and activities have other built-in capabilities useful for teachers. You can use them to review the activity or game with your class. These are the Check button (press it if you want to grade the activity), the Reset button (press it to delete the activity editions so you can start over), and the Solve button (press it to show the correct answers).

To access the Toolkit, go to your Gallery as shown in the previous section, and press Lesson Activity Toolkit 2.0. The folder opens with the following subfolders:

✔ Activities

✔ Examples

✔ Games

✔ Graphics

✔ Pages

✔ Tools

I briefly cover each of the content folders in the following sections. First, there are several general tips you should familiarize yourself with before you begin using the content in your lessons or presentations:

✔ To locate what you need, you can browse through each of the folders or use the Search box.

✔ To expand each folder, click the plus sign (+); to close each folder, click the minus sign (–).

✔ When you locate what you need for your lesson or presentation, drag the object to the page. It instantly becomes editable by selecting it. You see the editing box around the object when it's selected. (Refer to Chapter 8, which is all about working with objects.)

✔ Create your own folder in the Gallery where you can import the objects that you use frequently. You can easily drag and drop them, and they'll be there for you to use and reuse, saving you time searching for them.

Activities

The Activities folder contains templates for activities aimed at involving learners in a fun, interactive way. Use them to support your learning goals or as an ice breaker in a presentation. You can customize them for all ages. Activities include anagram, category sort, image match, keyword match, multiple choice, pairs, tiles, and word guess.

Examples

If you don't know where to begin, I recommend that you look at the Examples folder, which is filled with ideas on how to use a game or an interactive activity in a classroom and demonstrates creative ways some of the tools can be used (see Figure 10-2). This folder includes the following subfolders:

✔ **Activities:** Includes different examples you can use to create an activity.

✔ **Help:** Includes links to online help resources and instructional videos prepared by SMART Technologies.

✔ **Layering:** Has eight different files to help you use layering in your pages (for example, pull tabs, layer reveal, color reveal, and so on).

Here are two great examples:

✔ **Hot Spots game:** http://youtu.be/u-_9KCoPl7c

✔ **Pull tab tool:** http://youtu.be/O_Z3GSjVl5w

If you need more help using the Lesson Activity Toolkit, go to http://downloads.smarttech.com/media/trainingcenter/flash/tutorials/6_thelessonacttoolkit/lessonacttoolkit.htm.

Games

The Games folder gives you game pieces, enabling you to create games. This folder contains cards, checkerboards, dominos, Sudoku, crossword puzzles, and more. Look in the Examples folder to give you some ideas.

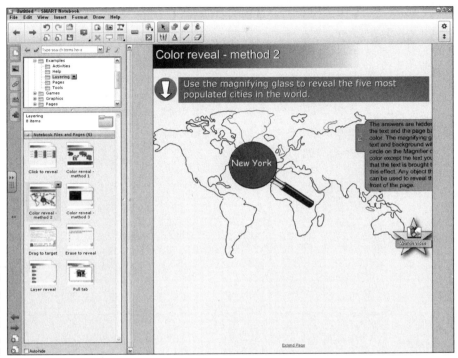

Figure 10-2:
A customized example.

Graphics

The Graphics folder includes images, borders, and a variety of icons to help you create fun and impressive designs. For instance, you can drag pull tabs and title bars right onto your notebook pages. The pull tabs and customized buttons help with the flow when you're accessing a variety of resources and look neater, more professional, and just plain cool.

Pull tabs are useful if you have lots of info you want to add to your page. They're like cards you can write in or add pictures to, and they have a little handle. The idea is that you add your content to the card, and then position it off the page so that only the handle (tab) remains visible on the page. This way the content is hidden, and you can pull it into view during your presentation when you need it and hide it when you don't.

To create a button that performs an action such as opening a website or playing a sound, you first need to pick an object and add a link to it. Follow these steps to create a button with a link:

1. **Add an object to your page, like one of the cool buttons (or create your own), and select it.**

   You see the select box around the object with a drop-down arrow.

2. **Press the drop-down arrow.**

   A menu appears.

3. **Press Link (see Figure 10-3).**

4. **Decide where you want to link the object (for instance, a page within the same file, another file, a website, or an attached file).**

5. **Add the info in the Address field, as shown in Figure 10-4.**

6. **Select the Corner Icon radio button.**

7. **Press OK.**

Pages

The Pages folder contains preset pages enabling you to create lesson activities or presentations. These work just like any template that includes a style, structure, and fields for text. All you have to do is add your content. Figure 10-5 shows a Title Page.

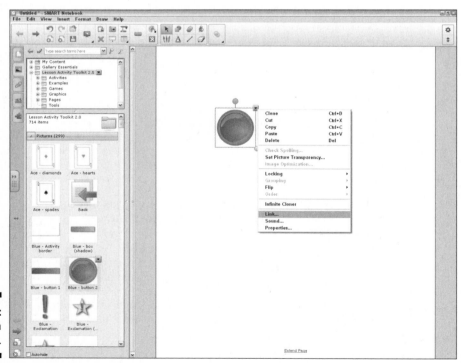

Figure 10-3:
Adding a link.

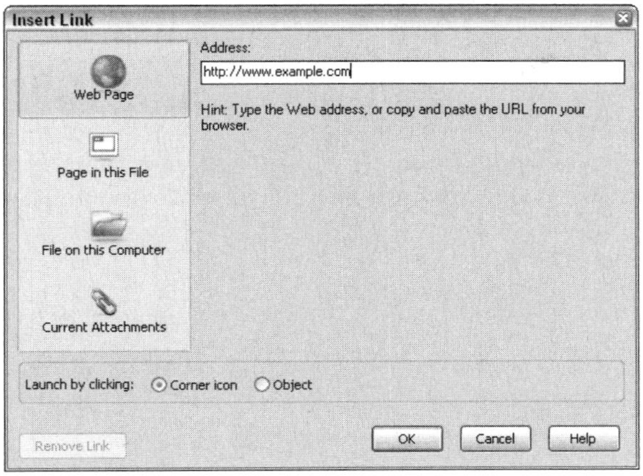

Figure 10-4:
The Address
field.

You can easily use any of the pages to change the text or add links and other objects like buttons. To change the text, highlight the template text and type over it. The pages include sections for lesson objectives and teachers' notes.

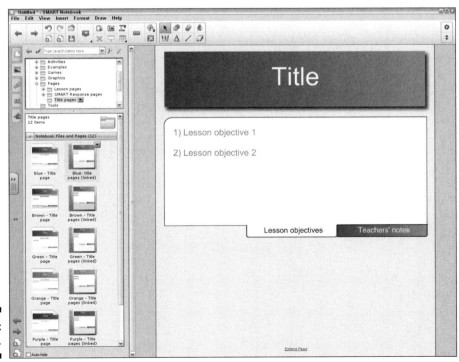

Figure 10-5:
A Title Page.

Tools

If you want to add interactive and multimedia activities to your lessons or presentations, then you must explore the Tools folder. It contains Adobe Flash tools you can use to create really sensational games and pages. There are dozens of tools for you to explore — here's a taste of what to expect:

- ✔ Press and reveal tools
- ✔ Keyword dice
- ✔ Random card
- ✔ Number and color generators
- ✔ Random group generators
- ✔ Scrolling text bar
- ✔ Vote tool
- ✔ Random word generator

Each of these tools is customizable. I encourage you to browse the tools, import one to your page, and play with it. To import a tool, follow these steps:

1. **Press the individual tool to select it.**

2. **Press the drop-down arrow.**

3. **Select Insert in Notebook (see Figure 10-6).**

The only drawback to these fantastic tools is that you may be asked to present more than you want to, or get a flood of colleagues wanting to know how you created the presentation. This is where you go to your boss and ask for a raise.

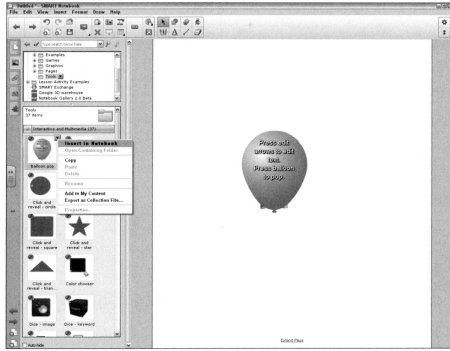

Figure 10-6:
Balloon Pop,
a press-
and-reveal
activity
you can
customize.

Finding and Using Content from the SMART Exchange

One of the best things about the Internet is that you can download and use material created by other experts. The SMART Exchange website (http://exchange.smarttech.com) is filled with lesson plans, presentations, and more tools for you to use, all free of charge, with no worries about copyright. Everything you find has been created by instructors, teachers, business professionals, or the experts at SMART Technologies. I highly recommend that you turn to the SMART Exchange website and explore what you have at your fingertips. I guarantee it will save you time, impress people, and inspire you with ideas for how to get creative with your own content.

You can access the SMART Exchange website from the Gallery tab. Click the SMART Exchange link (see Figure 10-7).

Click here to open SMART Exchange.

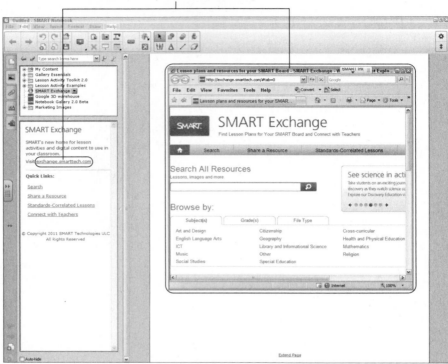

Figure 10-7:
The SMART
Exchange
link in the
Gallery.

The SMART Exchange folder contains the following:

✓ **Search:** Enables you to search the whole site for resources.

✓ **Share a resource:** This is where teachers, trainers, or anyone in the SMART community, including SMART Technologies staff, can show off their creativity and make it available to others to use. Remember to thank the creator, and if you develop something unique and you have great success with it, share it!

✓ **Standards-correlated lessons:** These resources are aligned with and approved for various curriculum standards in your chosen country or area. You can access lesson plans and other resources. It's a valuable resource aimed for the education market, but if you're a trainer in a company, I encourage you to look at this resource. Skills are transferable — what works for kids often works even better with adults.

✓ **Connect with teachers:** This link takes you straight to the Forum discussion and user groups. Create an account and search for ideas and answers. You'll be pleasantly surprised how much information is there.

You can subscribe to different user groups organized by states. Teachers like this because they can discuss and share tools to support statewide curriculum and standards.

Before you can find content at the SMART Exchange website, you first need to join the community. Follow these steps:

1. **Press SMART Exchange in the Gallery, and then click the SMART Exchange link.**

   You also can go to `http://exchange.smarttech.com` in your web browser. The SMART Exchange website opens.

2. **Sign in to your account (see Figure 10-8).**

   If this is your first time there, you'll need to press Join for Free, and then create an account.

3. **Browse and/or search the content until you find what you need.**

4. **Download the content into a folder on your computer.**

   I recommend that you create a SMART Exchange folder in your SMART Notebook folder (or wherever you keep your lessons or presentations) so that you can easily find the files when you import them. I talk about importing content into the Gallery in Chapter 9.

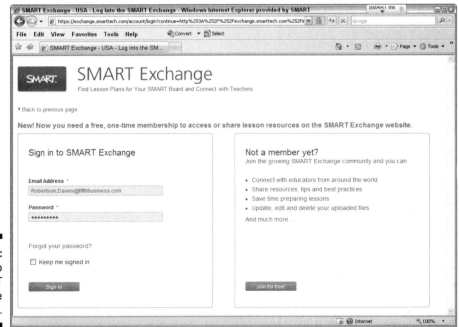

Figure 10-8: Signing in to the SMART Exchange website.

Chapter 11

Creating Your First Lesson or Presentation

In This Chapter

▶ Setting up your files for a successful presentation

▶ Considering your view options

▶ Using the tools at your disposal as you present

▶ Letting two people use the interactive whiteboard at the same time

*T*he previous chapters in this part give you all kinds of useful information that will make your presentations or lessons shine. In this chapter, I put the finishing touches on the part. Here, I walk you through setting up your files for a successful presentation. I introduce you to your view options and encourage you to go full screen. I walk you through the presentation tools available to you. And I tell you how to allow two people to use the interactive whiteboard at the same time (and why you might want to do that in the first place).

How to Set Up Files and Present to Your Audience

When you're getting ready to present to an audience, keep in mind the following tips:

✔ **Make sure the interactive whiteboard is set up with a computer and has access to the Internet (if you need to use content from the web).** If you're on a local area network (LAN), you can access your files via your profile. Otherwise, bring your files on a CD, DVD, or flash drive.

✔ **In your presentation, use the Full Screen view (see the next section).** Presenting your information on a huge board is impressive. Plus, you get more space to work, which is really useful if you have multiple people interacting with the board.

✔ **Prepare your links to outside resources or to other files in advance of your presentation or lesson.** It speeds up the process, and you don't have to lose focus on the topic you're discussing. I discuss attaching files and creating links in Chapters 6 and 9.

✔ **If your lesson or presentation contains too many pages, group them.** This way you can find info faster when you're jumping around or if someone asks you a question. I cover grouping pages in Chapter 7.

✔ **If you want to impress your audience, create objects that slowly fade, open a Magnification window, or open a Spotlight window with a magic pen to enhance and highlight specific content.** I discuss how to do all these things later in this chapter.

✔ **Another really impressive thing to do when you present is to hide objects before you present them.** You can get members of your audience or students in your classroom to reveal the objects. There are a number of different ways to hide and reveal objects, including the following:

- Add a Screen Shade to a page, and when you want to show the object or text, just remove the Screen Shade by touching it and sliding it away. I cover Screen Shades later in this chapter.

- Hide the object by using digital ink and then erase it to uncover what's below. I cover digital ink in Chapter 4.

- Cover an object with another object. I discuss stacking objects in Chapter 8.

Displaying Files in Different Views

You can give your presentation in several different views (see Figure 11-1):

✔ **Full Screen:** Full Screen view takes over the whole interactive whiteboard. When you're using Full Screen view, the SMART Notebook sidebar, menu bar, toolbar, and title bar are hidden.

✔ **Transparent Background:** Transparent Background view allows you to

- See your desktop windows behind the SMART Notebook window so you can interact with the transparent file.

- Draw in digital ink on a transparent page, and then save your notes in the file.

- Demonstrate measurement tools.

- Use screen capture.

- Interact with your desktop and non–SMART Notebook applications behind the SMART Notebook software window.

✔ **Dual Page Display:** Dual Page Display view enables you to display two pages side by side.

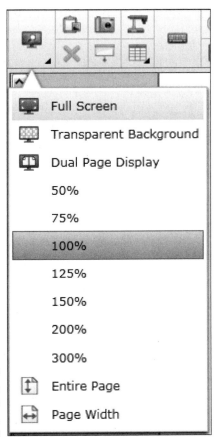

Figure 11-1:
Your view
options.

You also can set the view to 50%, 75%, 100%, 125%, 150%, 200%, 300%, Entire Page, or Page Width.

In the next few sections, I walk you through how to use Full Screen, Transparent Background, and Dual Page Display views.

Full Screen view

To use Full Screen view, do one of the following:

- ✔ Press the Full Screen button in the View Screens menu (refer to Figure 11-1).
- ✔ Press the Full Screen button on the Full Screen toolbar.
- ✔ Choose View⇨Full Screen.

The page you're working with expands to fill the whole screen. In addition, the Full Screen toolbar (shown in Figure 11-2) appears. Here's a guide to what's on the Full Screen toolbar:

✔ **Previous Page:** Takes you to the previous page in the current file

✔ **Next Page:** Takes you to the next page in the current file

✔ **More Options:** Opens a submenu of options enabling you to work with SMART Notebook tools

✔ **Exit Full Screen:** Returns you to normal view

✔ **Toolbar Options:** Displays another set of tools in a toolbar (see Figure 11-3):

  • **Blank Page:** Inserts a new page into your current file

  • **Undo:** Goes back one action and removes any new additions to the page

  • **Select:** Selects an object, allowing you to manipulate and edit it

  • **Magic Pen:** Lets you use the Magic Pen features (see the "Magic Pen" section, later in this chapter)

Transparent Background view

To use the Transparent Background view, press the Transparent Background button on the SMART Tools bar.

The SMART Notebook window and pages become transparent, allowing you to use what's on your desktop. Notice that the objects are still on the page — they just appear over your desktop (see Figure 11-4).

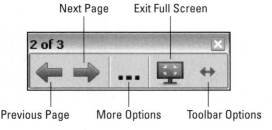

Figure 11-2: The Full Screen toolbar.

Next Page   Exit Full Screen

2 of 3

Previous Page   More Options   Toolbar Options

Blank Page   Select

Figure 11-3:
The Toolbar
Options.

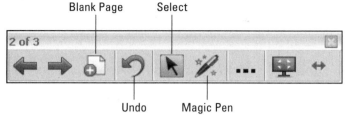

Undo   Magic Pen

Figure 11-4:
A
transparent
notebook
page with
objects.

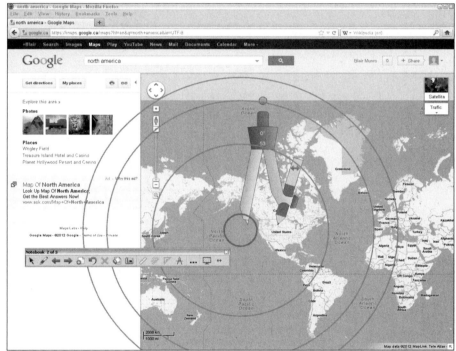

Notice the appearance of a new toolbar located at the bottom of your screen.
This toolbar enables you to interact with your SMART Notebook files and
toolbars. At the top of the toolbar, the pages in your file are displayed (for
example, 2 of 4). The toolbar icons are the same as outlined in Figure 11-2,
but the expanded toolbar options submenu has more functionality (see
Figure 11-5):

  ✔ **Blank Page:** Inserts a new page in your current file

  ✔ **Undo:** Goes back one action and removes any new additions to the page

   ✓ **Delete:** Deletes all the objects you selected on the page

   ✓ **Clear Page:** Erases all digital ink and deletes all objects from the page

   ✓ **Screen Capture:** Opens a toolbar enabling you to take screenshots

   ✓ **Ruler:** Inserts a ruler on a page

   ✓ **Protractor:** Inserts a protractor on a page

   ✓ **Geodreieck Protractor:** Inserts a Geodreieck protractor on the page

   ✓ **Compass:** Inserts a compass on the page

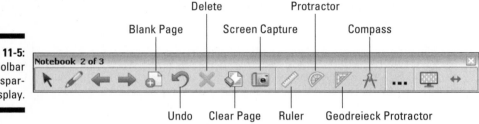

Figure 11-5:
The toolbar
for transpar-
ent display.

I discuss some of the tools later in the chapter.

Dual Page view

One of the cool things you can do with Dual Page view is to pin an area of a page and then view your other pages in the Page Sorter. Follow these steps:

1. **Press the Dual Page Display icon in the View Screens menu on the toolbar (refer to Figure 11-1), or choose View⇨Dual Page.**

   Another page appears on the right, with a red border. The red border indicates that the page is active.

2. **To pin a page, press the page you intend to interact with.**

   A red border appears around that page.

3. **Press View⇨Zoom⇨Pin Page.**

   Two pins appear on the page (see Figure 11-6).

To unpin the page, simply choose View⇨Zoom⇨Pin Page.

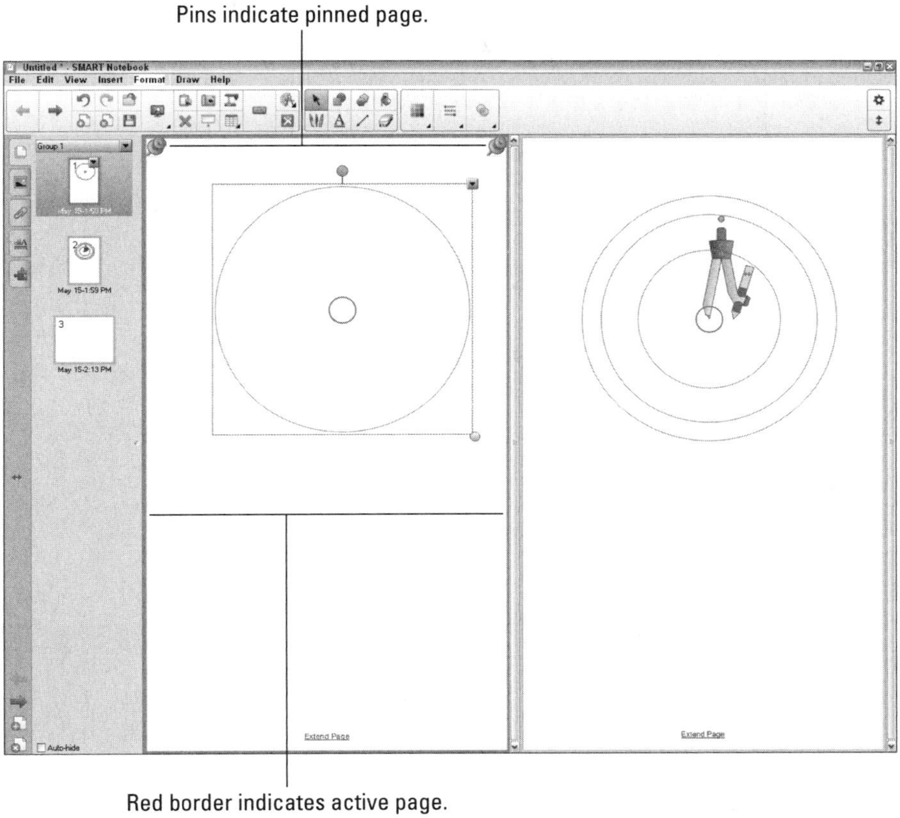

Pins indicate pinned page.

Figure 11-6:
A pinned
page.

Red border indicates active page.

Using Presentation Tools

SMART Notebook has a number of useful and clever presentation tools. If you use these tools in your lessons or meetings, everyone will think you spent hours creating your presentation. Little do they know that SMART Technologies has made it so easy.

In this section, I outline the presentation tools — Screen Shade, Magic Pen, and the measurement tools — and show you how to access them.

Screen Shade

The Screen Shade allows you to cover information and tease your students or audience by slowly revealing the content.

If you save a file with a Screen Shade, next time you open that file, the Screen Shade will cover the content.

Here's how to add a Screen Shade:

1. **Open the page you want to hide.**

2. **Press the Screen Shade icon on the toolbar or choose File⇨View⇨Screen Shade.**

3. **Drag the hand icon next to the small dot on the right side of the screen to the left to reveal the hidden page (see Figure 11-7).**

4. **To fully remove the Screen Shade from the page, press the Screen Shade icon, or the X at the upper-right side. To quickly cover everything again, double-press the Screen Shade icon.**

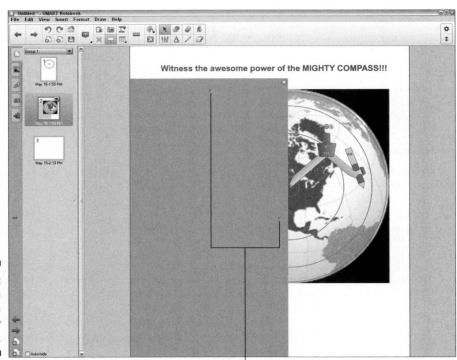

Figure 11-7:
A Screen Shade partially opened.

Drag the handles to reveal the image underneath.

Magic Pen

This is a wild tool that you can have loads of fun with. You can use it to make an object slowly fade, open a Magnification window, or place a spotlight on a window.

To begin, you need to select the Magic Pen. Here's how:

1. **Press the Pens icon on the toolbar.**

   The Pens tools appear.

2. **Press the Pen Types icon.**

   A submenu appears (see Figure 11-8).

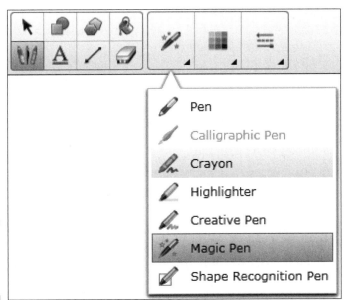

Figure 11-8:
The Pen
Types
submenu.

Pen

Calligraphic Pen

Crayon

Highlighter

Creative Pen

Magic Pen

Shape Recognition Pen

3. **Press the Magic Pen to select it.**

This is where the true fun begins! Open a new .notebook page or one of your existing pages and get ready to be impressed.

Creating fading objects

Fading objects are a great way to stun your audience when used as an ice-breaker. You can use this in place of those old cheesy jokes, and everyone will be grateful. Follow these steps:

1. **With the Magic Pen selected, use your finger (or SMART Pen Tray pen) to create something on the interactive whiteboard.**

2. **Watch what you wrote fade to get an idea of how fast the ink disappears.**

3. **To set the time on the Magic Pen, press Properties in the View menu list or on the SMART toolbar, press Fill Effects, and select the number of seconds in the Fade Time drop-down list.**

Fading objects are not saved in .notebook files.

You can change the default setting for the Pen by pressing Save Tool Properties before you close the Properties window.

Using the Magnification window

The Magnification window is a great tool to use with Google Earth or any file you have opened with finer detail that you can't enlarge. Follow these steps to use it:

1. **With the Magic Pen selected, open the website or file you want to magnify.**

2. **Use your finger (or SMART Pen Tray pen) to draw a square or rectangle on the interactive whiteboard.**

3. **To reduce the magnification size, press in the middle of the window and drag to the left.**

4. **To increase the magnification, press in the middle again and drag to the right.**

5. **To move the Magnification window, press somewhere near one of the edges and then drag it.**

Figure 11-9 shows the Magnification window in action.

Drag box by edges to move Magnification window.

Figure 11-9:
Using the
Magni-
fication
window.

Using the Spotlight window

The Spotlight window allows you to highlight portions of your screen, the way you might have years ago with a laser pen. Follow these steps to use it:

1. **With the Magic Pen selected, use your finger (or SMART Pen Tray pen) to draw a circle anywhere on the interactive whiteboard screen.**

   A spotlight appears (see Figure 11-10).

2. **Reduce the size of the spotlight by pressing in the middle of the circle and dragging to the left.**

3. **Increase the size of the spotlight by pressing in the middle of the circle and dragging to the right.**

4. **To move the spotlight, press somewhere near the edge and drag it.**

5. **To close the spotlight, press the X.**

Figure 11-10:
A spotlight
on an area
of the
interactive
whiteboard.

Measurement tools

The measurement tools (shown in Figure 11-11) are fantastic for all kinds of educational lessons. In this section, I summarize how you can use each measuring tool.

Figure 11-11:
The Mea-
surement
Tools menu.

The ruler

The ruler is very flexible and a great teaching tool. You can change the width, length, and rotation of the ruler; draw around the edges of the ruler; and use the ruler in art work.

To insert the ruler, press the Measurement Tools icon in the toolbar, and select the ruler from the submenu (refer to Figure 11-11). (You also can insert the ruler from the Insert menu.) Here's what you can do with the ruler:

- **Move the ruler.** Press in the middle of the ruler and drag it to the new location.

- **Resize the ruler.** Select the ruler by pressing or tapping it and drag the resize handle (the circle in the bottom-right corner).

- **Lengthen the ruler.** Press in the middle of the right edge between the drop-down arrow and the resize handle and arrows appear; drag to the right, away from the ruler. The scale stays the same.

- **Shorten the ruler.** Press in the middle of the right edge between the drop-down arrow and the resize handle and arrows appear; drag to the left, toward the center of the ruler, to shorten it. The scale stays the same.

- **Rotate the ruler.** Press the top or the bottom edge, and a circle with arrows appears; as you rotate, the rule changes to a different shade of blue. Degree or rotation is displayed by the left edge in a small circle located on the rule.

- **Reverse measurement on the ruler.** Press the flip symbol depicted by green arrows pointing in both directions, on the left side of the ruler, to move the inches from the bottom to the top of the ruler (or vice versa).

- **Draw with the ruler.** Press the Pen Types icon, select Standard Pen or Calligraphy Pen, select a line style, and draw along one of the edges of the ruler as you would when you place a rule on a sheet of paper. The digital ink line appears along the edge of the ruler the exact length you require.

- **Remove the ruler.** Select the ruler, press the drop-down arrow, and select Delete.

The protractor

To insert the protractor, press the Measurement Tools icon in the toolbar, and select the protractor from the submenu (refer to Figure 11-11). (You also can insert the protractor from the Insert menu.) Here's what you can do with the protractor:

- **Move the protractor.** Press in the inside of the protractor and drag it to the new location.

- **Resize the protractor.** Press the inner set of numbers and drag away to enlarge the protractor and toward the center to make the protractor smaller.

- **Rotate the protractor.** Press the outer set of numbers, and a blue arrow pointing in both directions appears. Move the arrow in the direction you need to rotate the protractor.

- **Display a complete circle.** Press the blue circle inside the 180-degrees mark; press it again to return to a semicircle.

✔ **Draw with the protractor.** Press the Pens Types icon, select Standard Pen or Calligraphy Pen, select a line style, and draw along the edges of the protractor as you would if you had the protractor on a piece of paper. The digital ink appears as an arc.

✔ **Display angles.** Select the protractor so that you see the green circle and arrow. Drag the green circle with the dark blue line until you identify the first two intersecting lines. Drag the white circle and light blue line until you identify the correct angle. Press the green arrow, and a separate object of the angle appears with the degrees.

✔ **Remove the protractor.** Select the protractor, press the drop-down arrow, and select Delete.

The Geodreieck protractor

The Geodreieck protractor is a complex tool, but being able to explain how it works on a large interactive whiteboard is very helpful to teachers. Students can come up to the board and use the measurement tool while you watch and explain what they're doing.

To insert the Geodreieck protractor, press the Measurement Tools icon in the toolbar and select the Geodreieck protractor from the submenu (refer to Figure 11-11). (You also can insert the Geodreieck protractor from the Insert menu.) Here's what you can do with the Geodreieck protractor:

✔ **Move the Geodreieck protractor.** Press in the inside of the Geodreieck protractor and drag it to the new location.

✔ **Resize the Geodreieck protractor.** Press the semicircle and drag away from the center to make the Geodreieck protractor bigger and inward to make it smaller.

✔ **Rotate the Geodreieck protractor.** Press outside the semicircle and drag the Geodreieck protractor where you want to rotate it. You see the rotation in degrees displayed in the center.

✔ **Draw with the Geodreieck protractor.** Press the Pens Types icon, select Standard Pen or Calligraphy Pen, select a line style, and draw along the edges of the protractor as you would if you had a protractor on a piece of paper. The digital ink appears as an arc.

✔ **Remove the Geodreieck protractor.** Select the Geodreieck protractor, press the drop-down arrow, and select Delete.

The compass

As with the protractors and ruler, you can manipulate the width, rotation, and location of the compass, and then you can use it to draw circles and arcs. The compass is the perfect teacher's assistant when it comes to actively involving students learning a new concept.

To insert the compass, press the Measurement Tools icon in the toolbar, and select the compass from the submenu (refer to Figure 11-11). (You also can insert the compass from the Insert menu.) Here's what you can do with the protractor:

- ✔ **Move the compass.** Press on the left arm that holds the spike and drag to the location on your page.

- ✔ **Widen the compass.** Press the right arm that holds the pen, and two blue arrows appear. Drag the arrows to change the angle between the left leg and the pen.

- ✔ **Flip the compass.** Press the compass flip symbol on the pen (the green arrows) and the compass flips.

- ✔ **Rotate the compass without drawing.** Press the rotation handle (the green circle above the drop-down arrow), and drag it in the direction you want to rotate the compass.

- ✔ **Draw with the compass.** Press the Pen tip on the compass, and the pen symbol appears. Drag the compass where you want the line to appear. To change the color of the compass, press the pen and select the color on the SMART Tools menu bar. You see the color appear on the body of the compass.

- ✔ **Remove the compass.** Select the compass, press the drop-down arrow, and select Delete.

Enabling Two People to Use the Interactive Whiteboard

Having two people share an interactive whiteboard is useful in brainstorming sessions or collaborating on projects.

To enable two people to use the interactive whiteboard at the same time, you need access to SMART Board D600 or 800 series (or some series of interactive flat panels). These are the only interactive whiteboards that are designed to allow two people to create and manipulate objects in SMART Notebook software at the same time.

Note: Some of the procedures described in this section vary between the D600 and 800 series. Some of the functionality available in one series may differ or be unavailable in the other.

As a presenter or teacher, you can set up many different types of exercises or interactive activities enabling two people to work together. Here are some ideas:

✔ When designing a plan, one person can draw and the other person can add the labels.

✔ You can have one person write questions on the interactive whiteboard. As the audience shouts out answers, the other person writes them down.

✔ People can play games together on the interactive whiteboard.

✔ You can have competitions using the interactive whiteboard. Whoever solves a problem first or solves a puzzle first, wins.

On an 800 series, Dual User mode is enabled when you pick up a pen from the Pen Tray. One user creates or manipulates objects with his or her finger ("the touch user"). The other user creates or manipulates objects with the pen ("the pen user").

To enable more than one person to share a D600 interactive whiteboard, you need to display the file in Dual User mode. Follow these steps:

1. **Press the View Screens button.**

2. **Press the Dual Write Mode button.**

3. **To return to Single User mode, press the Exit button.**

Here are a few hints and tips you may find helpful when two people are using the interactive whiteboard together:

✔ When it's set up in Dual User mode, the interactive whiteboard is activated as soon as a pen is picked up from the Pen Tray.

✔ Any combination is possible: finger/finger, finger/pen, pen/pen, finger or pen and eraser.

✔ Users can write anywhere on the interactive whiteboard. They aren't restricted to specific "owner" space.

✔ When one user selects or changes tools to touch, he must press the correct buttons on the toolbar or control in the properties with his finger. For instance, the user needs to make changes using his finger instead of picking up a pen.

✔ The pen user must change properties or tools with the pen.

✔ When the touch and pen users both select multiple objects on the screen, the dashed borders will be a different color for each user.

If the pen user makes a selection by pressing a button using his finger, whether it's in the properties selection or the toolbar, the change will be made for the user using his finger, not the pen. I can imagine that mischievous look in your eyes — you can have loads of fun messing with someone when he's writing: Just change his pen to disappearing ink when he doesn't know it, and watch what happens.

Part III

Adding Interactivity Tools and Collaborating Activities

The 5th Wave   By Rich Tennant

"Maybe we should break from this collaborative session so someone can explain to Marla in Toronto that we can see her doodles."

In this part . . .

Here I show you everything about the interactive tools and how you can be effective when preparing interactive and collaborative lessons or presentations. In Chapter 12, I explain how to use multimedia in your presentation. Chapter 13 shows you how to download and use Bridgit conferencing software, which lets you share files and programs anywhere in the world and deliver real-time lessons or meetings. Chapter 14 shows you how to share your desktop and schedule Bridgit meetings with the Smart Scheduler Outlook Add-in. In Chapter 15, I cover SMART Meeting Pro software and show you how to enhance teamwork and boost productivity; I also discuss screen capture in detail and show you how versatile and useful this tool is. Chapter 16 shows you examples and case studies, providing you with step-by-step guidelines to be able to prepare these activities. It's a real hands-on chapter in which I incorporate material from throughout the book.

Chapter 12

Adding Multimedia to Your Presentation or Lesson

In This Chapter

▶ Attaching sound to objects

▶ Using the SMART Video Player

▶ Recording with the SMART Recorder

*T*he ability to add multimedia to your presentations or lessons is one of the great features of SMART Notebook software. You can easily add sound to objects and videos or create your own. For example, you can use the video recorder to record a video of your lesson, and then post that video in your learning management system (LMS) or on TeacherTube (`www.teachertube.com`) or YouTube (`www.youtube.com`), allowing students who have missed a class to watch the lesson. You can even create a podcast from your presentations. (For more on creating podcasts, check out *Podcasting For Dummies,* 2nd Edition, by Tee Morris, Chuck Tomasi, and Evo Terra [Wiley].)

In this chapter, I show you how to use sound and video in your presentations. I also provide you with links to free resources enabling you to download files you can add to your objects and hints on how you can use media in your presentations.

Enabling and Using Sound

Sound can help make your presentations richer in a number of ways. For example, if your meeting or class can get heated and out of hand, you might use a sound to instantly grab everyone's attention and get them to take a deep breath. You might use sound to give the pronunciations of difficult words in a language lesson. You might use sound to congratulate the person who got a right answer or contributed something useful to the discussion.

All the objects work independently of each other, enabling you to add different sounds to different objects.

Finding sound files

If you want to use sound, it must be an MP3 file. The good news is, you can download many MP3 files free from sources such as the following:

- **Lit2Go:** http://etc.usf.edu/lit2go
- **SoundBible.com:** www.soundbible.com
- **Sound Jay:** www.soundjay.com
- **Soundzabound:** www.soundzabound.com
- **Soungle:** www.soungle.com
- **WavCentral.com:** www.wavcentral.com

If you find the perfect sound file, and it's a WAV file instead of an MP3, you can convert it to MP3 using Media Converter (www.mediaconverter.org) or Audacity (http://audacity.sourceforge.net).

Be sure to check out the copyright restrictions on any file you download. Just because a file is free to download on the Internet doesn't mean you can use it (especially if you're using it for commercial purposes). When in doubt, err on the side of caution and don't use anything unless you're certain you have the rights to use it.

Many of the Gallery objects in SMART Notebook software already have sound files included. You can tell that an item has a sound file because of the little sound icon located in the lower-left corner (see Figure 12-1).

Figure 12-1: An object with a sound file attached.

Sound icon

Adding sound to an object

In this section, I assume you have an object in a SMART Notebook page and you're comfortable with the menus (turn to Chapter 8 if you need a refresher).

You can add an existing sound file to an object, or record your own sound and add it to an object. In this section, I show you both options.

Adding a sound file to an object

To add a sound file to an object, follow these steps:

1. **Select the object.**

   You see a dotted line around it, with a drop-down arrow in the lower-right corner.

2. **Press the drop-down arrow.**

   A menu appears (see Figure 12-2).

3. **Select Sound.**

   The Insert Sound dialog box (shown in Figure 12-3) appears.

4. **Click the Browse button and select the sound file you want to use.**

5. **Select the Corner Icon radio button if you want the sound to appear as a corner icon and play when you press it; select the Object radio button if you want the whole object to be sound sensitive and for the sound to play anytime you press the object.**

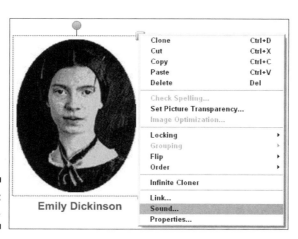

Figure 12-2:
The menu.

Figure 12-3:
The Insert
Sound
dialog box.

6. Press the Attach Sound button.

Figure 12-4 shows the new sound file attached as a corner icon.

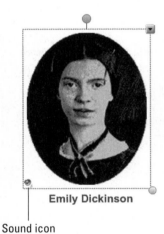

Emily Dickinson

Figure 12-4:
An attached
sound file.

Sound icon

Recording sound and adding it to an object

To record your own sound to an object, follow these steps:

1. Connect a microphone to your computer and turn it on.

If you're using a laptop, you probably have a microphone built in.

2. Select the object.

You see a dotted line around it, with a drop-down arrow in the lower-right corner.

3. **Press the drop-down arrow.**

   A menu appears (refer to Figure 12-2).

4. **Select Sound.**

   The Insert Sound dialog box (refer to Figure 12-3) appears.

5. **Press the Start Recording button.**

   You have only one minute. The recording will stop at the one-minute mark.

6. **When you're done recording, press the Stop Recording button.**

7. **Enter the name of the recording in the Recording Name field.**

8. **Click the Preview Sound button to listen to your recording.**

   Take this opportunity to listen to yourself and determine if you sound too silly before you attach the sound file to your object. If you think you sound awful and want to re-record, just press the Start Recording button again and start over.

9. **When you're happy with the sound you recorded, select the Corner Icon radio button if you want the sound to appear as a corner icon and play when you press it; select the Object radio button if you want the whole object to be sound sensitive and for the sound to play anytime you press the object.**

10. **Press the Attach Recording button.**

Removing sound from an object

If you need to remove the sound from an object, follow these steps:

1. **Select the object.**

   You see a dotted line around it, with a drop-down arrow in the lower-right corner.

2. **Press the drop-down arrow.**

   A menu appears (refer to Figure 12-2).

3. **Press Sound.**

   The Insert Sound dialog box (refer to Figure 12-3) appears.

4. **Press the Remove Sound button.**

Can't get much easier than this!

Inserting Internet browsers

You can insert a web page and access the Internet while working with objects. For example, if you want to download Audacity while you're working with your objects so that you can record your voice, or you want to insert a YouTube video or any other resource that you may want to use with SMART Notebook software over the Internet, you can add it as an object. Follow these steps:

1. **Choose Insert⇨Internet Browsers.**

   From the drop-down list select Internet Browsers and the internal web browser appears.

2. **Double-click the address bar and enter the web address you want to visit.**

3. **Press Go.**

You can pin the page you're browsing by pressing the Pin Page button on the Internet browser toolbar (it looks like a little pushpin). The next time you open the .notebook file, the pinned web page will open in the browser. You can open the pinned web page at any time by pressing the Return to Pinned Page button on the toolbar (it looks like a little pushpin with a green arrow on top of it).

To move the Internet browser toolbar, press the Move Toolbar button (it looks like an up and down arrow). You can toggle the toolbar between the top of the window and the bottom of the window.

Using the SMART Video Player

The SMART Video Player is part of the software and drivers that are included with the interactive whiteboard. You can use it to play DVDs, specific video files, or video on the Internet. Accessibility is very flexible — you can use a video hardware device that's connected to the computer or the DVD drive in the computer; you also can upload a video file or link to one on the Internet. Watching a video on the huge screen is impressive — the resolution and sound are fantastic. But that's not the coolest thing about the SMART Video Player. What adds another dimension is the capability to use SMART software to write over the videos on the interactive whiteboard.

Playing a video

You can open the SMART Video Player by doing one of the following:

✔ Selecting the SMART Board icon in the Windows notification area or Mac Dock and pressing Video Player.

✔ Customizing the Floating Tools toolbar so that the video player is on the toolbar.

After you've opened the SMART Video Player, follow these steps to play a video:

1. **Choose File➪Open or File➪Open URL if you're accessing the video from the Internet.**

2. **Press the Play button.**

   The video begins.

3. **To pause the video, press the Pause button.**

4. **Press the Stop button to stop the video.**

Figure 12-5 shows the Full Screen toolbar with all the buttons you can use to control the SMART Video Player. Here's what all the buttons do:

✔ **Play:** Plays the video.

✔ **Stop:** Stops the video.

✔ **Screen Capture:** Enables you to capture the current video frame with your notes and save them to your .notebook file.

✔ **Select Tool:** Enables you to select objects or other tools.

✔ **Pen Tool:** Enables you to write on the interactive whiteboard.

✔ **Pen Color:** Enables you to change the color of the digital ink.

✔ **Pen Width:** Enables you to change the width of the digital ink.

✔ **Clear Notes:** Clears your notes.

✔ **Full Screen View/Normal View:** Expands the video display to Full Screen view and restores it to Normal view.

   You may not be able to change the view to Full Screen or 200% if the computer that is connected to your interactive whiteboard doesn't have a video card that supports hardware accelerations.

✔ **Repeat:** Plays the video continuously. Press again to stop playing the video continuously.

You also can also access the control settings from the File menu at the top of the screen.

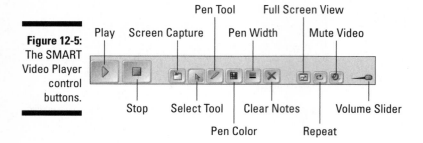

Figure 12-5:
The SMART
Video Player
control
buttons.

Writing and drawing over the video

You can write with the Pen tool or your finger on the video screen. Depending on your settings, you can pause or let the video play while annotating. When you finish with your notes, you can capture the screen and save it to your .notebook file. (I cover screen capture in greater detail in Chapter 15.)

To write or draw over the video, press the Pen Tool button on the toolbar if you want to use your finger or pick up the Pen tool and begin writing on the screen over the video frame. Depending on your video note settings, the video will either pause or continue to play as you write or draw.

You have several setting options for note taking. You can access them from the Settings menu. You can

✔ Pause the video when the pen is pressed or lifted.

✔ Allow the video to play continuously.

✔ Fade out notes after a set period of time.

 If you're playing your video using a VCR or DVD player when you write on the interactive whiteboard, the video will continue to play in the player even though it appears paused on the screen. You'll need to use the remote control and pause the video.

Customizing the video player

You can adjust the video player settings to meet your needs. You can alter the video player view, as well as change the window size.

Ways to use the SMART Recorder

How can you use SMART Recorder in your presentations or class? Here are a few ideas:

✔ Record yourself teaching a concept or a full lesson. Make use of the interactive whiteboard for examples, interactive activities, or explanations of resources as you surf the web. Everything you write or say will be captured by the computer and packaged into a single video file. Make the video available for students to take home on their own flash drives. Students who aren't good note takers will love it, and English as a second language learners will benefit as well.

✔ If you work at a college or university that services the military, mail your lecture to deployed soldiers taking your college courses or upload them to a learning management system such as Moodle. (Check out my other book, *Moodle For Dummies* [Wiley], for more on Moodle.)

✔ Make the video lectures available on TeacherTube (www.teachertube.com) or YouTube (www.youtube.com).

✔ Students can video their presentations and capture their notes. Then you as an instructor will have more time to go over the videos and mark the work or presentation.

✔ Use the SMART Recorder in a class that teaches students presenting skills.

These are just a few of the many uses presenters and teachers have found for the SMART Recorder. If you found a successful way to use the SMART Recorder, let people know by posting it on SMART Exchange (http://exchange.smarttech.com)!

Altering the video player view

You can view the movie at the regular size (100%), 200%, or full screen. If you view the video at 100% or 200%, you have access to the title bar, menu bar, toolbar, and status bar. In full-screen mode, you have access to the Full Screen toolbar (with the buttons listed in the "Playing a video" section).

You can drag the Full Screen toolbar anywhere on the screen or make it disappear after a set time. To hide the toolbar, follow these steps:

1. **Choose Settings⇨Video Player Settings.**

2. **Select Remove Toolbar in Full Screen Mode.**

3. **Enter the time period.**

4. **Press OK.**

Changing the window size

You can set the window size by going to the main menu and pressing View. Select 100%, 200%, or Full Screen. If you want the video player window to cover other applications, go to the main menu and select Settings. From the settings window, press Always on Top.

Making quality recordings

You can make high-quality recordings with the SMART Recorder, but if you're new to recording presentations (or even if you're a pro!), the following tips will start you off on the right foot:

✓ **Hide the toolbar while recording.** Your recording will look much more professional. To hide your recording, choose Menu⇨Hide to System Tray. You can press F8 to start and stop recording so that you don't need the toolbar.

✓ **Pay attention to the frame rate.** The recording length is displayed below the recording button. To the right of the menu is the status bar showing the rate of your recording. A faster frame rate indicates better quality. You can change the frame rate by accessing the configure options after you open Recorder.

✓ **Think about your disk space before you start recording.** If you run out of disk space during a recording, a warning message appears. Press the Pause button to stop recording, free up some disk space, and then start up again.

✓ **Use digital ink in the interactive whiteboard and use strong colors.** Strong colors show up better than lighter colors when you use a thin line style. If you really like your chosen color, you can change the style of the line so that the text lines are thicker.

✓ **Interact with your audience.** You can involve them by having them come up to the interactive whiteboard and annotating. It keeps the audience interested.

✓ **Prepare what you want to say ahead of time.** Try to avoid fillers like "um," "ah," and "you know."

✓ **If someone asks a question, repeat it.** This way, both the question and answer will be clear in the recording.

✓ **Don't use animation or special effects on the interactive whiteboard.** They don't transfer well to the recording; plus, they increase the file size.

✓ **Avoid using complex graphics.** Large graphic files or full-screen photos increase the file size. Use Word, Excel, and PowerPoint or SMART Notebook pages because the software is optimized for all SMART Board interactive whiteboard software.

Using SMART Recorder

The SMART Recorder enables you to record your on-screen actions presenting or delivering a lesson on your interactive whiteboard. You can use the SMART Recorder to create a step-by-step video tutorial every time you deliver a lecture, or you can create the tutorials, on your own, and then make them available to your audience. All you need is the SMART Notebook software and a microphone.

Be sure to back up the video on your own flash drive or computer if you're on a network and sharing the interactive whiteboard with colleagues.

Creating a recording

To create a recording, you only need yourself, access to your files, and a steady hand and voice.

You can always re-record if you find that your first recording is embarrassingly bad. You'll get better with practice.

To create a recording, follow these steps:

1. **Press the SMART Board icon in the Notification Area (Windows) or Dock (Mac), and then press Recorder.**

   The SMART Recorder opens (see Figure 12-6).

Figure 12-6: The SMART Recorder.

2. **If you don't want the SMART Recorder toolbar to appear in the recording, choose Menu⇨Hide to System Tray (see Figure 12-7).**

Figure 12-7: Hiding the SMART Recorder toolbar.

3. **If you need to record a certain window or screen area, press the arrow next to the Red Record button and select Record Window or Record Area (see Figure 12-8).**

   Recording only a small screen area keeps your file size down.

Figure 12-8: The Record drop-down menu.

4. **When you're ready to record, press the red Record button.**

   When you record, the time elapsed is displayed below the Record button. The colored dot indicates the quality of the recording, which is determined by the recorder settings.

   You'll need to connect a microphone to your computer if you require audio and your computer doesn't have a built-in mic.

5. **When you finish recording, press the Stop button.**

   Don't forget to save the file. After you save it, a dialog box appears showing the file size and the length of the recording. If you're unhappy with the recording, just press Cancel.

Changing the recorded video format

You may need to change the video format to play the video in another application or upload it to the Internet. Follow these steps to change the format:

1. **With the SMART Recorder open, select Options from the drop-down menu.**

   The Options dialog box appears (see Figure 12-9).

Figure 12-9:
The Options dialog box.

2. **Select the Video Format tab.**

3. **Select the format you require.**

   You have two options:

- Microsoft Video (*.wmv): Choose this option if you need the video to be viewed by Windows Media Player. This format uses 256 colors.

- SMART Recorder Video (*.avi): Choose this option to create a more compressed file. This format uses 16 million colors.

4. **Press OK to save your changes.**

Changing the recording quality

If you want, you can change the audio and video setting, experimenting with quality and file size. Follow these steps:

1. **With the SMART Recorder open, select Options from the drop-down menu.**

   The Options dialog box appears (refer to Figure 12-9).

2. **Select the Recording Quality tab.**

3. **Select the Sound Quality and Video Quality from the corresponding drop-down lists.**

   I recommend that you leave the settings set to the default options — Standard for Sound Quality and Automatic Selection for Video Quality — unless you have a specific reason for changing them.

Creating a file you can share on other platforms

When you record a fantastic lesson, lecture, or presentation to your team, you want the world to know about it! You can upload your recording to SMART Exchange (http://exchange.smarttech.com), TeacherTube (www.teachertube), or YouTube (www.youtube.com), or just carry it with you to share it with your family and friends.

To share your recordings, follow these steps:

1. **Before you record, select Options from the drop-down menu, select the Video Format tab, and make sure you select the SMART Recorder Video (*.avi) format.**

   After you make your recording, a message box will appear saying, "Recording Complete."

 2. **Select Share Recording and press OK.**

 The Share Recording Wizard opens.

 3. **Follow the steps in the Share Recording Wizard.**

 It guides you through a process to create either a .wmv (Windows Media) file or a self-extracting executable file (.exe). If you want to upload it to YouTube or another website, select .wmv.

 4. **Choose Menu⇨Share Recording.**

 The Share Recording dialog box appears.

 5. **Click Next.**

 6. **Browse to and select the file you want to share and then press Next.**

 Yon get a confirmation that a file was created.

 7. **Press Finish.**

 The file is created and can be shared.

Chapter 13

Collaborating with Your SMART Board Interactive Whiteboard

In This Chapter

▶ Downloading and using Bridgit conferencing software

▶ Getting ready for a Bridgit meeting

▶ Creating a meeting in Bridgit

*Y*ou've secretly been admiring your colleagues who talk about their video meetings with people halfway around the world. They talk about how fabulous the connection was, how they saved money not having to travel, how much they accomplished, and on and on. You secretly wish you had access to the state-of-the-art technology to collaborate, in real time, on projects. Well, now is your chance! You don't need fancy software, and you don't have to pay a third-party provider. Bridgit collaboration software, from SMART Technologies, interacts with your interactive whiteboard.

The brilliance of Bridgit software is its ability to let you work with your far-flung colleagues and students as though they were in the room with you, looking over your shoulder at your computer. More than that, Bridgit lets them actually interact with the files on your screen, adding notes, taking over control of your computer, collaborating, and communicating as though the thousands of miles that separate you were an illusion. Or perhaps you need to share your screen with a colleague down the hall or a telecommuter to demonstrate a visual concept. Bridgit also handles audio communication, so you can talk directly with your audience, narrating your presentation, facilitating discussions, and answering questions.

What's more, you can invite additional attendees on the fly, instantly e-mailing them an invitation that lets them join your presentation regardless of whether they have Bridgit on their computers.

Running the Audio Setup Wizard

The first time you run SMART Bridgit client software, you might have to run the Audio Setup Wizard. This wizard enables you to choose the volume level for your microphone, headphones, or speakers. Follow these steps:

1. **Attach your headphones (or speakers) and a microphone to your computer and turn them on.**

If you're working on a laptop, the speakers and microphone will likely be built in.

2. **Close every program that can play or record sound.**

3. **Click or press Next, and then follow the on-screen instructions.**

In this chapter, I explain how to download Bridgit, what's involved in a Bridgit meeting, how to prepare for a meeting, how to create a meeting, how to join a meeting, and how to leave a meeting. This chapter has everything you need to know about using Bridgit conferencing software.

Downloading Bridgit Software

Start by downloading the latest version of SMART Bridgit software at http://www.smarttech.com/software.

Check the system requirements on the download page to ensure your computer is up for the task.

Note: If you get invited to a Bridgit meeting but you haven't installed the software yet, you can download the "client" version by clicking a link in an e-mail invite. The *client* part of the name just means that you can attend meetings but not create them.

Bridgit Meeting Basics

You can create a meeting or attend a meeting set up by someone else. Before you get started doing either of these things, you need to consider what role you want to play in the meeting. You also need to know your way around the tools at your disposal in a Bridgit meeting. I cover both of these topics in this section.

To be or not to be: What role do you want to play?

When you participate in a meeting using Bridgit, you have one of three roles: owner, presenter, or participant. When you're in a meeting, the owner and the presenter are highlighted in the list of attendees.

Here's what each role is responsible for:

✔ **Owner:** The owner is the creator of the meeting on the SMART Bridgit Server. You can view this role as the boss or the person in charge. The owner can adjust the meeting settings. But, as the person in charge, the owner has specific powers no other role has, such as the ability to

- Adjust the audio
- Take over sharing of the desktop
- Draw on the desktop
- Talk in a meeting and share webcams
- Disconnect all participants and end the meeting

✔ **Presenter:** The presenter shares the desktop. This role is given to the person talking and presenting information. The presenter can disable the capabilities of participants, but not of the owner. The presenter can

- Adjust meeting settings
- Draw on the desktop
- Talk
- Share webcams

✔ **Participant:** Participants have a limited role. They can

- See everything on the shared desktop
- Listen to discussions and hear other participants in addition to the presenter
- View shared webcams

Participants can be given the ability to draw on the desktop, talk in the meeting, and share a webcam, but the owner or presenter has to enable those features.

Bridgit tools

When you enter a meeting, a set of tools is available to help you with your presentation. Figure 13-1 shows the Bridgit client toolbar. The toolbar has the following buttons (from left to right):

✔ Menu

✔ Audio window

✔ Video window

✔ Desktop sharing

✔ Select tool

✔ Pen

✔ Raise hand

✔ Participants List

The drop-down arrow to the right of the Menu button includes more capabilities (see Figure 13-2). You can

✔ Share your desktop or ask to take over sharing.

✔ Enable or request to control someone's desktop remotely.

✔ Select a set of writing tools and write over the shared desktop.

✔ Change meeting and audio settings (if you're the presenter and using VoIP [voice over Internet protocol]).

✔ Change the viewing options (if you're looking at someone's shared desktop).

✔ Change the language used in the software interface.

✔ Change to Full-Screen view.

✔ E-mail a meeting invitation.

During a meeting, you can make the menu appear by pressing Alt.

Colored border   Bridgit toolbar

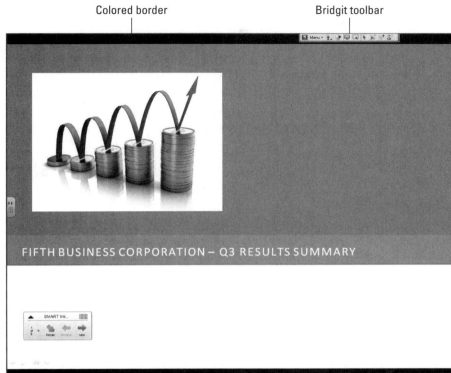

FIFTH BUSINESS CORPORATION – Q3 RESULTS SUMMARY

Figure 13-1:
The Bridgit
client
toolbar.

Figure 13-2:
Additional
options
accessed
via the
Menu
button.

What's in a color?

The bright border around the toolbar (refer to Figure 13-1) is more than decoration. It has specific functionalities related to the meeting. The border changes color when you share your desktop or when you view another participant's desktop. Here's what the colors mean:

✔ **Blue:** You're sharing your desktop and you're the presenter.

✔ **Green:** You're viewing the presenter's desktop, which is shared with any number of participants. All participants see a green border.

You can select the border and drag it vertically to reposition it on your desktop. If you want to move the toolbar horizontally, drag the handle right or left; the handle is the gray vertical bar to the right of the Participants List button.

The lobby screen

The lobby screen is your workspace in the meeting. It enables you to share your desktop, send e-mail invitations to participants, begin to talk in the meeting, or share your webcam. You can have access to the lobby even if no one present is sharing a desktop. Figure 13-3 shows the Windows lobby screen; Figure 13-4 shows the Mac lobby screen.

The participants window on the left lists all the participants in the meeting. It notes "owner" and "presenter" next to the names of the people taking on these roles. On the right side of the participants window is space for text to be entered if a participant wants to ask a question or make a statement. Below this window is the text field where participants can type their questions and answers.

The cool thing about the lobby screen is that you can use it to send e-mail to participants, inviting them to the meeting. To send invites from the lobby screen, follow these steps:

1. **Click the E-mail Invitation button at the bottom of the Participants List.**

   The Invite Participant dialog box appears.

2. **If the meeting is password protected, select the Include Password in E-mail check box.**

3. **Click Email.**

   You see your default e-mail client begin creating an e-mail invitation.

4. **Add the e-mail addresses of the invitees and send your e-mail.**

   Bridgit software includes a link in the body of the e-mail, which enables invitees to join the meeting.

Figure 13-3:
The Windows lobby screen.

Figure 13-4:
The Mac lobby screen.

Meeting etiquette

When you're holding or attending a meeting, observe these few rules of etiquette to make the experience pleasant for everyone involved:

✔ Place a do not disturb sign on your door when you're in the session.

✔ Ask attendees to turn off their handheld devices.

✔ Use participants' names when you address them. Ask all participants to identify them-selves before they speak or answer a question.

✔ If you're annotating on the interactive whiteboard, remind everyone that you'll capture the notes and make them available to all participants. There is no need for everyone to feverishly take notes while someone is annotating.

Preparing for a Bridgit Meeting

When you decide to set up a collaborative meeting or deliver a lesson or training session, preparation is critical. Here are some tips you may find helpful:

✔ **Contact all participants and give them the date and time of the tele-conference, specifying the time zone.** To avoid confusion, say something like, "The meeting will be held Wednesday, May 30 at 2 p.m. EST, 1 p.m. CST, 12 p.m. MST, 11 a.m. PST."

✔ **E-mail all participants information on how to join the meeting.** If they can dial in, give them the access code. I always include my contact details just in case any participant has difficulties joining the meeting.

✔ **Prepare an agenda and e-mail the agenda, along with any notes you may want to go over, so that participants can stay on track.** Also, give participants time to prepare — you'll avoid questions related to the purpose and/or structure of the meeting if they know it from the start.

✔ **Keep an eye on the clock.** Work out the timing and do your best to stick to it. If you organize your presentation and discussion and run it through once to time it, you can adjust the time frame. Bullet points and concise statements will help you avoid rambling.

✔ **If the purpose of the meeting is collaboration and ongoing relationships with colleagues or other students, prepare a short bio and relevant information on each participant and distribute it beforehand.** This information will speed up the meeting so participants don't have to spend time introducing themselves and questions can be targeted.

✔ **Start on time!** Don't wait for latecomers. Let them stroll in and then just acknowledge their presence. I usually just say, "Welcome, Pat," and continue.

✔ **At the beginning of the conference, acknowledge everyone involved with a quick hello.** If you have time, allow everyone to briefly introduce himself.

✔ **If you're on a tight timeline or running a class with younger students, outline some basic do's and don'ts.** For example, you might tell them how long they can speak before you'll interrupt, that they should pause and give other participants a chance to say something, and other basic etiquette considerations (see the nearby sidebar).

✔ **Prepare a list of all participants, and make notes on who is contributing.** You may need to engage the participants who have a quieter nature. The first time someone participates in a meeting, he tends to be hesitant to contribute. Coax that person out of his shell, and engage him by asking him a question.

✔ **If you're involved in a very important strategy meeting, consider recording the session.** Your interactive whiteboard can do this for you.

✔ **Schedule breaks.** If this is a long conference (say, over an hour), schedule a ten-minute break. Someone may really need that third cup of coffee.

✔ **Before you end the meeting, ask if anyone has any questions or comments.** Then summarize what you discussed, clearly state that the session is over, and end the session. If participants ask for more info or time, you can easily set up a forum discussion or ask them to e-mail you.

Creating a Bridgit Meeting

When you create a meeting, you're the owner of the meeting (see "To be or not to be: What role do you want to play?" earlier in this chapter), which means you control all the meeting options.

To set up a meeting, follow these steps:

1. **Open the Bridgit software by double-clicking the Bridgit icon on your desktop (Windows) or by clicking the Bridgit icon in your Dock (Mac).**

   The SMART Bridgit Software dialog box (shown in Figure 13-5) appears.

Figure 13-5:
The SMART
Bridgit
Software
dialog box.

2. **Select the Create New Meeting tab (see Figure 13-6).**

3. **Enter your name in the Your Name field.**

   The name you enter will appear in the Participants List.

4. **Enter a name for the meeting in the Meeting Name field.**

Figure 13-6:
The Create
New
Meeting
tab.

5. **If you want your meeting to have a password, enter the password in the Password field and again in the Confirm Password field.**

   If you don't password-protect the meeting, anyone who can view the list of meetings on your network can join the meeting.

6. **If your IT department has enabled VoIP and you want to use it, make sure you select the Automatically Open Microphones check box.**

   This enables participants' microphones to be opened when they join the meeting. If you aren't sure whether VoIP is enabled, check the Automatically Open Microphones box.

7. **Click the Create New Meeting button.**

   The software begins and connects to a Bridgit server.

   If for some reason you need to connect to a different server, click the server icon in the lower-left corner of the SMART Bridgit Software dialog box. A Server Information dialog box appears, where you can type the name of the server you want to connect to or select a server from a drop-down list.

8. **If you created a password for this meeting, enter the password in the Password dialog box and then click OK.**

   If your IT department set up your servers to require a creation password, you'll have to enter it after you create your meeting.

   The Bridgit lobby opens, and you can start your meeting.

Joining a Meeting

You have a few options for joining a Bridgit meeting. In this section, I walk you through each option.

Joining a meeting from an e-mail invitation

The easiest way to join a meeting is to click the link in an e-mail invite. To join a meeting from an e-mail invite, follow these steps:

1. **Select the link in the body of the e-mail.**

   If you haven't run the software, you'll need to run it. The Join Conference dialog box appears.

2. **In the appropriate fields, type your name and, if required, the password.**

   If a password is required, it will be included in the body of the e-mail that contained the link.

3. **Click OK.**

   The lobby screen opens and you're in!

Joining a meeting when cookies are disabled

If you try to join a meeting by clicking the link in your e-mail invite and a message appears telling you that you aren't able to join because cookies are disabled in your web browser, you have two options: Either enable the cookies (which may not be possible if you're on a network) or download the client software and manually enter the meeting information.

Follow these steps to download and enter the information manually.

1. **Click the link in the e-mail invite.**

   The File Download box appears.

2. **Click the Save button.**

3. **Browse to where you want to store the file on your computer and click Save.**

4. **Find the file saved on your computer, and double-click the icon to open the file.**

   The Open File Security Warning dialog box appears.

5. **Click Run.**

   The SMART Bridgit Loader starts.

6. **Type the name of the server in the Server Name box.**

7. **Click OK.**

   The SMART Bridgit dialog box appears.

8. **From the Meeting Name drop-down list, select your meeting.**

9. **Add your name and if prompted, the meeting password, and then click Join.**

   You see the lobby screen.

Note: These steps vary depending on your operating system.

As soon as you get your invite, try entering the meeting to see if you need to download and save the software. If you do, you'll be able to get the server name in advance.

Joining a meeting from Bridgit client software

To join through the client software, you need to have the software installed on your computer (see "Downloading Bridgit," earlier in this chapter). When you have the software on your computer, follow these steps:

1. **Double-click or press the Bridgit icon.**

2. **Select the meeting you want to join.**

   Choose carefully because there may be a number of meetings scheduled.

3. **If VoIP has been enabled, select Yes or No.**

   VoIP is voice over Internet protocol, and it can be enabled to use audio software on your computer.

4. **Click Join Meeting.**

If you need to change the server you're connected to, click the server icon in the bottom-left corner of the SMART Bridgit Software window, and select the server from the drop-down list or enter it into the field; then click Connect.

Searching for a meeting

If you know the name of the meeting, you can search for it in the SMART Bridgit Software window. Simply type the name of the meeting in the Meeting Name box (as shown in Figure 13-7) or, from the menu, select the meeting from the drop-down list.

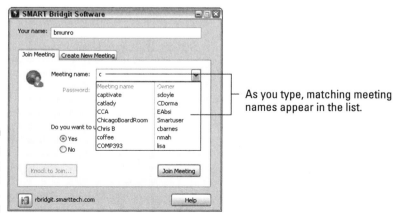

Figure 13-7: Searching for a meeting.

As you type, matching meeting names appear in the list.

Leaving a Meeting

When you finish a meeting, you need to exit it. Here's how:

1. **Click the arrow next to the Menu button.**

2. **From the drop-down list, select Exit Smart Bridgit (Windows) or Quit (Mac).**

   If you're the owner of the meeting, you'll be asked whether you want to disconnect all participants.

3. **Click Yes.**

Chapter 14

Taking Advantage of Remote Collaboration and Other Conferencing Tools

. . . .

In This Chapter

▶ Using voice conferencing

▶ Presenting and participating in meetings using Bridgit software

▶ Sharing a desktop

▶ Scheduling meetings with the SMART Scheduler Outlook Add-in

. . . .

*T*his chapter empowers you with a tool set that helps you make distance education and remote collaboration or meetings a snap. Here I walk you through how to set up a meeting or lesson, invite participants, and add notes to presentation materials that every participant can see. All this can be done in a few simple steps.

In this chapter, I explain how to use Bridgit conferencing software, how to present and participate in meetings, and how to use the SMART Scheduler Outlook Add-in to simplify and speed up the process of inviting participants to a meeting. Soon you'll wonder why you would ever want to get in your car and travel to a meeting.

Using Voice Conferencing

When you use Bridgit software, participants can interact with the presenter by typing questions and answers into a text box or using the software's voice feature. The Voice over Internet Protocol (VoIP) feature allows participants to talk to each other during a meeting. The meeting owner administers this functionality. (Refer to Chapter 13 for more on the various roles — owner, presenter, participant — of meeting attendees.)

Talking in a meeting

Before your participants are able to talk in a meeting, they first need to run the Audio Setup Wizard, which allows them to set the volume levels of their speakers or headphones and microphone (see Chapter 13).

To be able to talk in a meeting, or to enable your participants to talk, follow these steps:

1. **Press or click the Open My Mic button on the Audio Controls toolbar.**

   If you can't see the Open My Mic button, click the Show/Hide Audio Controls button (see Figure 14-1). The participants should be able to hear you when you speak into or near the microphone.

Click here to view these controls.

Figure 14-1:
The Show/
Hide Audio
Controls
button.

2. **Adjust the volume by sliding the slider located on the Audio Controls toolbar.**

   This volume control adjusts both the microphone and the headphones or speakers.

3. **When you finish speaking, click Close My Mic.**

   You have to close the mic in order for other participants to be able to talk. This functionality prevents participants from interrupting the presenter.

If the owner of the meeting selected the Automatically Open Microphones check box when setting up a meeting, the microphones automatically open for the first four participants who join the meeting.

The owner of the meeting can show or hide the audio controls. If you have a chatty bunch that can't contain their excitement, it may be in your best interest to hide the audio control. This will encourage participants to use the texting option instead. To hide the audio control, click the Audio icon and press the Show/Hide Audio Controls button (refer to Figure 14-1). The owner and/or presenter can still talk to the participants.

Seeing what the owner, presenter, and participants can do with audio

Only four participants can talk at any one time. By default, the capability is given to the first four participants who enter the meeting. In order to allow other participants to talk, follow these steps:

1. **Close another participant's microphone by clicking or pressing the Participants List button (shown in Figure 14-2).**

   The Participants List appears (see Figure 14-3).

2. **Click or press the green microphone icon next to the participant's name.**

Participants List button

Figure 14-2:
The
Participants
List button.

Figure 14-3:
The
Participants
List.

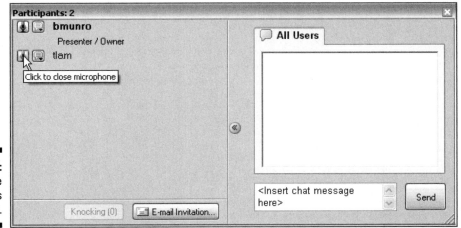

You also can select Others Must Request to Talk, which changes the participant's Open My Mic button to a Request Mic button, depicted by a raised hand icon. To enable participants to talk, click the raised hand icon; it changes back to the Participants List icon. Click the same raised hand icon next to a participant's name to enable an individual participant to talk.

As the owner of a meeting, you can enable all participants to have microphone capabilities at all times during the session, or you can set it up so that when a participant wants to speak, he makes the request and you enable him to speak. I strongly recommend that, if you're giving a timed lecture, lesson, or presentation, and you want to control when you take questions, you require participants to request a microphone. You do this from the Meeting Settings tab of the Options/Preferences window (which you access by choosing Menu⇨Options [Windows] or Menu⇨Preferences [Mac]), shown in Figure 14-4. Select the Require Others to Request Microphone check box. In order for participants to be able to talk, they have to click the microphone button (once it's enabled) and click the Request Mic hand button to enable the microphone. A message pops up on the shared desktop informing the presenter of the request. The participant won't be able to speak until the presenter clicks the microphone icon.

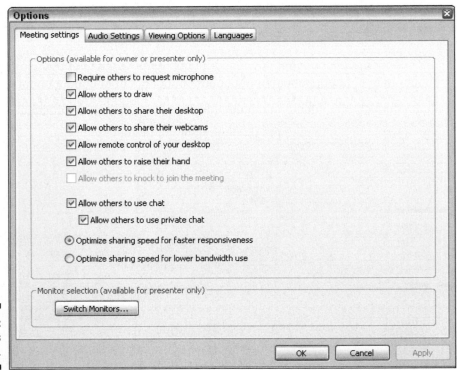

Figure 14-4:
The Options
window.

Using a third-party voice system

Bridgit software can be used with a third-party voice bridge. It works the same as joining a Bridgit meeting, but you have to use a telephone and the conference code provided by the third party.

You can join the meeting by clicking a link sent to you in an e-mail or from the Bridgit client software, but you also need to use your telephone to dial the number and enter the code. If you're already sharing your desktop, you may be able to see the telephone number and conference code in the Participants List.

Presenting and Participating in Meetings

Presenting and collaborating is a shared activity. People often learn or accomplish goals and tasks best by collaborating with others. The beauty of Bridgit software is that it supports multifaceted communication, giving you and your participants many devices and tools to help you present and collaborate on documents or other presentation materials.

With Bridgit software, you can

- ✔ Use editing and drawing tools and pointers
- ✔ Talk and listen to participants
- ✔ Chat via text
- ✔ Share and view a webcam
- ✔ Move the toolbar and change the shared area of your desktop
- ✔ Change sharing options
- ✔ Monitor a meeting's performance
- ✔ View the list of participants
- ✔ Enable remote control options to control participants' computers

Setting meeting options

You can set a variety of options for your meeting in the Options/Preferences window (refer to Figure 14-4). Here are the settings:

✔ **Require Others to Request Microphone:** Selecting this check box requires participants to make a request before they can talk. The presenter and owner receive an alert of the request, and they can grant or deny the request. If you don't select this check box, a participant will be able to talk by clicking the Open Mic button.

✔ **Allow Others to Draw:** Selecting this check box enables participants to use their drawing/writing tool to annotate information. This is selected by default. If you want to be the only one with this capability, uncheck this box.

✔ **Allow Others to Share Their Desktop:** Selecting this check box enables participants to ask to take over sharing and making their desktops visible instead of yours. You can decline the request. This is selected by default. If you don't want participants to have this capability, uncheck this box.

✔ **Allow Others to Share Their Webcams:** Selecting this check box enables participants to share their webcams. Only four participants can share their webcams at the same time. This is selected by default. If you want only your webcam to be available, uncheck this box.

✔ **Allow Remote Control of Your Desktop:** Selecting this check box enables participants to request to control the presenter's desktop by clicking Request Remote Control. The presenter can always regain control.

✔ **Allow Others to Raise Their Hand:** Selecting this check box lets participants inform the presenter or owner that they want to speak by "raising" their digital hand in the form of a pop-up, which the presenter or owner can acknowledge.

✔ **Allow Others to Knock to Join the Meeting:** Selecting this option lets anyone on your server "knock" to join your meeting without being invited. As a presenter or owner, you see a pop-up message, and you can click to allow the person access. This saves you from having to provide the password to other people.

✔ **Allow Others to Use Chat:** Selecting this check box enables participants to use text messaging in the Participants List. Conversations are visible to all participants.

✔ **Allow Others to Use Private Chat:** Selecting this check box enables one-on-one text messaging conversations. Texting isn't visible to anyone else.

✔ **Optimize Sharing Speed for Faster Responsiveness:** This option is available only when sharing a desktop. Bridgit software captures the shared screen at regular intervals so participants see updates.

✔ **Optimize Sharing Speed for Lower Bandwidth Use:** This option is available only when sharing a desktop. Bridgit software captures the shared screen less frequently to use less bandwidth.

Sharing your desktop

Before you begin any type of activity, you need to make sure you can share your desktop with participants. Sharing your interactive whiteboard adds that extra dimension to collaboration that you don't have in teleconferencing.

After you create and/or join your meeting, follow these steps to share your desktop:

1. **Click the Share My Desktop button in the lobby screen.**

   Refer to Chapter 13 for a screenshot of the lobby screen. If multiple displays are used, the Select Monitor Window list will appear.

2. **To share a single monitor, select the monitor and click OK. To share more than one monitor, hold down the Ctrl key, select the monitors you want to share, and click OK.**

   A "preparing desktop" message briefly appears. Then the Bridgit toolbar with a blue border appears. This means that anyone in the meeting can see your screen. Meeting participants see one enlarged display, which is the presenter's screen (see Figure 14-5).

To stop sharing your desktop, press the Start/Stop Sharing My Desktop button located on the Bridgit toolbar (see Figure 14-6).

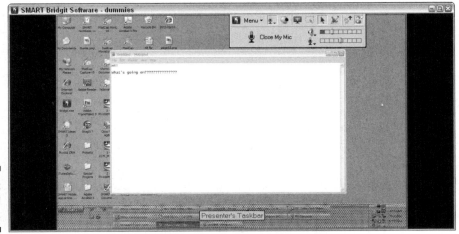

Figure 14-5:
A shared desktop.

Start/Stop Sharing My Desktop

Figure 14-6:
The Start/
Stop
Sharing My
Desktop
button.

In order for participants to share their desktops so other participants can see them, they have to make a request to the owner of the meeting, and the owner has to grant permission. This capability is only available if the owner or presenter hasn't disabled it. To take over the screen sharing as a participant, click the Start/Stop Sharing My Desktop button. The presenter sees the request and will either grant you permission or not. (If he doesn't, you'll continue to view the current desktop.)

The owner doesn't need the presenter's permission to take over the screen.

Sharing a webcam

In the previous section, I show you how to share your computer screen only. But unless you enable the webcam on your laptop, your participants won't be able to see *you*. If your participants have webcams and enable them, you'll be able to view them as well. Only four participants can share their webcams at one time.

As the owner or presenter, you can enable and disable remote webcams. If you disable them, participants will still be able to see you from your webcam, but you won't be able to see them.

If any other program on the computer is using the webcam, make sure you disable it first.

To share a webcam, follow these steps:

1. **Click the webcam icon located on the Bridgit toolbar (it's between the microphone and the screen buttons).**

   The video window appears.

2. **Click the Start My Webcam button on the bottom-left side of the screen.**

   Your image is displayed to participants.

If the webcam is shared with other participants, a small thumbnail image shows at the bottom of the larger image. If you hover your mouse or finger over the thumbnail images, you see a message showing the name of the person sharing that particular webcam. Click the smaller images to expand them.

You can hide or show the webcam by clicking the webcam icon.

To stop the webcam, click Stop My Webcam.

Reviewing the Participants List

The Participants List informs you of all the participants, their names, and their status. Your own name should appear in bold, with the word *owner, presenter,* or *participant* next to it. You can access the Participants List by clicking the Participants List icon in the Bridgit toolbar (it looks like a little figure with a speech bubble).

You also can see the Participants List in the Bridgit lobby screen (see Chapter 13).

Here is a rundown of the buttons associated with the Participants List:

- ✔ **Microphone:** This button indicates whether the participant has the capability to talk in the conference. Clicking this button opens and closes the capability. The Open Microphone button has a green microphone in it, with a blue box around the microphone; the Closed Microphone button is just a gray microphone with no box around it.

- ✔ **Request to Talk:** If you see this hand, it indicates the participant is requesting to talk. Clicking the button enables communication. The hand appears only if you've selected Require Others to Request Microphone in the Options/Preferences window when you set up your meeting.

- ✔ **Chat:** This button indicates whether chat is enabled. When chat is enabled, the speech bubble is yellow with a blue box around it; when chat is disabled, the speech bubble is gray and there is no blue box. If chat is enabled, you receive a message and the hand changes color. If there is a waiting time during a meeting, an hourglass appears over the icon.

- ✔ **Microphone Requested:** The button with a microphone inside a blue speech bubble indicates that a participant is requesting to speak in the meeting. To allow the participant to speak, click the button. The Participants window opens. Click the icon beside the name of the requesting participant.

The chat window: Letting your fingers do the talking

Another way that you can communicate with your participants is to use chat. The chat feature in Bridgit software is similar to other online chat or instant messaging software, like Google Chat or AIM.

You have two options to chat: You can use the chat window in the Participants List or in the lobby screen. As the owner or presenter, you have to enable chat before it can be used. To enable chat, click the Allow Others to Use Chat check box on the Meeting Settings tab of the Options/Preferences window (refer to Figure 14-4).

A number of neat functions and options are included with Bridgit Chat that you may want to explore:

✔ You can send a message to every participant by opening the Participants List or lobby screen, clicking the All Users tab, typing the message, and pressing Send.

✔ To chat with only one participant, open the lobby screen or the Participants List, and click the chat button next to the participant's name. The participant is added to a private conversation. Select Create a New Conversation with Participant. A tab appears in the chat window with the participant's name. Now you can communicate with this participant one-on-one. You'll know the message is headed to a particular participant because the tab will be opened.

You can create a number of tabs for different participants so you can switch between numerous one-on-one conversations. If you have multiple conversations and a message arrives for a conversation not currently selected, the chat balloon icon will appear next to the participant who sent the message. You'll always be informed when a text message arrives.

✔ To add more participants to a conversation, click the chat button next to the names of the participants you want to add, and select Add Participant to Selected Conversation.

✔ If you receive messages when you aren't present, the notification bubble appears next to your name in the list, flashes three times, and stays green until you return and open the message. When you return, just click the bubble to open the chat window and read the message.

✔ When you want to end a conversation, click the X on the tab you want to close. The participants in the chat will see a message that you've left. Participants can continue to chat even though you aren't present.

Writing on a shared desktop

Bridgit software allows you to draw and write notes on your screen when it's shared. You also can use SMART Ink or Ink Aware tools (see Chapter 4) and capture what you've created using the screen-capture software bundled with the interactive whiteboard. (I talk about Screen Capture in Chapter 15.)

To access the drawing tools when you're sharing a desktop, choose Menu➪Tools and select the tool you want. I cover the tools in the following sections.

The Screen Pointer

The Screen Pointer is a great tool when you're walking through a procedure or trying to show everyone something on a busy screen. I find it useful to point to bullet points to keep participants on track. To use the Screen Pointer, from the shared desktop, choose Menu➪Tools➪Screen Pointer. The Screen Pointer flashes red for a few seconds to let you know that it has been added to the presentation screen and a new participant has become active. The name of the participant using a pointer appears below the pointer.

When you want to move the Screen Pointer, click the arrow head and drag it. You see the standard editor circular arrows while moving it, informing you that you can alter the pointer in any direction. To move the Screen Pointer without changing the direction, select the rear half of the arrow, not the arrowhead, and drag it.

To stop using the Screen Pointer, double-click it.

Several participants can use the Screen Pointer at the same time. When you're presenting in a meeting, and you want to see only one Screen Pointer, double-click the others to make them disappear.

The Pen tool

The Pen tool allows you to write notes and add them to documents or presentation materials. Every participant has access to the Pen tool by default, unless the owner disables the writing tools.

To write on a shared desktop, follow these steps:

1. **Click the Pen button in the Bridgit toolbar.**
2. **Click and drag with the Screen Pointer.**
3. **When you finish, click the Screen Pointer again.**

When you draw on the shared desktop, the ink and notes are visible to all participants sharing your desktop. You aren't limited in terms of how many people write on the same screen.

Presenters can clear notes placed on the desktop. Just take the Screen Pointer, and click anywhere on the shared desktop. Before clearing notes, you may want to take a screen capture and save them first.

When you select the Pen tool, you have a default color when you join the meeting. If you hate the color you're assigned, no worries — you can change the color, line width, and transparency. To customize the Pen tool, follow these steps:

1. **Choose Menu⇨Tools⇨Customize Pen.**

   The Customize Pen dialog box appears.

2. **Select the color you want.**

   If you can't find the color you need, click More.

3. **Select a width from 1 to 32 pixels.**

   The default is 3 pixels.

4. **If you need to use the pen as a highlighter, select the Transparent option.**

5. **Click OK.**

The Eraser

As easy as it is to write on a shared desktop, it's even easier to erase the content. To erase what you've written, choose Menu⇨Tools⇨Eraser. Drag the Eraser tool over any notes you want to erase. When you're done, just click the Screen Pointer anywhere.

Remotely controlling other people's desktops

Being able to control someone else's desktop is, well, quite satisfactory if you're a control freak. Even if you aren't, it's useful and satisfying when you need to make a point or show where your participants made mistakes. Remote control is enabled by default, allowing participants to click the shared desktop to take control or request remote control of the presenter's desktop.

If you can't control a shared desktop, you need to enable it either from the shared desktop or on the Meeting Settings tab of the Options/Preferences window:

- ✔ From the shared desktop, choose Menu⇨Enable Remote Control. To disable it, choose Menu⇨Disable Remote Control.

- ✔ From the Meeting Settings tab, choose Menu⇨Options (Windows) or Menu⇨Preferences (Mac), select the Meeting Settings tab, and select the Allow Remote Control of Your Desktop check box. (To stop it, uncheck this box.)

To gain control of the presenter's desktop, click the presenter's desktop. If the presenter wants to regain control, he can move the mouse or press the keyboard. Users won't be able to take control for three seconds.

To change the shared area, just select the Screen Pointer and hover it over the border until it changes into a horizontal, vertical, or diagonal resize pointer. Then drag the border until it engulfs the area you intend to share. The participants will be able to view this area only.

To share the whole desktop, hover the mouse pointer as above and double-click the border. The whole desktop will be surrounded by the border.

Using the SMART Scheduler Outlook Add-In

In Chapter 13, I cover inviting participants to a Bridgit meeting via e-mail. The participant receives an e-mail with a link to the meeting. This task is very simple if you have the SMART Scheduler Outlook Add-in because it integrates the SMART Bridgit Server with the Microsoft Exchange Server and Outlook clients, enabling you to schedule single or recurring meetings. When you create a meeting, all participants are automatically invited.

Before you can use the SMART Scheduler Outlook Add-in, you need to make sure you have the right system requirements on your network. See the Bridgit page at www.smarttech.com/downloads to review the requirements.

The add-in can be used on any computer that is communicating with your Bridgit software. When you're sure you have all the system requirements, get your friendly system administrator from the IT department to download and install the .msi file. Now you can set up your first meeting making the requests from Outlook.

To set up a Bridgit meeting, follow these steps:

1. **Open Outlook and switch to Calendar view.**

2. **Click the arrow on the New button and select Meeting Requests.**

   An untitled meeting request form appears.

3. **Enter the meeting information.**

   Don't forget to add time in the correct time zone.

4. **Select the This Is a SMART Bridgit Meeting check box to use Bridgit for your meeting.**

   Your invitees are e-mailed an invitation.

The beauty of the software is that when you create a meeting, all participants receive an invitation containing the link and log-in information and the user ID and password.

Chapter 15

Using SMART Meeting Pro Software

. . . .

In This Chapter

▶ Understanding the functionality of SMART Meeting Pro software

▶ Using SMART Meeting Pro software to accomplish your goals

. . . .

SMART Meeting Pro software is designed to deliver easy business solutions by enhancing the use of your interactive whiteboard and content sharing through Bridgit conferencing software. SMART Meeting Pro includes a bundle of tools to make it easy to share content and capture everything you do on the desktop or interactive whiteboard. This software includes SMART Ink, which allows you to annotate PDFs, Microsoft Office files, web pages, or anything else on your screen. You can then send those notes and images by e-mail to your meeting participants or save them, right from within the meeting. It also includes easy-to-use templates and meeting resources.

Getting Started with SMART Meeting Pro Software

The true strength of SMART Meeting Pro software lies in its simple interface and the fact that you're only one or two steps away from performing specific actions to create or add to your presentations. There are many business packages out there, but most aren't integrated with an interactive whiteboard that supports every business function you can think of, including conferencing software.

Unless you already have the software installed on the computer that is connected to the interactive whiteboard, you'll need to download it. Go to www.smarttech.com/downloads to do that.

System requirements

Here are the system requirements for SMART Meeting Pro software on single- or dual-display systems:

- ✔ Windows XP Service Pack 3 or Windows 7
- ✔ 2.0 GHz dual core processor or faster (quad-core recommended)
- ✔ 1GB RAM for Windows XP, 2GB RAM for Windows 7 (4GB recommended)
- ✔ 1GB free hard disk space for minimum installation (additional free space required during installation)
- ✔ DirectX 9–capable video card with discrete 256MB VRAM
- ✔ At least 10 Mbps wired network or 802.11 a/g/n (100 Mbps recommended)

The system requirements for SMART Meeting Pro software on multiple-display systems are as follows:

- ✔ Windows XP Service Pack 3 or Windows 7
- ✔ 3.0 GHz dual core processor or faster (quad-core recommended)
- ✔ At least 4GB RAM
- ✔ 1GB free hard disk space for minimum installation (additional free space required during installation)
- ✔ DirectX 9–capable video card with discrete 256MB VRAM
- ✔ At least 10 Mbps wired network or 802.11 a/g/n (100 Mbps recommended)

Available tools

SMART Meeting Pro software has a set of tools enabling you to work with any type of digital file, save everything you annotate on the interactive whiteboard (even a web page), and write content using digital ink. This treasure chest of tools enables your lessons, meetings, or collaboration activities to run effectively and efficiently. Plus, it adds an element of fun and enjoyment.

Here are some of the features of SMART Meeting Pro software:

- ✔ Automatic setup for Bridgit software (see Chapter 14)
- ✔ A very simple, intuitive interface
- ✔ Meeting tools that allow you to hold your meeting with ease, including tools to help you monitor the meeting time

✔ SMART Ink digital ink to add or annotate any type of page or file, including web pages and your desktop

✔ Business Content Gallery, which is similar to the SMART Notebook Gallery but filled with tools for business presentations

✔ The ability to e-mail all your notes by choosing File⇨Email Notes

✔ All the interactive whiteboard features you're used to

✔ The ability to save anything you do in a number of different formats

✔ The ability to organize your notes

✔ The ability to move notes and documents between screens and write on more than one interactive whiteboard simultaneously

✔ Integration with Microsoft Exchange, allowing you to manage your calendar, meetings, and meeting requests

✔ SMART GoWire™ auto-launch cable, enabling guests to use SMART Meeting Pro without having to install it on their laptops

Using SMART Meeting Pro Software

Some of the tools and features of SMART Meeting Pro software are similar to those found in SMART Notebook software.

To get started, turn on your interactive whiteboard and launch SMART Meeting Pro by doing one of the following:

✔ Double-pressing the SMART Meeting Pro icon on your desktop

✔ Choosing Start⇨All Programs⇨SMART Technologies⇨SMART Meeting Pro (*Note:* This procedure varies depending on your operating system.)

Your workspace and all your tools

As soon as you open SMART Meeting Pro software, you'll be delighted to see that everything you need, and more, is right in front of you. The layout is bright, clear, simple, and neat.

When you have SMART Meeting Pro open, you should see the active workspace (shown in Figure 15-1). Here, notice the following:

Whiteboard menu   Bridgit Collaboration toolbar   Whiteboard area

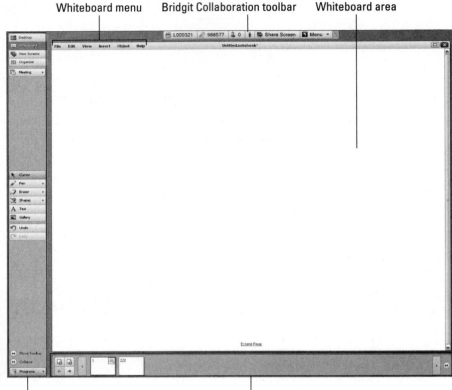

Figure 15-1:
The SMART
Meeting Pro
workspace.

SMART Business toolbar   Page Sorter

✔ The whiteboard annotating/drawing area in the center, which changes when you choose one of the viewing modes

✔ The main SMART Business toolbar on the left, which includes four different viewing and working options: Desktop, Whiteboard, View Screens, and Organizer

✔ The Page Sorter at the bottom, which acts like the Page Sorter in SMART Notebook software

✔ The main Whiteboard menu with various options and access to other tools

✔ The Bridgit software meeting/collaboration toolbar, which includes all the information you need to join a meeting and run it

Whiteboard

When you first open SMART Meeting Pro, the default screen opens in Whiteboard mode. The whiteboard area is used to display your page where you work with objects, write, and draw. The functionality and options are very similar to the SMART Notebook page. Use the tools to annotate; draw; add text, shapes, and art; work with templates; and use activities from the Gallery.

The Whiteboard mode is very similar to the SMART Notebook workspace. You use the main area to create pages that can be used for any type of activity — taking notes during your meeting that you can distribute at the end, extending presentation slides, displaying graphics and charts, brainstorming, and more. All your drawing and interaction tools are in the toolbar, located on the left side. The tools are similar to the Floating Tools toolbar in SMART Notebook.

Desktop

The Desktop mode enables you to view your computer's desktop so you can open and interact with your Windows applications and any files you have stored on your hard drive, network, external disc drives, or thumb drive. You also can access the Internet or any Microsoft Office files, use SMART Ink to write on the files or add to the files, and then save the files in your whiteboard presentation or use Screen Capture. You have every option possible to support your business and presentation needs.

To access the desktop, press the Desktop button in the SMART Business toolbar (see Figure 15-2). You see the workspace change to your desktop. You can interact with the desktop as you would normally, but you have all the editing tools available for you to add and annotate your files or web pages.

Figure 15-2:
The SMART
Business
toolbar.

The best way to learn an application is to play with it, so try this:

1. **In Desktop mode, open one of your existing files (for example, a Word document).**

2. **Pick up a pen.**

The SMART Ink or Ink Aware toolbar appears.

3. **Add a figure or circle a sentence in Word, and place a note on the side (see Figure 15-3).**

4. **Select Screen Capture and save your page to your notes area at the bottom of the screen.**

View Screens

You use View Screens mode when you're connected to any number of screens of participants in a meeting using SMART Meeting Pro or Bridgit software. Note that the participants need to have the software running on their computers or they need to be using a SMART Board interactive whiteboard running the software in order for you to be able to share the screens and view participants' screens.

If you're in a Bridgit meeting and you want to view the screen of someone sharing her desktop, simply press View Screens and her broadcast appears.

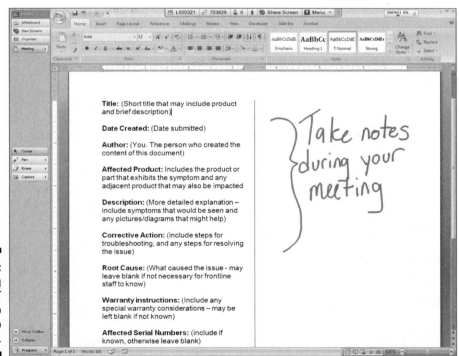

Figure 15-3:
Working with SMART Meeting Pro in Desktop mode.

Organizer

Organizer mode gives you a bird's-eye view of everything you're working with in SMART Meeting Pro — all the pages and files, as well as Microsoft Exchange (if you've integrated it) and your favorite accessories. The cool thing about Organizer mode is being able to jump from one file to another. This capability is most useful when you're in a remote meeting and need quick access to the Internet, files, and SMART Meeting Pro tools.

Everything you need to run a meeting

SMART Meeting Pro software allows you to schedule a meeting or set up a meeting at random. All you have to do is log into a room resource computer.

In order to be able to use all the features of a scheduled meeting, the meeting owner must log into the room resource computer with his network credentials. You can use SMART Meeting Pro software, Microsoft Exchange, or Bridgit software (see Chapter 14).

Scheduling or starting a meeting

The easiest way to start a meeting is to log into the room resource computer. After SMART Meeting Pro software starts, you can use the Meeting Notification window and the Bridgit Collaboration bar to organize and manage any meeting.

Meetings can be scheduled, ad hoc, or you can start them manually. A scheduled meeting is simple — it begins automatically when the meeting owner logs into the room resource computer. An ad hoc meeting can be started if a room resource is available for 30 minutes.

To begin a meeting manually, press Meeting and select Start Meeting. If you're the owner of the meeting, it starts immediately. If the meeting is scheduled, you aren't the owner, and you haven't been invited, you see a prompt asking for your network login. If the meeting is unscheduled and you find that the room resource is available, press Book Room to manually start an ad hoc meeting.

To book a room, follow these steps:

1. **Press Organizer on the SMART Business toolbar.**

2. **Select the Meeting tab (see Figure 15-4).**

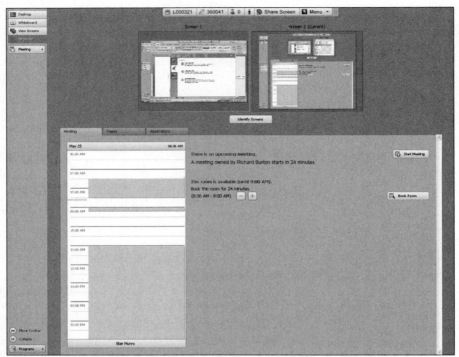

Figure 15-4:
The Meeting
tab.

You see the following:

- A calendar showing the availability of the room
- The room resource's availability status highlighted in blue
- The length of time you can use the resource
- Options to increase or decrease the time and to book the room resource (press the + or – signs to increase/decrease time)

3. **Press the Book Room button.**

   Note: This button is available only if the meeting room isn't booked already.

   SMART Meeting Pro starts an ad hoc meeting.

You can monitor the meeting's time and activities in the Meeting Notification window (see Figure 15-5). The Meeting Notification window provides three alerts:

Meeting Progress bar (green indicates over 15 minutes left)

Status messages

Additional options

Figure 15-5:
The Meeting
Notification
window.

✔ **Status messages:** These messages keep you informed about what's hap-
pening with your meeting. You see a status message when a meeting
starts, when a meeting is in progress, when the meeting has five minutes
left, when the meeting has passed its scheduled time, and so on.

✔ **Meeting Progress bar:** The Meeting Progress bar is a clock that changes
color depending on the time. It's green if you have over 15 minutes left
in the meeting; orange if you have 15 minutes or less left in the meeting;
and red if you have only 5 minutes left.

✔ **Five-minute reminder:** When you have only five minutes left in a meeting, you're reminded in the Meeting Notification window and given the
following options:

  • Extend the meeting for 30 more minutes by pressing the Extend
    button.

  • Press the Reminder button to get another five-minute warning.

  • Press the red X to ignore the reminder.

  • Press the red rounded arrow to end your meeting.

If another meeting is scheduled, you won't be able to extend the meeting
any longer than scheduled. At the end of the five-minute warning, the
meeting will be terminated.

✔ **Reset Room button:** When you're done with your meeting and you need
to close your files quickly and clear out for the next people to come in,
pushing this button lets you close all your open files, e-mail your notes,
and log off.

Adding a guest's laptop to your presentations

If you've set up a session and a new participant runs in to join the meeting
with a laptop under her arm, no problem. If she's using SMART Meeting Pro

or Bridgit already, all she has to do is use Bridgit to join the meeting (see Chapter 14). If you have wireless Internet in your meeting room, even if she doesn't have SMART Meeting Pro, she can still easily download Bridgit and join the meeting in about a minute (see Chapter 14).

If she doesn't have SMART Meeting Pro, she can connect using a physical cable called a SMART GoWire auto-launch cable. See www.smarttech.com/support for more information on the SMART GoWire.

Managing your meeting

One of the most useful and timesaving features of SMART Meeting Pro software is that it's designed to integrate with Microsoft Exchange and Bridgit software, allowing you to automate the whole process of conferencing. When you do this, the people invited to your meeting in Outlook receive, as part of the standard meeting invitation, the Bridgit information that allows them to join the meeting remotely. That means you can book one meeting to conference with your sales office in Tokyo, your branch manager in Cairo, and your field office in Houston, all at once.

It works by using your Outlook calendar to schedule and send meeting invitations, as you do with standard meetings. But unlike standard meetings, you need to add, in Outlook, the in-room resource in your invitation. When you book your meeting in Outlook, invite the SMART Meeting Pro software–equipped room as your room resource. After you start the meeting from one location, SMART Meeting Pro software automatically joins remote room participants to the owner's Bridgit session.

In order to be able to sync Outlook, you must enable Microsoft Exchange integration. To enable Microsoft Exchange integration follow these steps:

1. **Open SMART Meeting Pro.**
2. **Press SMART Settings.**
3. **Press SMART Meeting Pro Settings.**

   The log-in dialog box appears.

4. **Enter your password or, if your network administrator hasn't set up a password or if you don't know it, click OK (by default, there is no password).**

   The SMART Meeting Pro Settings dialog box appears.

5. **Select the Microsoft Exchange tab.**
6. **Select the Enable Microsoft Exchange Integration check box.**
7. **Type your meeting room resource e-mail in the field.**
8. **Press OK.**

That's all there is to it — the synchronization will be done for you.

The next thing you need to do is enable automatic starting of scheduled meetings. Follow these steps:

1. **Follow steps 1 through 4 in the preceding list to access the SMART Meeting Pro Settings dialog box.**

2. **Select the Microsoft Exchange tab.**

3. **Select the Auto Start Scheduled Meeting at Log On or Auto Book Ad Hoc Meeting at Log On check box.**

4. **Press OK.**

There are a number of other settings you can explore.

If you need help, click the Help icon. SMART Technologies has extended online help that's easy to read and use.

The Screen Capture tool

The Screen Capture tool is an incredibly useful addition that you'll love. This tool enables you to take a screen capture of part of the image on the interactive whiteboard or the whole screen. It automatically saves the image into a `.notebook` file, or you can save it as a web page, graphic image, PDF, or PowerPoint file.

For example, if you're brainstorming with colleagues in a meeting, going over charts, annotating as you go, you can save everything on the interactive screen. Prior to this capability, I found myself feverishly taking notes on some device or paper. But with this technology, you can easily capture each page and save it as a file that you can share with all the attendees or anyone else who needs it.

Follow these steps to take a screen capture:

1. **Open SMART Meeting Pro.**

   The SMART Business toolbar appears. The Screen Capture menu is halfway up the toolbar (see Figure 15-6).

Figure 15-6:
The Screen
Capture
menu on
the SMART
Business
toolbar.

2. **Open a file or web page.**

3. **With your finger or interactive whiteboard pen, place a few arrows to change the flow, circle something, and add a note (as shown in Figure 15-7).**

4. **Press Screen Capture on the SMART Business toolbar and then select one of the following options: Full Screen Capture, Rectangle Selection, or Freehand Selection.**

   Full Screen Capture takes a screen capture of — you guessed it! — the full screen. Rectangle Selection takes a screen capture of a rectangle, the size and position of which you set. And Freehand Selection lets you select and shape the area you want to take a screen capture of.

5. **Select the area of the screen that you want to capture (if applicable).**

   The image of the captured area appears on a page in Whiteboard mode. Press Whiteboard on the SMART Business toolbar, and your new image is in the Page Sorter area at the bottom (see Figure 15-8).

In addition to saving your notes as a `.notebook` file to be used in SMART Meeting Pro, you can save the notes and images you captured on your annotated interactive whiteboard by exporting your screen captures into one of four formats:

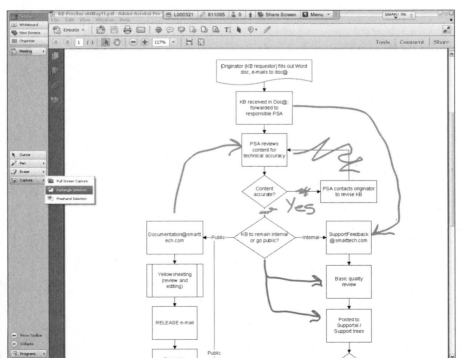

Figure 15-7:
An anno-
tated
document.

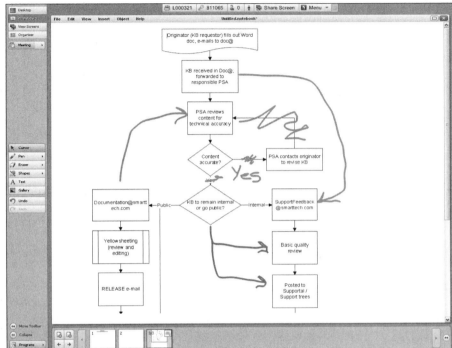

Figure 15-8:
A screen
capture
of an
annotated
flowchart in
Whiteboard
mode.

- ✔ Web page (HTML)
- ✔ Graphics file (JPG, BMP, PNG, or GIF)
- ✔ Adobe document (PDF)
- ✔ Microsoft PowerPoint file (PPT or PPTX)

Just follow these steps:

1. **In Whiteboard mode, choose File⇨Save As.**
2. **Browse to the location where you want to save the file.**
3. **Enter a filename.**
4. **From the Save As Type drop-down list, select the format you want to save it in.**
5. **Press Save.**

   The file is saved.

Enjoy this great tool!

E-mailing notes

At the end of your meeting, with the press of a button, SMART Meeting Pro sends the minutes, markups, images, and notes you worked on to all the participants of the meeting. This feature has made the role of the meeting secretary obsolete — or rather, it's just made it far easier and more efficient for the meeting secretary to accurately capture and electronically distribute everything that was discussed and decided on in the meeting. No more woolly action items or conflicting opinions about what was said and done. Now that's progress!

Note: To use the e-mail feature, you must have Microsoft Exchange integration enabled or your computer's default e-mail client configured.

Better still, you have the option to send the notes as a `.notebook` file, a PDF, or a PowerPoint presentation, in case your attendees don't have SMART Meeting Pro software.

To e-mail your meeting notes, follow these steps:

1. **In Whiteboard mode, choose File⇨Send To⇨Mail Recipient (as Attachment).**

   The E-mail Notes window appears (see Figure 15-9).

2. **Select a file type under E-mail the Following File(s).**

3. **If you want, select Add Attachments to attach additional files to your e-mail.**

4. **Press E-mail [Your Name] to send the file only to yourself (if you set up the meeting, your name appears) or E-mail All Attendees (to send the notes to all the invitees), or press Cancel to cancel the operation and return to your file.**

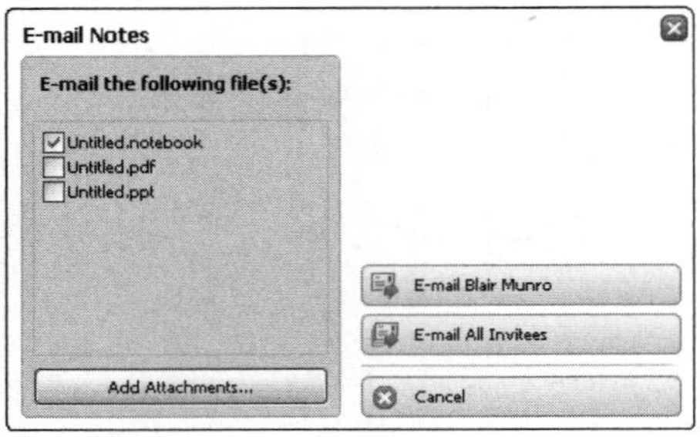

Figure 15-9:
The E-mail
Notes
screen.

E-mail Notes

E-mail the following file(s):

☑ Untitled.notebook
☐ Untitled.pdf
☐ Untitled.ppt

E-mail Blair Munro

E-mail All Invitees

Add Attachments...   Cancel

Chapter 16

Putting It All Together: Some Great Examples

● ●

In This Chapter

▶ Taking your lessons and lectures to the next level

▶ Kicking your presentations up a notch

● ●

*T*he best way to learn a new product is to sit down with it and start creating something. This chapter dives into showing you how to set up activities you can use in your lessons, training sessions, or meetings. Although the examples focus on education or business, you can adapt them to fit your unique presentation goals.

Be sure to visit the SMART Exchange website (`http://exchange.smart tech.com`) for templates, files, and ideas you can use in your own lessons and presentations. Appendix A includes links to other useful websites, too.

If you have SMART Meeting Pro Software, you'll find similar activities and building tools aimed at the business sector — workflows, graphs, processes, and so on.

Scrolling Banners

A scrolling banner is a neat way to capture people's attention or distract them at a specifically timed moment. You might, for example, have a particular message scroll across the screen to highlight an important date or remind people of a key takeaway.

To create a scrolling banner, follow these steps:

1. **Open SMART Notebook and open a file or a new page.**

2. **Press the Gallery tab and select Lesson Activity Toolkit.**

   A menu appears.

3. **Press Tools**.

4. **In the lower half of the Gallery tab, expand Interactive and Multimedia.**

   You see loads of different objects.

5. **Scroll down until you find the scrolling text banner.**

6. **Drag the scrolling text banner to your page.**

7. **Double-click the banner to edit the text, and then type the message you want to scroll (see Figure 16-1).**

8. **Use the handles at the lower right to resize the banner and then place it where you want.**

9. **Click OK.**

Type your scrolling message here.

Figure 16-1:
Creating a
scrolling
banner.

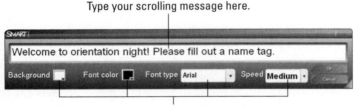

Use these options to customize the appearance.

Pull Tabs

Pull tabs (see Figure 16-2) enable you to store extra information around the page. You can include text, graphics, links to websites, or sound. The advantage is that if you want to include a lot of information in one page, and you don't want to have to jump around from one page to another, you can just pull out the tab you need.

To access and play with the example shown in Figure 16-2, follow these steps:

1. **Open SMART Notebook.**

2. **Press the Gallery tab, and select Lesson Activity Examples.**

3. **Select Interactive Techniques.**

4. **In the lower pane of the Gallery tab, scroll down until you find Pull Tab.**

5. **Drag the pull tab to your page, or select the arrow on the thumbnail and from the drop-down list, select Insert in Notebook.**

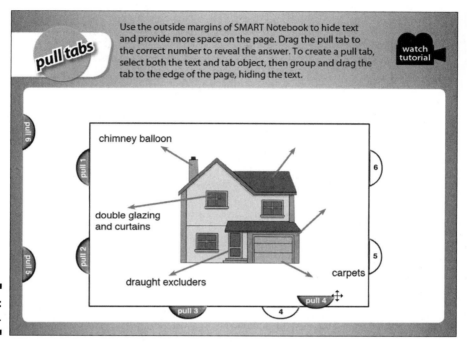

Figure 16-2:
Pull tabs.

Drag the pull tabs from the edge of the
screen, and drop them into their slots.

There are many other templates in the Interactive Techniques folder. Be sure
to experiment with them. Here are just a few examples:

- ✔ Erase to reveal
- ✔ Drag to target
- ✔ Object animation
- ✔ Layer and reveal

Tiles

There are five different tile examples you can customize. You're probably
familiar with games where you flip over a card and find the answer underneath or where you matched pictures. SMART Notebook software re-creates
these games, enabling you to use them any way you need.

This kind of activity can be especially useful in training sessions. For example, if you're training a group in emergency-response procedures, you can set up this activity by having the group identify the order of a procedure. Write the procedure on top of the tile and the step number behind the tile.

Teachers use the tiles in many ways. For example, you can list states or countries on top with the capital cities behind the tiles (see Figure 16-3). The beauty in this activity is the simplicity. All you have to do is ask the question, and then when someone answers, touch the tile, and the answer is revealed.

A good ice breaker and a great way to learn everyone's name is to list pictures of participants and their names. Everyone can try to learn the name of the group. Give out a prize for the winner.

Here's how to set up tiles in your presentation:

1. **Open SMART Notebook.**

2. **Press the Gallery tab, select Lesson Activity Toolkit, and select Examples.**

3. **Select Activities.**

   In the lower half of the tab, you should see Notebook files and Pages (23).

4. **Expand Activities and scroll down until you see Tiles.**

   You see five different types. Open all five and see which is best for your activity. In this example, I chose Tiles 1, which is a capital cities exercise.

5. **Drag the object to your page.**

6. **Press the tiles to see the answer under each tile.**

7. **To customize the activity, click Edit in the top-left corner.**

   You have a number of options to create your activity:

   • The Tiles tab enables you to set the number of tiles and whether you want random colors.

   • The Text tab enables you to set the font of the text the student sees on the top. You have options for font and size. *Note:* If you uncheck the Text box, you'll have color tiles. This is good for hidden pictures or examples.

   • The Objects tab is where you have an answer as text or image.

   Make sure that if you drag the objects over the tiles, you send them to the back (right-click and choose Order⇨Send to Back); otherwise, they'll be in front of the answers.

   • The Options tab gives you options to enable interactions and manual versus random tile selection.

8. **When you finish, click OK.**

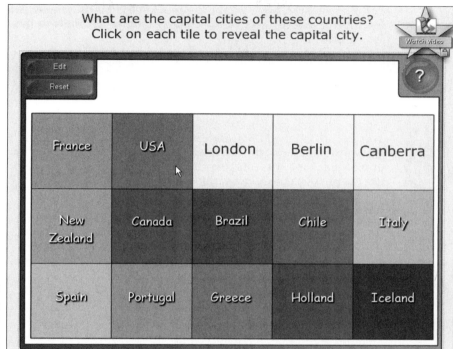

Figure 16-3:
The Tiles
game.

Brainstorming

One of the most powerful things you can do with the interactive whiteboard is to allow your participants to use it in collaborative activities and brainstorming sessions. Set them up either with one blank page in Word or a page in SMART Notebook software, and let them problem-solve.

One rule I have in brainstorming sessions is that nothing is erased or deleted. Here's one of my brainstorming strategies you may want to try:

1. **Open SMART Notebook.**

2. **Create a number of different pages, letting each group choose how many pages they want.**

3. **Name the pages by pressing the date under the page thumbnail in the Page Sorter, or press the drop-down arrow next to the page and select Rename Page.**

4. **Show students where the themed backgrounds, graphs, and other objects are located (in the Gallery tab), or ask them to import their notes.**

5. **Let them brainstorm by writing on the page with the Pen Tray pens, telling them that the only rule is that they can't delete or erase anything.**

6. **Export the session as a PDF.**

You can upload the PDF to SlideShare (www.slideshare.net). You can even get some code from SlideShare and embed the PDF in your personal website or blog, enabling students to continue to work with their ideas. You also can use Google Docs (see the nearby sidebar).

This process works well for any problem-solving exercise where it's useful to show problem-solving strategies. An engineering professor used this process and posted the results to demonstrate how students came to a conclusion.

Games, Puzzles, and More

Editable game templates are bundled in the SMART Notebook software. In addition, the SMART Exchange website (http://exchange.smartech. com) has more free downloads than you can imagine. These games were created by the community of teachers, instructors, and business professionals who use SMART Notebook, and they're all available free of charge.

Generally, the games fall into one of three categories:

✔ **Games:** Examples include board games, checkers, dominos, chess, dice games, card games, Spin to Win (see Figure 16-4), tic-tac-dough, Hangman (see Figure 16-5), and Brain Battle (see Figure 16-6)

✔ **Puzzles:** Examples include crossword puzzles, word searches, and Sudoku

✔ **Game shows:** Examples include Deal or No Deal, Guess Who, Concentration, Hollywood Squares, Jeopardy! (see Figure 16-7), Are You Smarter Than a 5th Grader, Who Wants to Be a Millionaire?, and Wheel of Fortune

Posting your presentation to a blog

Posting to a blog is a great way to share lectures or classroom notes.

Follow these steps to post your SMART Notebook presentation to a blog. *Note:* You need to have a Google account before you can do this.

1. **Export the SMART Notebook file to PowerPoint by choosing File⇨Export⇨To PowerPoint.**

   Save the file somewhere you'll remember, like your desktop, because you'll be uploading it.

2. **Go to** `http://docs.google.com` **and log in (if you aren't logged in already).**

3. **Choose File⇨Presentation.**

4. **In your Google Presentation, choose File⇨Upload a File.**

5. **Select the file you just saved.**

6. **Click OK.**

   When the presentation is uploaded to Google Presentation, you see a blue Share button.

7. **Click the Share button, and you see the code to link to and share that file.**

Figure 16-4:
Spin to Win.

Figure 16-5:
Hangman.

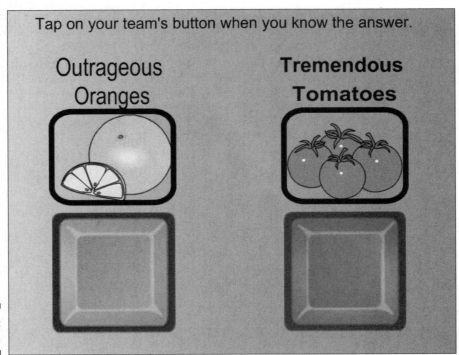

Figure 16-6:
Brain Battle.

Capital cities	Geography	Famous Bobs	Film	Animals
$100	$100	$100	$100	$100
$200	$200	$200	$200	$200
$300	$300	$300	$300	$300
$400	$400	$400	$400	$400
$500	$500	$500	$500	$500

◀- - Drag a blue tile over used squares!

Figure 16-7:
Jeopardy!

Most of the games have two main goals:

✔ To engage the audience

✔ To meet your needs as a presenter or educator by being very easy to modify and customize

Many of these games have been developed for K–12 education, but adults can easily benefit from the games as well. Because you can easily modify and add your own content to the games, you can use them to engage your audience in ways you may not have been able to in the past. Even the most boring of training topics can be made more interesting with a game.

You can download a game from the SMART Exchange website, and then add it to your My Content folder in the Gallery. There are a number of games already ready to be customized in the Gallery.

To add a game to your presentation, from the Gallery, follow these steps:

1. **Open SMART Notebook.**

2. **Press the Gallery tab.**

3. **Press Lesson Activity Toolkit.**

4. **Open the Games folder.**

5. **Select Crossword.**

6. **In the folder in the bottom part of the screen, expand Notebook Files and Images.**

   It opens with one crossword object inside.

   You can download many different types of crosswords from the SMART Exchange website.

7. **Drag the thumbnail to your page or select it and press the down arrow and select Insert in Notebook.**

   You see a big button on the left with a question mark.

8. **Select the question mark button.**

   You see instructions telling you how to input text.

9. **Select the question mark again.**

   You return to the editing screen.

10. **Choose your input method by selecting pencil or typed text.**

11. **Click the Edit button.**

   You're given a template field page where you place your word and clue.

12. **Select Generate when you finish.**

   Your game is created (see Figure 16-8).

The value of learning to present

At Saint Martin's University, Professor Chickering requires his students to present their business projects using the SMART Board interactive whiteboard. He believes that the students will have an instant advantage when they're looking for jobs if they have experience with the technology and can confidently present to a group of professionals using it. I sat in on the presentations and was impressed. One of the students mentioned that using the interactive whiteboard is easy and intuitive. All the students were receptive to the possibilities and realized the advantages they'll have if they know how to present and set up interactive presentations engaging their audience.

Two students, Michael Grosso and Theo Porter, used the interactive whiteboard to present their project about the company Research In Motion (RIM), maker of the BlackBerry. They started with a PowerPoint presentation, which they imported into SMART Notebook software (see Chapter 6). They used SMART Notebook pens and objects to annotate and add notes to each slide and highlight and explain concepts. During their presentation, they had another window open to the Internet; they accessed websites for additional information (company position in the market, company websites, and so on), and used the transparent layer to annotate information on the websites. At the end of the presentation, they got the group involved in a *Jeopardy!*-style game related to what was discussed in the presentations.

The class liked the format and felt they were part of the presentation. The concepts used in the game reinforced the points and highlighted the key goals of the presenters.

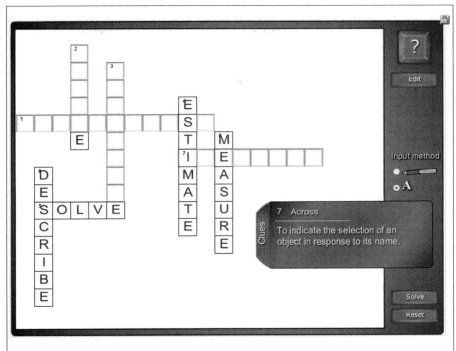

Figure 16-8:
Crossword
puzzle.

Part IV
The Part of Tens

The 5th Wave   By Rich Tennant

"Although the SMART Board comes with interactivity tools, feel free to add one of your own."

In this part . . .

*I*n true *For Dummies* style, and with great excitement, I include the Part of Tens, which is all about that little extra something. These little chapters pack a powerful punch. In Chapter 17, I cover ten frequently asked questions about the SMART Board interactive whiteboard. Chapter 18 is all about ten of the coolest accessories. Chapter 19 gives you ten ideas, tips, and shortcuts for using the interactive whiteboard. And Chapter 20 provides ten creative ways to involve your audience in using the interactive whiteboard.

Chapter 17

Ten (Or So) Frequently Asked Questions

In This Chapter

▶ Getting answers to common questions

▶ Finding out how the interactive whiteboard works

▶ Using other software with the interactive whiteboard

*W*hen you're getting started with any new technology — whether your interactive whiteboard or a new computer or smartphone — you're bound to have questions. And the questions you'll have are likely similar to the questions lots of other new users have. In this chapter, I answer ten (or so) frequently asked questions about SMART Board interactive whiteboards.

Can I Hide the Image on My Interactive Whiteboard but not on My Computer?

The simplest way to hide the image on your interactive whiteboard but still display it on your computer is to turn off — or "picture mute" — your projector. Most projectors have a button on the remote control to "mute" the image or an option in the display menu to turn off the image.

If you're using SMART Notebook software, instead of turning off or "muting" the projector, you can use the Screen Shade tool, which enables you to conceal all or part of the image (see Chapter 11). This solution may not be ideal if you're relying on your computer for notes, however, because it also conceals the image on your computer.

Can I Use Other Software with a SMART Board Interactive Whiteboard?

Yes, you can. Because the interactive whiteboard is an input/output device (like your monitor and mouse in one), you can use any point-and-click application you have on your computer — including web browsers, spreadsheets, interactive CD-ROMs, Microsoft Office programs, OpenOffice programs, NetMeeting, and graphics applications such as CorelDRAW and Adobe Photoshop.

How Does a SMART Board Interactive Whiteboard Actually Work?

The technology behind your SMART Board interactive whiteboard is pretty cool. The interactive whiteboard is connected to a computer via a USB cable, which provides power. The *driver* (software that lets your computer talk to peripheral hardware) automatically switches on when the computer is turned on, and as long as the driver is running, the interactive whiteboard is active. A digital projector is connected to your computer and projects the computer image onto the interactive whiteboard. If you're using a SMART Board interactive flat panel (which is just like an interactive whiteboard but based around a TV instead of a projector), the computer image appears on the display panel and the drivers are able to convert contact with the display into mouse clicks and/or electronic ink. This is the cool part, because it allows you to use your fingers to write on the interactive surface and write over applications such as Excel spreadsheets, PowerPoint slides, or SMART Notebook pages.

What's the Difference between an Interactive Whiteboard and an Electronic Whiteboard?

Interactive whiteboard is a generic term for hardware that's connected to your computer and displays your computer's desktop, allowing you to interact with the information at the interactive whiteboard instead of on your computer. So, you can open applications, surf the web, write on the interactive surface, write over your notes, save the notes, watch videos, record sound, and use the camera attached to the interactive whiteboard.

Electronic whiteboard is also a generic term for hardware that's connected to your computer, but all you can do with an electronic whiteboard is use dry-eraser markers on the board and then save the notes to your computer. You can't display your computer desktop or any other software on an electronic whiteboard, or use your finger or other tools to control or interact with your software.

How Can I Show My Notes to Someone without an Interactive Whiteboard?

You can share your notes in a number of different ways with someone who doesn't have a SMART Board interactive whiteboard. The easiest method is to save your notes as a PDF, HTML, or JPG file. These file formats are standard and can be viewed across all platforms. (For more on saving your notes in these formats, turn to Chapter 6.)

If you need to collaborate and share your SMART Notebook software files with someone else, that person can download the software. A free 30-day trial of the software is available, enabling your colleagues to open, edit, and save any SMART Notebook files. Go to www.smarttech.com/downloads to check it out.

What Programs Does Ink Aware Work With?

The Ink Aware software (which I cover in greater detail in Chapter 4) can be used with a number of different applications:

- Adobe Connect
- AutoCAD
- CorelDRAW
- Microsoft Office, including Microsoft Excel, Microsoft PowerPoint, and Microsoft Word
- Microsoft Office Live Meeting
- Microsoft OneNote
- Microsoft Paint
- Microsoft Windows Imaging
- Microsoft Visio
- OpenOffice

Newer versions of SMART software (for instance, SMART Notebook software version 11 and SMART Meeting Pro software version 3) come with SMART Ink software, which lets you write and save digital notes over virtually anything on your screen, regardless of what program you're using. It's almost like making your entire computer "Ink Aware"!

What Is the Attachment Tab and Why Would I Need It?

You can attach copies of files, shortcuts to files, and links to web pages using the Attachments tab. Attaching files or web pages enables you to find and open these items easily while presenting a `.notebook` file.

Attachment tabs are very useful if you're delivering a presentation or a lesson and you're using a number of different files or objects. The tabs are impressive — you can position them on either side of the interactive whiteboard, use colors or images as tabs, and set them up to slide out when you tap or press on them.

Why Should I Use the Gallery Essentials Collection?

The Gallery Essentials collection is one of the most fabulous resources that SMART Technologies bundled in the SMART Notebook software. It contains over 6,000 learning and presentation objects, which you can insert into your SMART Notebook files. This resource enables you to quickly develop lessons or presentations with rich graphics and media. You have pictures, interactive multimedia files, icons, images, backgrounds, and themes — all free for you to use any way you want.

You can find what you need using the drop-down menus on folders and subfolders. The files are organized into clear themes and logical groupings. You also can use the search box to find what you're looking for. Before you start searching for free resources online or creating charts or images from scratch, explore the Gallery Essentials collection.

One very useful Gallery Essentials resource is a collection of pull tabs you can add to your presentations. To find the pull tabs, follow these steps:

1. **Open SMART Notebook.**

2. **Tap the Gallery icon in the Page Sorter (the menu on the left).**

3. **In the upper pane, choose Lesson Activity Toolkit➪Graphics➪Pull Tabs.**

   A collection of resources appears in the lower pane. Here, you'll find pictures and multimedia tabs you can add to your presentation. To find out how to add these tabs to your files, turn to Chapter 16.

How Does the Interactive Whiteboard Know Which SMART Pen Tray Tool I'm Using?

The SMART Pen Tray's built-in optical sensors detect when a tool is lifted from the tray. As soon as the tool is lifted, information is sent to the computer. The program then waits for that particular tool to make contact with the whiteboard. It knows the chosen color (if it's a pen), and it knows to erase (if it's an eraser). The LEDs on the Pen Tray indicate which tool is active.

I know what you're thinking: What if more than one pen and/or eraser is removed from the tray? How does the interactive whiteboard know which one to use? The very clever designers at SMART Technologies understand that presenters and instructors don't put things back in the same places when they're in the middle of presentations, so they made sure that the last tool that's selected is the active one. Brilliant!

Even more mind-bendingly cool is the Touch Recognition feature in some newer SMART Board interactive whiteboards. On these models, the digital cameras that track your touches on the screen can actually tell whether you're using a pen, using your finger as a pen, using an eraser, or using the palm of your hand as an eraser — all based on the size of contact with the surface. What will they think of next?

How Can I Tell if the Interactive Whiteboard Is Communicating with the Computer?

On the lower-right side of the border of the interactive whiteboard, you see a light. Here's what the light means:

- ✔ **Red:** There is no communication between the interactive whiteboard and your computer.
- ✔ **Flashing red:** The interactive whiteboard is starting up.
- ✔ **Green:** The interactive whiteboard is turned on.
- ✔ **Flashing green:** There's a software issue.

You can find lots more information about the light and what it means in your interactive whiteboard's user's guide. Go to www.smarttech.com/support to find out more.

What Do I Do When I Get a "Clean Filter" Warning?

Many projectors need their filters cleaned after a certain number of hours of use. Some projectors are programmed to remind you to clean the filter. If you don't clean the filter, you run the risk of the device overheating, which will shorten the life span of the lamp and the projector.

When the "clean filter" warning comes on, follow these steps:

1. **Call your information technology (IT) department to see if you can bribe someone who's responsible for the equipment to clean it.**

2. **If you can't get someone from IT to clean the filter for you, find the user's guide for your specific interactive whiteboard system and/or projector and follow the instructions there.**

   There are dozens of projectors out there — SMART Technologies alone produces about half a dozen, each with its own cleaning requirements — so it's impossible to give a quick, easy solution to cleaning in this book.

   If you have a SMART projector (one that came with your interactive whiteboard), go to www.smarttech.com/support and search the knowledge base or browse through the product pages to find your system's user's guide. If your projector isn't made by SMART, go to the manufacturer's website for more info.

You may need to orient the interactive whiteboard after you've cleaned the filters (see Chapter 3).

Can I Lock the Interactive Whiteboard to Prevent Other People from Using My Computer?

You can lock your SMART Board interactive whiteboard in just a few simple steps:

1. **Press the SMART Board icon in the Windows notification area (Windows) or Dock (Mac).**

2. **Choose Other SMART Tools⇨Lock All SMART Devices.**

   The All Devices Locked floating tool appears.

3. **Click the All Devices Locked floating tool.**

To unlock the interactive whiteboard, just click the All Devices Locked floating tool again.

 This procedure varies a bit depending on what version of software you're using. It's pretty similar from one version to the next, but if these instructions aren't quite right, try poking around the menus. If you can't figure it out, go to your SMART software's Help system and search for "locking your interactive product."

 You can't use the interactive screen to unlock the devices. In order to unlock SMART devices, you must use a connected mouse to click the All Devices Locked floating tool.

Chapter 18

Ten (Or So) Cool Accessories

. . . .

In This Chapter

▶ Looking at accessories that can take your interactive whiteboard up a notch

▶ Exchanging and sharing presentations with ease

. . . .

*Y*our SMART Board interactive whiteboard is a killer tool on its own, but when you see how incredibly useful it is, you'll want to do as much as you possibly can with it — and that's where this chapter comes in. Here, you find ten (or so) accessories that you can use to get the most out of your interactive whiteboard and make your presentations and lessons even more impressive.

The SMART Response Interactive Response System

The SMART Response interactive response system (shown in Figure 18-1) uses a remote "clicker" device that communicates with software that is integrated with SMART Notebook software, enabling students to answer questions from their desks. Can't get much cooler than this. If you use the SMART Response system with your classes, I guarantee that you'll be seen as the most interesting, most innovative, and coolest teacher ever!

The advantage is that when you ask questions or give quizzes using the interactive whiteboard, students can answer using the remote and see answers right away — they can see how they're doing in comparison to the rest of the class. As the instructor, you can view answers anonymously or see which student answers. You can collect answers and automatically push data to a report. The brilliant aspect of this device when it's used as a learning tool is that you can instantly see students' performance and alter your lesson based on summative or formative assessment.

There are five different models that are tailored for various target groups, including K–12, special needs, and advanced math and science. The XE model is a handheld response system like a BlackBerry or iPhone, which includes a full keyboard, enabling instructors to pose questions that require more advanced math or science responses, and the VE system actually lets you use your BlackBerry, iPhone, or other mobile Internet device. I've spoken with several teachers who use the system, and they all say that their students love it, are much more engaged, and often more careful. As far as a teaching tool, one teacher said that he no longer uses any other type of assessment activity — Response does it all for him. For more information on this product, go to www.smarttech.com/response.

Figure 18-1:
The SMART Response interactive response system.

SMART Notebook Math Tools

Math Tools (shown in Figure 18-2) is an add-on to SMART Notebook software. It includes everything a math teacher would ever dream of having. If you teach math or science, I highly recommend that you check out this killer app.

The combined tools in SMART Notebook Math Tools enable you to create, teach, and evaluate math concepts that support a variety of learning styles. You'll be able to create math lessons that are interactive, engaging, and fun. The software even includes a launcher for Texas Instruments emulators. If you aren't convinced that this tool will make a difference, let the quiz and test results show you how useful it is.

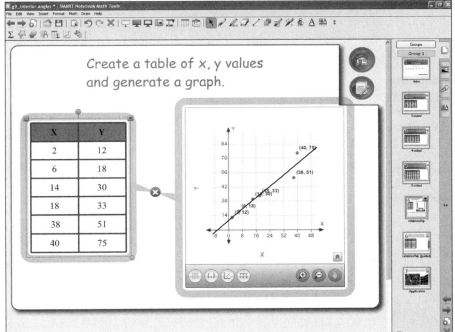

Figure 18-2:
SMART
Notebook
Math Tools.

SMART Document Camera and Mixed Reality Tools

SMART Document Camera (shown in Figure 18-3) is a convenient way to display and explore images of objects anytime — including 3D content — without losing the momentum of your lesson. You can hold physical objects under the document camera and display them on your SMART Board interactive whiteboard, or use the included Mixed Reality Tools for in-depth exploration of 3D content. This will blow your audience's mind.

Figure 18-3:
SMART
Document
Camera
and Mixed
Reality
Tools.

The document camera lets you zoom in to show even the smallest details of objects and automatically focus images and adjust the document camera's brightness for varying light conditions. But the real jaw dropper is Mixed Reality Tools. This lets you manipulate a physical object — a small cube — that is linked with a three-dimensional graphic on your interactive whiteboard. You can rotate it, manipulate it, and look at it in a completely new light. (There's also loads of free content available from the Google 3D warehouse at http://sketchup.google.com/3dwarehouse/.) Words don't do it justice — check out the video at www.smarttech.com/mixedreality for something truly amazing.

SMART Slate™ Wireless Slate

Formerly called the AirLiner™ Wireless Slate, the SMART Slate (shown in Figure 18-4) is an ideal gadget if you enjoy walking around in the audience, getting closer to students and participants, and asking questions or explaining concepts. If you also like to dazzle and look impressive, the SMART Slate is a must! The slate enables you to control all SMART applications on your interactive whiteboard, wirelessly. You can stand in the back of the room and write on the slate and, like magic, what you write appears on the interactive whiteboard. You can stand in front of a room full of students, showing them how to work out a math problem, and everyone can view what you're doing.

The SMART Slate is quite versatile. If you don't want to use it with an interactive whiteboard, it connects wirelessly to your computer from over 32 feet away. Some of the models boast an impressive 54 feet.

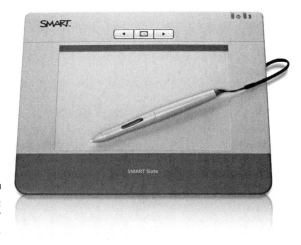

Figure 18-4:
The SMART Slate wireless slate.

SMART Exchange Website

The SMART Exchange website (shown in Figure 18-5) is a community of shared information, lessons, forums, and Help files. Each new lesson uploaded is featured and reviewed. Before you start developing your own lessons and presentations, visit the site and see what's out there for you to use. Participate in the forum discussions, and share with others what has worked or hasn't worked for you. If you develop something absolutely brilliant, why not post it for thousands of people to see and use?

You can access SMART Exchange right from SMART Notebook or SMART Meeting Pro. Visit `http://exchange.smarttech.com` to see what it's all about. You'll find everything — I mean everything — you need for a great lesson or presentation.

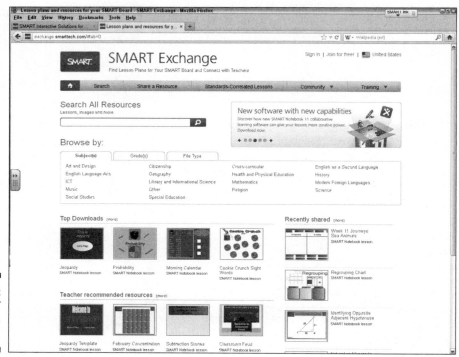

Figure 18-5:
The SMART
Exchange
website.

SMART GoWire Auto-Launch Cable

If you're using SMART Meeting Pro software and you're a regular meeting presenter or participant, the SMART GoWire (shown in Figure 18-6) is a must. It enables you to connect any laptop to your interactive whiteboard and work with your desktop and files. You can access every functionality of SMART Meeting Pro, even digital ink, and have full capabilities to manipulate and save objects.

With SMART GoWire, you also can give your clients and guests access to your SMART Board interactive whiteboard without installing all the software. All they have to do is plug in, wait a couple seconds, and they're good to go. When they unplug the SMART GoWire, the applications no longer exist. I know what you're thinking: "How can this be?" The way it's done is quite slick — the SMART Meeting Pro software is embedded in a USB drive inside the SMART GoWire cable and automatically launches when connected to any laptop. Cool!

Figure 18-6:
The SMART
GoWire
auto-launch
cable.

SMART Sync™ Classroom Management Software

SMART Sync classroom management software (shown in Figure 18-7) helps you organize material and keep students focused by providing thumbnail views of all computers in a class. It's available as part of the SMART Classroom Suite.

Knowing students assigned to specific computers will help you guide their learning progress and engage, one-on-one, with them. They'll see that you're watching them, so they won't be able to be on Facebook or YouTube, play games, and do their classroom work all at once. You also can interact, collaborate, and communicate with students as a group and guide their activities. You can even broadcast videos and demonstrations to their desks.

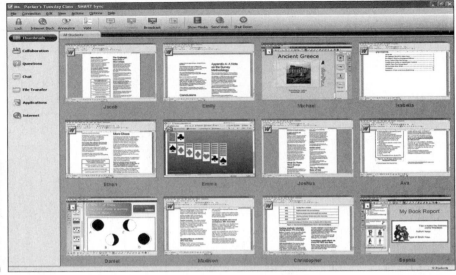

Figure 18-7:
Viewing
screens
with SMART
Sync
software.

If you need a tool that allows you to assist individual learners, help small-groups and observe whole-class in a single lesson, this is the tool for you. Visit www.smarttech.com/sync and explore. You're sure to be impressed.

SMART Ideas® Concept Mapping Software

If you need a fabulous tool for plotting out processes, creating organization charts, or helping students visualize abstract concepts and complex ideas, get a hold of SMART Ideas concept mapping software. It's bundled with activities and tools enabling you to create visual maps and charts quickly. Instructors, presenters, students, or participants in a conference can drag colorful shapes and connectors to create a concept map. If you're a teacher, you have access to templates and a bundle of curriculum-specific and inter-active clip art, free of charge, to assist you in creating visual maps to help explain topic-related concepts. One of the great things about using this soft-ware with students is allowing them to use the tools and learn to help build a concept map (as shown in Figure 18-8).

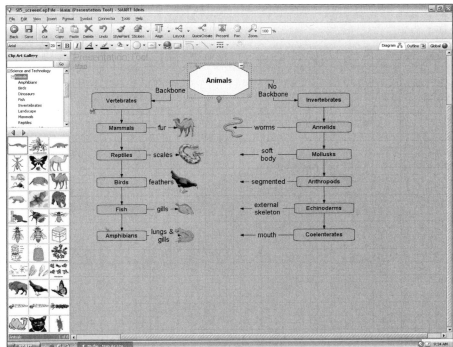

Figure 18-8:
A SMART
Ideas
concept
map.

Here are just a few of the many features you'll love:

- ✔ **Style collections:** Enable you to create concept maps by dragging and dropping symbols, basic and complex connectors, images, and interactive clip art.

- ✔ **Curriculum-specific clip art gallery and clip art objects:** Give you access to over 2,000 resizable pieces of clip art to add to your maps and lessons. The beauty is that they're all grouped in categories according to curriculum topic.

- ✔ **Legend creation:** Allows you to create legends to explain and highlight the meaning of symbols and how they relate to information you're presenting or explaining.

- ✔ **Multilevel diagrams:** Allow you to create multilevel diagrams and then export maps to create web pages that you and your students can easily navigate.

- ✔ **Multimedia linking:** Provides you with the tools to link or attach map objects to files, websites, and/or other diagrams or levels within diagrams.

CoreFocus

If you're a preschool, kindergarten, or primary grade teacher, you'll be interested to know that SMART Technologies has teamed up with experts to deliver CoreFocus interactive whiteboard content (shown in Figure 18-9). Hatch, Inc., provided a team of experts in core curriculum, and together with SMART Technologies, they designed child-focused, fun, and engaging lessons and tools you'll find invaluable. The two companies even developed input devices to help little fingers or children with disabilities get the most out of the activities and learn in a fun way. Check it out at `http://tinyurl.com/corefocus`.

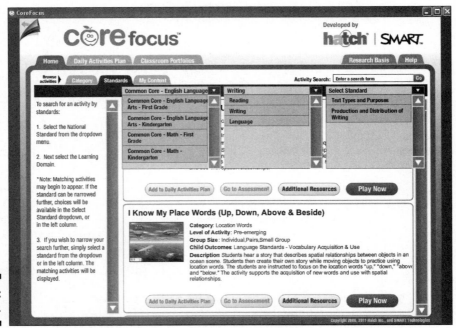

Figure 18-9:
CoreFocus.

Trimble SketchUp

Trimble SketchUp (`http://sketchup.google.com`; see Figure 18-10), formerly known as Google SketchUp, is one of the most popular 3D modeling tools in the world! It's a great tool to use with the interactive whiteboard because it allows your audience to interact and view how something is built in the most visible and versatile way. This software is used for education, geo-modeling, movie making, engineering, architecture, design, construction, game design, and more.

Using the interactive whiteboard to bring a project to life is an awesome experience. What's more impressive is if two participants use the software and together construct something. SketchUp Gallery comes with hundreds of incredible images and models you can use. For instance, you can quickly design a bathroom or engage a physics class in building a bridge. Visual gaming is especially cool. The neat thing about SketchUp is that people around the world share and build together. Give it a try!

Quizlet

Quizlet (www.quizlet.com; see Figure 18-11) is the largest flash cards and study games website on the Internet. It includes over 12 million free sets of flash cards on just about every subject you can think of, including every language. Sound is available for all flash cards, and there is a step-by-step how-to guide, a blog, and answers to frequently asked questions. (I even found flash cards about SMART Board interactive whiteboards.) Students can use and create new flash cards on the interactive whiteboard. Try it out!

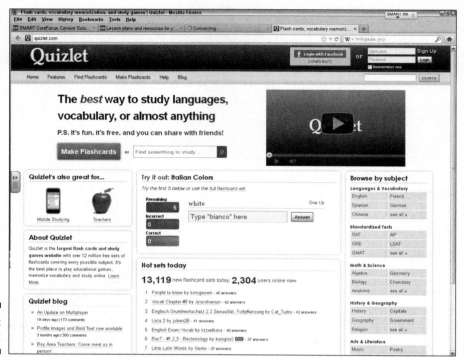

Figure 18-11:
Quizlet.

Chapter 19

Ten (Or So) Hints, Tips, and Shortcuts

In This Chapter

▶ Giving great presentations

▶ Using hardware and software better

▶ Using other software with the interactive whiteboard

This chapter is all about giving you ideas, tips, and shortcuts that I've found useful in working with my interactive whiteboard. Some of these may seem obvious, but sometimes the most obvious solutions are easy to overlook!

Enhancing Your Presentations with Technology

One of the most important aspects of presenting or teaching using technology is to avoid trying to fit your learning or presentation goals to the technology. Instead, you need to identify what you're trying to achieve first, and then think about how the technology can enhance what you're doing.

Bloom's Digital Taxonomy

If you're an educator, you're familiar with Bloom's Taxonomy. But did you know that Bloom's students have revised the taxonomy for the 21st-century digital generation, calling it, more appropriately, Bloom's Digital Taxonomy? For more information on Bloom's Digital Taxonomy, check out the following resources:

✔ www.usi.edu/distance/bdt.htm

✔ www.techlearning.com/article/ 44988

Letting Your Fingers Do the Walking

You don't need a mouse, a keyboard, or a SMART Pen Tray pen to work with your interactive whiteboard — all you need is your finger. Pressing on an interactive whiteboard is the same as left-clicking with a mouse. For example, to open an application such as a web browser or Microsoft Word, double-press the application icon with your finger.

The more you use your finger, the less you'll want to use anything else. The only drawback is that when you come to your computer, you'll forget and start pressing on the screen!

Testing, Testing, 1, 2, 3

The last thing you want is to prepare a lesson or walk into a large presentation and have the technology let you down. It's happened to all of us at one time or another. You'll save yourself time and embarrassment if you go to the room where you'll be presenting 15 minutes early; turn on the interactive whiteboard; and make sure all the cables are connected, the sound system works, the light bulb hasn't burned out, you can access the Internet if you need to, and the board is oriented correctly.

Make sure that the files you'll be using are backed up. If they're on a network, back up on a thumb drive. If they're on your computer, back up on a network or a thumb drive.

Erasing a Large Area

You don't need to use the eraser to try to rub out lots of different annotations or objects. Here are two quick ways to erase large areas:

✔ Press the eraser on the Floating Tools toolbar. Draw a large circle around the area you want to erase. Then with your finger, tap inside the circle. All digital ink disappears.

✔ Pick up the eraser, make a large circle around the area you want to erase, and tap inside the circle.

Filling an Empty Pen Tray Slot

No matter how careful you or your colleagues are, at some point, the pen from the SMART Pen Tray will disappear. You'll have to find something to replace the empty slot; otherwise, the interactive whiteboard gets a message that you're using it when you press on the interactive whiteboard. You can fill that tray with any marker or object that covers the sensor. A favorite around the office is a sticky note.

Sending Text from Another Application into a SMART Notebook File

You know how easy it is to export files or pages from SMART Notebook software to other applications, but what about the reverse? You'll be please to hear it's equally simple. Here's how:

1. **In the other application (for example, Microsoft Word), select File⇨Print.**

2. **Select SMART Notebook Print Capture as your printer.**

   Note: This might be called SMART Notebook Document Writer, depending on the version you're using.

3. **Click OK.**

   Each page of the text will appear as an object on an individual SMART Notebook page, and the formatting will stay the same.

Quickly Accessing the Orientation Screen

If you need to orient the screen quickly on a 600 series interactive whiteboard, press and hold both buttons on the Pen Tray. That will activate the orientation screen, enabling you to go through the quick synchronization points. On an 800 series, just press the Orientation button.

Trying the Transparent Layer

A really cool tool you should try is the Transparent Layer. This tool allows you to write on anything with digital ink, including all files (such as the desktop or web pages). To activate the Transparent Layer, pick up a pen from the SMART Pen Tray or select the Pen icon on your Floating Tools toolbar. As soon as you pick up the pen, an invisible layer is placed over your current page, and you can write on it. To stop using the Transparent Layer, press the red X that appears in the upper right-hand corner of your layer.

Right-Clicking

If you need to right-click, just press and hold your finger on the interactive whiteboard until you see the right-click menu. You also can press the Right Mouse button on the Pen Tray, and your next press on the interactive whiteboard will be a right-click. If you want to go back, press the interactive whiteboard again and it reverts back.

Chapter 20

Ten Creative Ways to Involve Your Audience

In This Chapter

▶ Engaging your audience

▶ Thinking creatively

Knowing your audience is the first step in an interactive process. Involving them right from the start is the next step. When you involve participants in some kind of activity, you've grabbed their attention. The SMART Board interactive whiteboard has many different ways to involve your audience. I can't begin to list them all, but in this chapter I give you ten different ways you can use the interactive whiteboard tools to engage your audience, whether they're school-age children, college students, or business associates. All the activities are simple to develop and are sure to engage even the most stubborn participant.

If you try any of these suggestions and you're inspired to build on, improve, and create your own engaging activity, upload the resource to SMART Exchange (`http://exchange.smarttech.com`).

Have Them Sign Their Names as They Arrive

Open a SMART Notebook page, put the pens in view, and write on the board, "Please sign in." Have every student or participant sign his or her name upon entering the room. If you want, you can use the Pen tool with all the fun options (crayon, smileys, stars, rainbow colors, line types, and so on) and let participants' creative sides take over. Adults and kids alike can have fun with the bright and versatile pens.

For adult audiences, ask them to write why they came to the meeting or a question they may want answered during the presentation. You can use a table or spreadsheet and instantly collect data. Then you can save the page and e-mail it to the participants after the meeting, if appropriate.

Play Games

Download one of the games from SMART Exchange, the Gallery, or the web and display it on the interactive whiteboard. You can easily start a simple game like Hangman, word search, Sudoku, Scrabble, or a puzzle, and ask students or audience members to add to it. For children, get the map of a continent, scramble the countries, and ask them to put it together; have a list of names of countries and have them drag and drop where they belong.

You can get really creative with a map. For example, if you're teaching the states on the U.S. map, display the map with a sound behind it. If the correct state is placed in the map, add a clapping sound; if the wrong state is placed in the map, have a "Try again" sound played. You can open a window to access the Internet and ask students to fill in facts about states, such as the capital city, population, state bird, and so on.

Puzzles and games are great as ice breakers or teaching tools. Pictionary is a great one! Ask someone to draw a picture and have the rest of the group guess what it is. If it's a learning activity, you can have a set of words on one of the SMART Notebook pages — perhaps vocabulary words learned during the week — and ask students to draw the words.

Flip the Classroom

You're probably doing blended learning with your classes — using technology in your classroom to enhance your learning goals. Well, here's an idea that's being tested within education academic circles: flipping the classroom.

For example, an instructor videotapes her instruction, such as a lecture, which the students then watch at home, and the homework is done in the classroom instead. This gives the teacher more time to interact with the students and provide one-on-one help while they do their homework. The theory is that making use of the classroom for key learning activities and help sessions may turn out to be a more productive use of face-to-face time. The SMART Board interactive whiteboard has all the tools you need to be able to record your instruction.

Although this type of learning is still experimental, I bet we'll be seeing data in the next year or two reporting on how effective this method is. Try it, experiment, and see how your students respond!

Use Sound Effectively

You can use sound files to help students pronounce words or indicate correct and incorrect answers. You can create a SMART Notebook page for each student and record each student's voice. Or use video and surprise your students. For example, let students choose an animal or a place, and link the image to a video opening up from *National Geographic,* the BBC, PBS, or any other online video resource you use.

Stage Your Own Game Show

You can find templates for games such as Jeopardy!, Are You Smarter Than a 5th Grader?, The Weakest Link, Who Wants to Be a Millionaire?, and more. If you can find them in the SMART Notebook Gallery, you can download templates from SMART Exchange (`http://exchange.smarttech.com`). The formats, including music files, are usually in PowerPoint, and you can add the content in SMART Notebook pages.

A group of MBA students at Saint Martin's University, where I work, presented their final project and used the Jeopardy! game template as part of the presentation. They used the topics in the unit and involved the whole class, including the professor — it was a hoot, and they got an A! You can download Jeopardy! templates from SMART Exchange at `http://exchange.smarttech.com/search.html?q="jeopardy"`.

Play with Faces and Photos

Use shapes and add pictures of yourself, your audience, or your students. You can find images of cities or other interesting places and add them in the background. Participants can add text bubbles about themselves, or use the art tools to add to their faces. A fun icebreaker activity can be built around this concept.

Give People a Task

Don't waste a minute! As soon as your learners arrive, give them a task. Make it as direct as you can, in great big bold letters stating something like, "TAKE ACTION NOW! THIS IS DUE!" Your goal is to get their attention. Add sound that will play every few seconds or at your touch. On another page or area of the board, have the assignment instructions.

Communicate with People around the World

Take advantage of your interactive whiteboard's conferencing capabilities (see Part III). If you don't have Bridgit software, it doesn't matter — you can still communicate through Skype (www.skype.com) or VoiceThread (www.voicethread.com). Both are free and don't require extra software to install. In no time, you can be talking and sharing work with another classroom anywhere in the world!

Take a Trip with Google Earth

There are numerous activities to involve your students or presenters using Google Earth (http://earth.google.com). You can plan a trip, take a virtual trip, take a trip through a story, use it for model making, and more. Google Earth activities look very impressive when you use the whole interactive whiteboard. You can find more ideas at http://tinyurl.com/5t7rcrs.

Write Stories as a Group

Involve your students in writing a story. Each student can take on a character and contribute one or two sentences. Start with a topic or theme, and ask every student to take a turn at the interactive whiteboard and add to the story. If your interactive whiteboard enables more than one person (up to four people with the 800 series) to work on the interactive whiteboard at the same time, you can assign one person to write, while other people illustrate, link to information, enter data, or organize other objects. By using a variety of objects and graphical and multimedia files, the story can come to life. You can move text around, ask writers to use different colors and pen styles, have them serve as editors, and in the end, have a document everyone can be proud of.

You can capture everything the students write and save it to your .notebook file.

Part V
Appendixes

The 5th Wave   By Rich Tennant

HERPETOLOGISTS PARTICULARLY LIKE THE ABILITY TO WRITE WITH ANYTHING ON A SMART BOARD

FROGS: AMPHIBIA
GOOD EYESIGHT
GOOD H'
POWER'
DISTINCTI

"That pretty much covers the frog. Now, let's look at the newt."

In this part . . .

In this part, I offer up some fantastic resources where you can turn for more information on your SMART Board interactive whiteboard. I also provide some trouble-shooting tips to help you out of a jam.

Appendix A

Resources

● ●

A wealth of information about the interactive whiteboard is available online, both from SMART Technologies and from the user community. Because so much is out there, I've sifted through hundreds of links and listed those that I think are most valuable. If you're looking for more information on working with the interactive whiteboard, you can't go wrong with any of these resources.

SupportLink: SMART's Services and Support Publication

SupportLink is a bimonthly publication that provides tips, tricks, and technical advice to get the most from your SMART hardware and software products. This no-cost electronic bulletin is for teachers, administrators, technology specialists, and support staff around the world who use and maintain SMART products.

Go to www.smarttech.com/supportlink and click Subscribe Now to receive the e-mail and check out previous issues.

Technical Support

If you're looking for technical support with your SMART Board interactive whiteboard, your first stop should be SMART Technologies itself. You can contact them online at www.smarttech.com/contactsupport. You also can call them at 866-518-6791 (toll-free in the U.S. and Canada) or 403-228-5940.

If you have the SMART Support iPhone app, you can contact SMART through the app. Download it from the iTunes Store.

You also can find useful tech support answers on the SMART Technologies forums: `http://exchange-forum.smarttech.com`.

Outside of SMART Technologies, you can find help from SmartEd Services (`www.teachsmart.org/Support Services/FAQs.aspx`); this site, which is not affiliated with SMART Technologies, has excellent FAQs. An excellent tutorial on how to install the SMART Board interactive whiteboard is available at `www.digitalsparkles.com/example/smartboard_install/smartboard_install.html`.

The main training site for SMART Technologies is at `www.smarttech.com/trainingcenter`. If you want further training offered by the experts, contact one of the groups or look at the resources they have to offer. You can find training for education, business, and more.

Inspiration

SMART Exchange (`http://exchange.smarttech.com`) is a great place to search and browse for all types of resources for education and business. It's mainly aimed at education, but many of the tools, lessons, templates, and games are easily adaptable to business situations. The site also includes forum discussions and a direct link to support staff at SMART Technologies. This should be your number-one place to visit!

You also can access SMART Exchange from SMART Notebook and SMART Meeting Pro software.

Education resources

If you're looking for more interactive whiteboard resources for your work as an educator, check out the following:

- **Blossom Learning (`www.blossomlearning.com/Resources.aspx`):** This site has lots of free lessons, how-to guides, and troubleshooting.

- **Educational Origami (`http://edorigami.wikispaces.com/Bloom%27s+and+ICT+tools`):** Describes the Bloom's revised taxonomy and offers an abundance of education resources.

- **56 Interesting Ways to Use an Interactive Whiteboard in the Classroom (`https://docs.google.com/present/view?id=dhn2vcv5_106c9fm8j`):** This site is an excellent resource and includes links to more resources.

- ✓ **SMART Board Revolution (http://smartboardrevolution.ning.com):** Started by educators, this site includes loads of useful information, including shared files and Help files. You can post questions and get answers from other members of the community. Use the Search box to find what you're looking for.

- ✓ **SMART Board Tricks (www.smartboardtricks.com):** This is a website and blog dedicated to the SMART Board interactive whiteboard.

- ✓ **Teachers Love SMART Boards (www.teacherslovesmartboards.com):** This site is a great resource for the SMART Board classroom. You can find games to download and much more.

- ✓ **TeacherTube (www.teachertube.com):** This site is a fab teaching resource and a community for teachers and instructors. It isn't specifically devoted to the SMART Board interactive whiteboard, but you can find content on this site dedicated to the interactive whiteboard.

- ✓ **Teaching Resources Blog (www.lauracandler.com/strategies/smartboard.php):** This site is full of ideas and links to resources and downloadable games and lessons.

Business solutions

If you're using your interactive whiteboard in the business world, you can adapt many of the education resources in the preceding section to meet your needs. But you don't have to stop there. Freestorm™ collaboration solutions, from SMART Technologies, offers business solutions videos, case studies, software, and support. Check it out at www.smarttech.com/freestorm.

Sharing

When you want to share your presentations or lessons beyond your classroom or conference room, check out the following tools:

- ✓ **SlideShare (www.slideshare.net):** SlideShare allows you to share presentations.

- ✓ **YouTube (www.youtube.com):** You can embed YouTube videos in your blog, learning management system (like Moodle), or web pages.

Subscribe to the SMART Classrooms YouTube channel to stay in the loop with official SMART-created videos: www.youtube.com/user/SMARTClassrooms.

Appendix B

Troubleshooting

• •

*1*f you've run into a problem using your SMART Board interactive white-board, you've come to the right place. This appendix troubleshoots the most frequent problems. If you don't find the answers you need here, or if you're still having trouble, contact SMART Technologies for technical support (see Appendix A for contact information).

There are three general troubleshooting tips that will solve many problems you may experience:

- ✔ **Restart your computer.** When in doubt, just restart. Sometimes a simple restart is all it takes to get things working properly again.

- ✔ **Check to make sure that all cables are properly connected.** Follow the cable(s) from the wall socket to the device that isn't working, whether that's your computer, interactive whiteboard, projector, or something else. Unplug the cable, wait at least ten seconds, and then plug the cable back in (making sure it's fully plugged in). That may solve your problem.

- ✔ **Update your SMART software to the latest versions.** SMART regularly releases bug fixes and improvements to its software. Choose Help⇨Check for Updates in your software.

Hardware Problems

The main hardware problem you may encounter is also the most basic: trouble turning on the interactive whiteboard. You often can diagnose the problem you're having using the Ready light (see Figure B-1 for the Ready light location on the 600 series and Figure B-2 for the Ready light location on the 800 series).

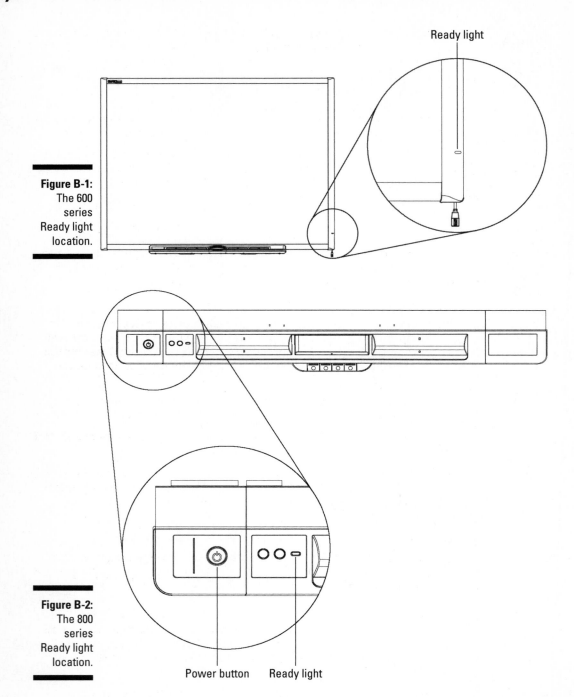

Ready light

Figure B-1:
The 600
series
Ready light
location.

Figure B-2:
The 800
series
Ready light
location.

Power button   Ready light

If you have a 600 series interactive whiteboard (the most common model), check out this troubleshooting flowchart: www.smarttech.com/kb/117615. If you have an 800 series, see www.smarttech.com/kb/156537.

Here's what the Ready light means:

> ✔ **If the Ready light is red:** Your SMART Board interactive whiteboard is not communicating with the computer. Follow these suggestions in order:
>
> 1. Make sure your computer is turned on. ***Remember:*** Turning on the interactive whiteboard is a two-step process — both the computer and the interactive whiteboard need to be turned on.
>
> 2. Make sure that the USB cable, power cord, and any other cords and cables are all fully connected. It's easy for cables to come loose, so do a quick check to make sure that hasn't happened.
>
> 3. Unplug the USB cable, wait ten seconds, and plug it back in. If the light doesn't turn green, restart the computer.
>
> 4. Try plugging the USB cable into a different USB port on the computer.
>
> 5. Use a pen to press the interactive whiteboard's Reset button for three seconds *or* unplug the interactive whiteboard from the wall socket, whichever you prefer. (Figure B-3 shows the Reset button on the 600 series, and Figure B-4 shows the Reset button on the 800 series.)
>
> 6. Reinstall or update the SMART Product Drivers (choose Help⇨Check for Updates in your SMART software).
>
> If the Ready light is still red after trying all these options, contact SMART Technologies technical support.
>
> ✔ **If the Ready light is flashing green:** The interactive whiteboard is communicating with the power source and computer, but the software may not be working. Follow these suggestions in order:
>
> 1. Reinstall or update the SMART Product Drivers (choose Help⇨Check for Updates in your SMART software).
>
> 2. Unplug the USB cable, wait ten seconds, and plug it back in.
>
> 3. Try plugging the USB cable into a different USB port on the computer.
>
> 4. Use a pen to press the interactive whiteboard's Reset button for three seconds *or* unplug the interactive whiteboard from the wall socket, whichever you prefer. (Refer to Figures B-3 and B-4 for the location of the Reset button on the 600 series and 800 series, respectively.)
>
> If the Ready light is still flashing green after trying all these options, contact SMART Technologies technical support.

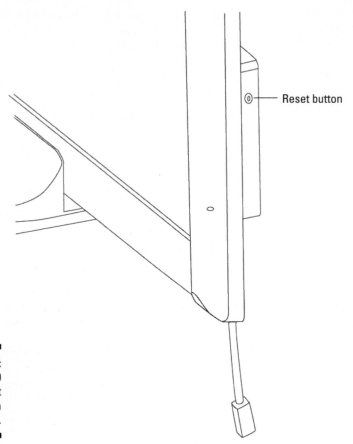

Reset button

Figure B-3:
The 600
series Reset
button
location.

Reset button

Figure B-4:
The 800
series Reset
button
location.

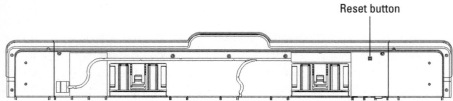

✔ **If the Ready light is solid green, but the interactive whiteboard doesn't work:** The interactive whiteboard is working correctly, but there are problems associated with other devices or software. Follow these suggestions in order:

1. If the computer applications such as SMART Notebook software have frozen, force quit the software by pressing Ctrl+Alt+Delete (Windows) or by choosing ⌘⇨Force Quit (Mac). Shut down the computer and wait approximately ten seconds. Turn the computer back on. If this doesn't solve the problem, there may be other issues.

2. Reinstall or update the SMART Product Drivers (choose Help⇨Check for Updates in your SMART software).

3. Restart the computer and the interactive whiteboard.

If the interactive whiteboard still isn't working properly, contact SMART Technologies technical support.

Sometimes the hardware issue you're having can't be detected by looking at the Ready light. Here are several common hardware-related problems and how to solve them:

✔ **Another user may have reassigned the pen, eraser, or Pen Tray button functions, or the tools may not work as expected.** If this happens, try either of the following suggestions:

- You can return to default operation by using the SMART Control Panel (also called SMART Settings) to change SMART hardware settings. To access the SMART Control Panel, click the SMART Board icon in the Windows notification area (Windows) or in the Dock (Mac) and select Control Panel or SMART Settings from the SMART Board Tools menu.

- Reset the interactive whiteboard. Use a pen to press the interactive whiteboard's Reset button for three seconds *or* unplug the interactive whiteboard from the wall socket, whichever you prefer. (Refer to Figures B-3 and B-4 for the location of the Reset button on the 600 series and 800 series, respectively.)

✔ **When you press a button, write with your finger, or write with pens, the point may be off from the target (that is, misaligned).** If this happens, you need to orient the interactive whiteboard. Chapter 3 walks you through the process.

✔ **You may see irregularities, spots, or obstructions on the interactive whiteboard.** If you're seeing spots or lines on the interactive whiteboard, dust particles or dirt may be on the camera lens or reflective tape. Take a soft cloth and wipe the reflective lens; check for dirt sticking to the lenses.

Be extremely careful when cleaning your projector's lens or reflective mirror. Read and understand all the warnings, cautions, and instructions in your product's user's guide. If you're using a SMART projector, go to www.smarttech.com/support to find relevant documents.

Software Problems

Before I dive into some specific software problems you may encounter, here are some great places to turn for specific information on different SMART software products:

- **SMART Notebook Version 11:** Download the user's guides at the following URLs:
  - Windows: www.smarttech.com/kb/170138
  - Mac: www.smarttech.com/kb/170139
- **SMART Notebook Version 10.8:** Download the user's guides at the following URLs:
  - Windows: www.smarttech.com/kb/123570
  - Mac: www.smarttech.com/kb/124143
- **Bridgit software:** Download the user's guide at www.smarttech.com/kb/170181.

To access the Help system for any SMART software, choose Help➪Contents.

Here are some specific software problems you may encounter and how to solve them:

- **The digital ink features may not be working correctly or the toolbars may not be displayed in Microsoft Office applications:** These issues are most likely caused by SMART Ink not being fully installed. Try reinstalling the SMART Ink plug-in for Microsoft Office. *Note:* This issue doesn't occur on Macs.

To install the plug-in on a computer running the Windows 7 operating system, follow these steps:

1. **Choose Start➪Control Panel➪Programs and Features.**

   The Programs and Features window appears.

2. **Select SMART Ink from the drop-down list.**

3. **Click Repair.**

   The SMART Ink plug-in installation wizard appears.

4. **Follow the on-screen instructions.**

   The SMART Ink plug-in for Microsoft Office is installed.

To install the plug-in on a computer running the Windows XP operating system, follow these steps:

1. **Choose Start⇨Control Panel⇨Add or Remove Programs.**

   The Add or Remove Programs window appears.

2. **Select SMART Ink.**

3. **Select Click Here for Support Information.**

   The Support Info for SMART Ink window appears.

4. **Click Repair.**

   The SMART Ink plug-in for Microsoft Office is installed.

Note: You may need to log in as an administrator to perform these procedures.

✔ **You may have very large files that include media and/or pictures and they run slowly.** If this occurs, you need to reduce size of your files. You can find suggestions on how to do that in the SMART Notebook user's guide or Help system (choose Help⇨Contents in SMART Notebook software). See the topic "Reducing file sizes" or search the Help for "large pictures."

✔ **SMART Notebook toolbar buttons described in the book may not appear on your toolbar.** If there is a drop-down arrow on the right side of the toolbar, press it to see if other buttons are available. If so, you can drag those buttons to the toolbar.

If the drop-down arrow isn't there, one of your colleagues probably customized the toolbar. For instructions on customizing the toolbar, turn to Chapter 3.

Also, remember that you may have a different version from the one used in the figures in this book. If you poke around, you'll usually find the tool you need!

✔ **Two users may be writing and manipulating objects on the interactive whiteboard, one using a finger and the other using a pen, when all of a sudden the participant using a pen can't write.** This can happen on the 800 series interactive whiteboards because they recognize whether you're touching the surface with a finger or a pen. They "assume" that any settings that you change using a finger or a pen apply to the user using that tool. If one user is using a finger and another user is using the pen, the person using the pen probably changed the pen style using his finger, giving different information to the interactive whiteboard. If a pen is picked up, then all actions need to be with the pen. Ask the pen user to press the styles or any other button with the pen only.

✔ **You may not be able to resize an object.** This problem happens because the object is locked. For instructions on locking and unlocking the object, turn to Chapter 8.

Index

• P •

Notes

Notes

Notes

Notes

EDUCATION, HISTORY & REFERENCE

978-0-7645-2498-1

978-0-470-46244-7

Also available:
- ✔ Algebra For Dummies
  978-0-7645-5325-7
- ✔ Art History For Dummies
  978-0-470-09910-0
- ✔ Chemistry For Dummies
  978-0-7645-5430-8
- ✔ English Grammar For Dummies
  978-0-470-54664-2

- ✔ French For Dummies
  978-0-7645-5193-2
- ✔ Statistics For Dummies
  978-0-7645-5423-0
- ✔ World History For Dummies
  978-0-470-44654-6

FOOD, HOME, & MUSIC

978-0-7645-9904-0

978-0-470-67895-4

Also available:
- ✔ 30-Minute Meals For Dummies
  978-0-7645-2589-6
- ✔ Bartending For Dummies
  978-0-470-05056-9
- ✔ Brain Games For Dummies
  978-0-470-37378-1

- ✔ Gluten-Free Cooking For Dummies
  978-0-470-17810-2
- ✔ Home Improvement All-in-One Desk
  Reference For Dummies
  978-0-7645-5680-7
- ✔ Wine For Dummies
  978-0-470-04579-4

GARDENING

978-0-470-58161-2

978-0-470-57705-9

Also available:
- ✔ Gardening Basics For Dummies
  978-0-470-03749-2
- ✔ Organic Gardening For Dummies
  978-0-470-43067-5

- ✔ Sustainable Landscaping For
  Dummies 978-0-470-41149-0
- ✔ Vegetable Gardening For Dummies
  978-0-470-49870-5

GREEN/SUSTAINABLE

978-0-470-84098-6

978-0-470-59678-4

Also available:

- Alternative Energy For Dummies
  978-0-470-43062-0
- Energy Efficient Homes For Dummies
  978-0-470-37602-7
- Green Building & Remodelling For
  Dummies 978-0-470-17559-0
- Green Cleaning For Dummies
  978-0-470-39106-8
- Green Your Home All-in-One For
  Dummies 978-0-470-59678-4

HEALTH & SELF-HELP

978-0-471-77383-2

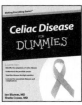

978-0-470-16036-7

Also available:

- Borderline Personality Disorder For
  Dummies 978-0-470-46653-7
- Breast Cancer For Dummies
  978-0-7645-2482-0
- Cognitive Behavioural Therapy For
  Dummies 978-0-470-01838-5
- Emotional Intelligence For Dummies
  978-0-470-15732-9
- Healthy Aging For Dummies
  978-0-470-14975-1
- Neuro-linguistic Programming For
  Dummies 978-0-7645-7028-5
- Understanding Autism For Dummies
  978-0-7645-2547-6

HOBBIES & CRAFTS

978-0-470-28747-7

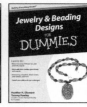

978-0-470-29112-2

Also available:

- Crochet Patterns For Dummies
  97-0-470-04555-8
- Digital Scrapbooking For Dummies
  978-0-7645-8419-0
- Knitting Patterns For Dummies
  978-0-470-04556-5
- Oil Painting For Dummies
  978-0-470-18230-7
- Quilting For Dummies
  978-0-7645-9799-2
- Sewing For Dummies
  978-0-7645-6847-3
- Word Searches For Dummies
  978-0-470-45366-7

HOME & BUSINESS COMPUTER BASICS

978-0-470-49743-2

978-0-470-48953-6

Also available:
- Office 2010 All-in-One Desk Reference For Dummies 978-0-470-49748-7
- Pay Per Click Search Engine Marketing For Dummies 978-0-471-75494-7

- Search Engine Marketing For Dummies 978-0-471-97998-2
- Web Analytics For Dummies 978-0-470-09824-0
- Word 2010 For Dummies 978-0-470-48772-3

INTERNET & DIGITAL MEDIA

978-0-470-44417-7

978-0-470-39062-7

Also available:
- Blogging For Dummies 978-0-471-77084-8
- MySpace For Dummies 978-0-470-09529-4
- The Internet For Dummies 978-0-470-12174-0

- Twitter For Dummies 978-0-470-47991-9
- YouTube For Dummies 978-0-470-14925-6

MACINTOSH

978-0-470-27817-8

978-0-470-58027-1

Also available:
- iMac For Dummies 978-0-470-13386-6
- iPod Touch For Dummies 978-0-470-50530-4
- iPod & iTunes For Dummies 978-0-470-39062-7

- MacBook For Dummies 978-0-470-27816-1
- Macs For Seniors For Dummies 978-0-470-43779-7

PETS

978-0-470-60029-0

978-0-7645-5267-0

Also available:
- Cats For Dummies
  978-0-7645-5275-5
- Ferrets For Dummies
  978-0-470-13943-1
- Horses For Dummies
  978-0-7645-9797-8

- Kittens For Dummies
  978-0-7645-4150-6
- Puppies For Dummies
  978-1-118-11755-2

SPORTS & FITNESS

978-0-471-76871-5

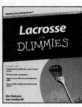

978-0-470-73855-9

Also available:
- Exercise Balls For Dummies
  978-0-7645-5623-4
- Coaching Volleyball For Dummies
  978-0-470-46469-4
- Curling For Dummies
  978-0-470-83828-0
- Fitness For Dummies
  978-0-7645-7851-9
- Mixed Martial Arts For Dummies
  978-0-470-39071-9

- Sports Psychology For Dummies
  978-0-470-67659-2
- Ten Minute Tone-Ups For Dummies
  978-0-7645-7207-4
- Wilderness Survival For Dummies
  978-0-470-45306-3
- Yoga with Weights For Dummies
  978-0-471-74937-0